I0003955

PyTorch Deep Learning

Build and Deploy Models from CNNs to Multimodal Architectures, LLMs, and Beyond

Written By

Dr. Maxwell Brooks

Copyright

Table of Content

Chapter 1: Advanced PyTorch Foundations

1.1 PyTorch Core Principles – A Quick Refresher

PyTorch is celebrated for its **dynamic computation graph**, which builds itself on the fly as you execute your code. This flexibility—allowing you to use native Python control flow and debug interactively—makes PyTorch a favorite in both research and production environments. In this refresher, we will review the essential principles behind PyTorch's operation: from tensor management and autograd to performance optimizations and best practices that empower you to write efficient, production-ready code.

Tensors and Operations

At the heart of PyTorch is the **tensor**: a multi-dimensional array similar to a NumPy array but with support for GPU acceleration and automatic differentiation.

Key Concepts:

- **Creation:** Tensors can be instantiated from Python lists, NumPy arrays, or using built-in initializers.
- **Attributes:** Each tensor has a **dtype** (data type) and a **device** (CPU or GPU). By default, tensors reside on the CPU unless moved explicitly.
- **Operations:** PyTorch provides a rich suite of operations—arithmetic, linear algebra, indexing, slicing, and reshaping—that are highly optimized and can be executed on both CPU and GPU.

Example:

```python
import torch

# Creating tensors
x = torch.tensor([[1.0, 2.0], [3.0, 4.0]])        # 2x2 tensor
```

```
y = torch.arange(6).reshape(2, 3)
# 2x3 tensor

# Basic operations: broadcasting and elementwise
arithmetic
z = x + y.float()   # y is converted to float and
broadcast to match x's shape
print("Tensor z:", z)
```

Remember:

- **Indexing & Slicing:** Use standard Python slicing (`tensor[0, 1]`, `tensor[:, 0]`) to access parts of tensors.
- **Reshaping:** Methods like `.view()` or `.reshape()` let you change tensor dimensions without data duplication.
- **Broadcasting:** Enables operations on tensors of different shapes by automatically expanding dimensions without extra memory overhead.

Computational Graph and Autograd

One of PyTorch's standout features is its **automatic differentiation engine (autograd)**. It dynamically constructs a **computation graph** as you perform operations on tensors marked with `requires_grad=True`.

How It Works:

- **Forward Pass:** As you execute tensor operations, PyTorch records the operations as nodes in a dynamic graph.
- **Backward Pass:** When you call `.backward()` on a scalar loss, PyTorch traverses this graph in reverse to compute gradients using the chain rule.
- **Gradient Accumulation:** Gradients are stored in the `.grad` attribute of leaf tensors (usually model parameters). Always remember to zero gradients before the next backward pass.

Example:

python

```
# Create tensors with gradient tracking
x = torch.tensor(2.0, requires_grad=True)
```

```
y = torch.tensor(3.0, requires_grad=True)

# Build a simple computation graph
z = x * y + y ** 2   # z = 2*3 + 3^2 = 15

# Compute gradients
z.backward()
print("dz/dx:", x.grad)   # Expected: 3.0
print("dz/dy:", y.grad)   # Expected: 2.0 + 2*3 =
8.0
```

Tips:

- **No Gradient Tracking:** For inference or evaluation, wrap your code in a `with torch.no_grad():` block to reduce memory overhead.
- **Detaching Tensors:** Use `tensor.detach()` when you need to break the computation graph and work with tensor data without tracking gradients.

Optimized Tensor Operations

Leveraging hardware acceleration is crucial for high-performance deep learning. PyTorch provides straightforward tools for **GPU acceleration** and **mixed precision training**.

GPU Acceleration:

- **Moving Data:** Transfer tensors and models to a GPU using `.to(device)` after checking availability.
- **Asynchronous Execution:** CUDA operations are asynchronous. Use `torch.cuda.synchronize()` to ensure accurate performance measurements.

Mixed Precision Training:

- **AMP (Automatic Mixed Precision):** Reduces memory usage and speeds up training by using FP16 precision where appropriate. Use `torch.cuda.amp.autocast()` to automatically cast operations and `torch.cuda.amp.GradScaler` to maintain numerical stability.

Example:

```python
python

device = torch.device("cuda" if
torch.cuda.is_available() else "cpu")
tensor = torch.randn((1000, 1000), device=device)

# Simple GPU operation: matrix multiplication
result = torch.matmul(tensor, tensor.T)
print("Result shape:", result.shape)
```

Performance Pointers:

- Utilize vectorized operations rather than Python loops.
- Consider using data loader optimizations such as
  `pin_memory=True` for faster CPU-to-GPU data transfers.

Best Practices and Troubleshooting

To maintain efficiency and robustness in your PyTorch code, adopt these best practices:

- **Reproducibility:** Set seeds using `torch.manual_seed()`,
  `np.random.seed()`, and, for multi-GPU setups,
  `torch.cuda.manual_seed_all()`.
- **Training vs. Evaluation Modes:** Switch between
  `model.train()` and `model.eval()` to control behaviors like
  dropout and batch normalization.
- **Gradient Management:** Reset gradients each iteration with
  `optimizer.zero_grad()`. Use gradient clipping if you
  encounter exploding gradients.
- **Debugging:** Utilize
  `torch.autograd.set_detect_anomaly(True)` to catch
  and debug problematic operations.
- **Efficient Data Loading:** Use `DataLoader` with multiple workers
  to parallelize data fetching, minimizing CPU-GPU data transfer
  bottlenecks.

Hands-On Code Example

Below is a complete, runnable script that demonstrates many of the concepts covered:

```python
import torch

# --- Setup and Reproducibility ---
torch.manual_seed(42)
device = torch.device("cuda" if
torch.cuda.is_available() else "cpu")
print("Running on:", device)

# --- Create Sample Data ---
# A simple linear relationship: y = 2x - 1, with
added noise
X = torch.linspace(-1, 1, steps=100).unsqueeze(1)
# Shape: (100,1)
y = 2 * X - 1 + 0.2 * torch.randn_like(X)
# Add some noise
X, y = X.to(device), y.to(device)

# --- Define a Simple Linear Model ---
model = torch.nn.Linear(1, 1).to(device)
loss_fn = torch.nn.MSELoss()
optimizer = torch.optim.SGD(model.parameters(),
lr=0.1)

# --- Training Loop ---
for epoch in range(5):
    model.train()
    optimizer.zero_grad()
    predictions = model(X)
    loss = loss_fn(predictions, y)
    loss.backward()
    optimizer.step()
    print(f"Epoch {epoch+1}: Loss =
{loss.item():.4f}")
```

```
# --- Evaluation ---
model.eval()
with torch.no_grad():
    test_input = torch.tensor([[0.5]],
device=device)
    test_output = model(test_input)
print("Prediction for input 0.5:",
test_output.item())
```

This script walks through:

- Reproducible setup and device configuration.
- Data creation for a simple regression problem.
- A straightforward model definition and training loop with proper mode management.
- A quick evaluation that uses the no-grad context.

Exercises

1. **Tensor Broadcasting Challenge:**
   Create a tensor of shape `(2, 3)` and another of shape `(3,)`. Perform an elementwise multiplication and explain how PyTorch applies broadcasting. Then, rewrite the code by explicitly expanding the smaller tensor.

2. **Autograd Exploration:**
   Define a function $f(x)=x^3-2x+5$ using PyTorch tensors (with `requires_grad=True`). Compute its derivative at a chosen value (e.g., x=4) both manually and using `.backward()`. Compare your results.

3. **GPU Performance Test:**
   Create two large random tensors (e.g., 5000×5000) and measure the time taken for matrix multiplication on both CPU and GPU. Use `torch.cuda.synchronize()` for accurate GPU timing. Document the speedup achieved.

4. **Mixed Precision Experiment:**
   Modify the training loop from the hands-on code example to use automatic mixed precision (AMP). Compare the training time and memory usage with and without AMP. How does AMP impact your results?

5. **Debugging Practice:**
   Intentionally remove the call to `optimizer.zero_grad()` in a

training loop. Observe and document the effects on training loss and gradient accumulation. Then, use `torch.autograd.set_detect_anomaly(True)` to identify any issues when introducing an in-place operation on a tensor that requires gradients.

This refresher lays a solid foundation by revisiting core PyTorch concepts, while also preparing you to tackle more complex architectures and deployment scenarios in later chapters. By understanding these principles deeply, you'll be ready to build, optimize, and troubleshoot advanced deep learning models with confidence.

1.2 Advanced Tensor Operations and GPU Acceleration

As deep learning models become more complex, efficient tensor operations and leveraging GPU acceleration become critical for performance and scalability. This section delves into advanced tensor operations—beyond basic arithmetic—to include sophisticated indexing, reshaping, broadcasting, and in-place modifications. We then explore how to seamlessly offload these operations to a GPU, harnessing parallelism to speed up computations significantly.

Advanced Tensor Operations

1.2.1 In-depth Look at Tensor Manipulation

Advanced Indexing & Slicing:
PyTorch supports a variety of indexing methods:

- **Slicing** (e.g., `tensor[:, 1:3]`),
- **Integer indexing** (e.g., `tensor[[0, 2]]`),
- **Boolean indexing** (e.g., `tensor[tensor > 0]`).

These allow fine-grained selection and manipulation of tensor data without copying memory unnecessarily.

Reshaping and Transposition:
Changing the shape of a tensor without altering its data is central to deep learning:

- Use `.reshape()` or `.view()` to alter the tensor's dimensions.
- For permutation of dimensions, methods like `.transpose()` or `.permute()` come in handy.

Example:

python

```
import torch
# Create a tensor with shape (2, 3, 4)
tensor = torch.arange(24).reshape(2, 3, 4)
# Permute dimensions: new shape (3, 2, 4)
permuted_tensor = tensor.permute(1, 0, 2)
print("Original shape:", tensor.shape)
print("Permuted shape:", permuted_tensor.shape)
```

Broadcasting and Elementwise Operations:
Broadcasting is a powerful feature allowing elementwise operations on tensors of different shapes without explicit expansion. It minimizes memory footprint by conceptually "stretching" the smaller tensor.

Example:

python

```
a = torch.tensor([[1, 2, 3],
                  [4, 5, 6]])
b = torch.tensor([10, 20, 30])
result = a + b   # b is broadcast to shape (2,3)
print("Result of broadcasting addition:", result)
```

In-place Operations:
For memory efficiency, PyTorch provides in-place operations (e.g., `tensor.add_()`). However, use them cautiously since they modify data directly, which may interfere with gradient tracking if applied on tensors requiring gradients.

GPU Acceleration

1.2.2 Leveraging GPU for Performance

GPU acceleration is a game-changer in deep learning, offering thousands of cores to perform large-scale tensor operations in parallel.

Device Management:

- **Determining the Device:**
  Use `torch.cuda.is_available()` to check if a CUDA-enabled GPU exists.
- **Transferring Tensors to GPU:**
  Use the `.to(device)` method to move tensors and models to the GPU.

Example:

python

```
device = torch.device("cuda" if
torch.cuda.is_available() else "cpu")
tensor = torch.randn((1000, 1000)).to(device)
print("Tensor is on device:", tensor.device)
```

Asynchronous Execution and Synchronization:
CUDA operations are asynchronous. This means the Python interpreter does not wait for the GPU computation to finish. For accurate performance timing or debugging, use `torch.cuda.synchronize()`.

Example:

python

```
import time
start = time.time()
result = torch.matmul(tensor, tensor.T)
torch.cuda.synchronize()  # Wait for GPU to finish
print("Matrix multiplication time:", time.time() -
start)
```

Mixed Precision Training:

Leveraging lower-precision (FP16) operations via Automatic Mixed Precision (AMP) can boost throughput and reduce memory usage, especially on modern GPUs with Tensor Cores. The `torch.cuda.amp` module provides:

- `autocast()`: Automatically casts operations to FP16 where beneficial.
- `GradScaler`: Scales gradients to avoid numerical issues with FP16.

Example snippet within a training loop:

```python
from torch.cuda.amp import autocast, GradScaler

scaler = GradScaler()
for data, labels in dataloader:
    data, labels = data.to(device), labels.to(device)
    optimizer.zero_grad()
    with autocast():
        outputs = model(data)
        loss = loss_fn(outputs, labels)
    scaler.scale(loss).backward()
    scaler.step(optimizer)
    scaler.update()
```

Best Practices and Troubleshooting

Efficient Tensor Computation:

- **Vectorize Operations:**
  Avoid Python loops; always use batch operations for speed and memory efficiency.
- **Memory Management:**
  Use in-place operations judiciously, and transfer tensors in batches to reduce host-to-device overhead.
- **Pin Memory:**
  When using DataLoader, set `pin_memory=True` to speed up CPU-to-GPU transfers.

Debugging GPU Code:

- **Synchronize for Timing:**
  Always synchronize (`torch.cuda.synchronize()`) before timing GPU operations.
- **Monitor Memory:**
  Use `torch.cuda.memory_allocated()` and `torch.cuda.memory_cached()` to monitor GPU memory usage.
- **Handle Exceptions:**
  CUDA errors can be cryptic. Wrap sections of code in try-except blocks to catch and log errors, which is particularly useful when debugging complex models.

Hands-On Code Example

Below is an end-to-end script that demonstrates advanced tensor operations combined with GPU acceleration. This example includes reshaping, broadcasting, and a matrix multiplication on the GPU.

```python
import torch
import time

# --- Device Setup ---
device = torch.device("cuda" if
torch.cuda.is_available() else "cpu")
print("Using device:", device)

# --- Advanced Tensor Operations ---
# Create a tensor and reshape
tensor = torch.arange(0, 24,
dtype=torch.float32).reshape(2, 3, 4)
print("Original shape:", tensor.shape)
permuted_tensor = tensor.permute(1, 0, 2)
print("Permuted shape:", permuted_tensor.shape)

# Demonstrate broadcasting: add a tensor of shape
(4,) to each row of the last dimension
broadcast_tensor = torch.tensor([1.0, 2.0, 3.0,
4.0])
```

```
result = tensor + broadcast_tensor
print("Result shape after broadcasting addition:",
result.shape)

# --- GPU Acceleration ---
# Move a large tensor to GPU and perform matrix
multiplication
large_tensor = torch.randn((1000, 1000),
device=device)
start = time.time()
matmul_result = torch.matmul(large_tensor,
large_tensor.T)
torch.cuda.synchronize()  # ensure completion for
accurate timing
print("Matrix multiplication completed in: {:.4f}
seconds".format(time.time() - start))
```

Exercises

1. **Advanced Indexing Challenge:**
   Create a 3-dimensional tensor with random values. Use advanced
   indexing to extract a sub-tensor that selects every other element along
   one dimension and a specific range along another. Describe how the
   slicing and indexing are applied.
2. **GPU Performance Benchmark:**
   Write a script that multiplies two large matrices (e.g., 5000×5000) on
   both CPU and GPU. Use `torch.cuda.synchronize()` to
   measure GPU time accurately. Document the speed difference and
   analyze why GPU provides a significant speedup.
3. **Mixed Precision Exploration:**
   Modify the provided matrix multiplication example to include a
   simple training loop using AMP. Observe the differences in
   computation time and GPU memory usage when AMP is enabled
   versus standard FP32 computation.
4. **Debugging In-place Operations:**
   Create a scenario where an in-place operation on a tensor with
   `requires_grad=True` leads to an error. Use
   `torch.autograd.set_detect_anomaly(True)` to identify
   the problematic operation, and then refactor the code to resolve the
   error.

This section equips you with the advanced tensor manipulation techniques and GPU acceleration strategies essential for scaling deep learning models. By mastering these techniques, you can achieve substantial performance gains and efficient memory management, setting a strong foundation for the subsequent advanced topics in this book.

1.3 Custom Autograd Functions

PyTorch's dynamic computation graph and automatic differentiation engine (autograd) allow you to compute gradients automatically for most operations. However, there are situations where you need to implement custom forward and backward passes—either to optimize performance, support non-standard operations, or simply to experiment with novel gradient computations. In these cases, you can define your own custom autograd functions by subclassing **`torch.autograd.Function.`**

Custom autograd functions give you full control over how the forward pass computes its output and how the backward pass computes gradients with respect to the inputs. This level of control is particularly valuable when working with cutting-edge research or optimizing performance-critical components in your model.

Implementing a Custom Autograd Function

1.3.1 Structure and Key Concepts

A custom autograd function in PyTorch is implemented by subclassing `torch.autograd.Function` and defining two static methods:

- **`forward(ctx, ...):`**
    - Performs the forward computation.
    - Accepts input tensors and returns output tensors.
    - Uses the context object (**`ctx`**) to save any information (using `ctx.save_for_backward()`) needed later for computing gradients.
- **`backward(ctx, grad_output):`**
    - Receives the gradient of the loss with respect to the function's output (**`grad_output`**).
    - Retrieves saved values from the context.
    - Computes and returns gradients with respect to each input of the forward function.

Key Steps:

1. **Subclassing:** Create a new class that inherits from `torch.autograd.Function`.
2. **Forward Pass:**
   - Define the static `forward(ctx, input1, input2, ...)` method.
   - Perform your custom operation.
   - Save any intermediate results needed for the backward pass using `ctx.save_for_backward(...)`.
3. **Backward Pass:**
   - Define the static `backward(ctx, grad_output)` method.
   - Retrieve the saved values.
   - Compute the gradient of the output with respect to each input.
   - Return gradients in the same order as the inputs received by the forward function.

Example: Custom Square Function

Let's illustrate by implementing a simple custom function that computes the square of a tensor. Although squaring is built-in, this example demonstrates the mechanism clearly.

Code Example:

```python
python

import torch

class SquareFunction(torch.autograd.Function):
    @staticmethod
    def forward(ctx, input):
        # Save the input for backward computation
        ctx.save_for_backward(input)
        # Compute the forward pass: output =
input^2
        return input ** 2

    @staticmethod
    def backward(ctx, grad_output):
```

```
        # Retrieve the saved tensor from the
context
        (input,) = ctx.saved_tensors
        # The derivative of x^2 is 2x
        grad_input = grad_output * 2 * input
        return grad_input

# Use the custom function
x = torch.tensor([2.0, 3.0, 4.0],
requires_grad=True)
# Apply the custom square function
y = SquareFunction.apply(x)
print("Output y:", y)

# Compute gradients
y.sum().backward()   # Sum to get a scalar output
for backward()
print("Gradient of x:", x.grad)
```

Explanation:

- **Forward Pass:**
  The `forward()` method receives the input tensor, saves it for later use, and returns its square.
- **Backward Pass:**
  The `backward()` method retrieves the input from the context.
  Given the derivative $\frac{d}{dx}x^2=2x$, it computes the gradient for each element and multiplies by **grad_output** (the gradient from subsequent layers).

Advanced Example: Custom Function with Multiple Inputs

Sometimes, you need a function with multiple inputs. Consider a custom function that computes the product of two tensors and, in the backward pass, calculates gradients with respect to both inputs.

Code Example:

```python
python

class MultiplyFunction(torch.autograd.Function):
```

```python
    @staticmethod
    def forward(ctx, a, b):
        # Save both tensors for backward
computation
        ctx.save_for_backward(a, b)
        return a * b

    @staticmethod
    def backward(ctx, grad_output):
        a, b = ctx.saved_tensors
        # Derivative with respect to a: grad_output
* b
        grad_a = grad_output * b
        # Derivative with respect to b: grad_output
* a
        grad_b = grad_output * a
        return grad_a, grad_b

# Use the custom multiply function
a = torch.tensor([3.0, 4.0], requires_grad=True)
b = torch.tensor([5.0, 6.0], requires_grad=True)
c = MultiplyFunction.apply(a, b)
print("Output c:", c)

# Compute gradients by summing the output
c.sum().backward()
print("Gradient of a:", a.grad)
print("Gradient of b:", b.grad)
```

Best Practices and Troubleshooting

- **Context Management:**
  Use `ctx.save_for_backward()` to store only what's necessary. Avoid storing large intermediate results if not needed, as it increases memory usage.
- **Multiple Outputs:**
  If your forward function returns multiple tensors, ensure that your backward returns gradients for each input in the same order.
- **Error Handling:**
  If your backward pass returns None for any input, it implies that the input is not differentiable. Make sure to document and handle such cases clearly.

- **Testing Your Function:**
  Validate your custom function using simple tests (like comparing numerical gradients with analytical ones) to ensure correctness. PyTorch's built-in functions like `torch.autograd.gradcheck()` can be used for this purpose.
- **Performance Considerations:**
  Custom autograd functions are powerful but can be a source of performance bottlenecks if not implemented carefully. Use vectorized operations and minimize Python-level loops.

Exercises

1. **Implement a Custom Cubic Function:**
   Create a custom autograd function that computes $f(x)=x^3$ and verifies that its backward pass correctly computes $3x^2$.
2. **Extend to a Non-Linear Function:**
   Design a custom function for a non-linear operation such as $f(x)=\sin(x)$ where you manually implement the backward pass using $\cos(x)$.
3. **Combine Multiple Operations:**
   Write a custom function that takes two inputs and computes a non-trivial combination, such as $f(a,b)=a^2+\log(b)$, and derive the gradients for both inputs.
4. **Gradient Check:**
   Use `torch.autograd.gradcheck()` to validate the gradients computed by your custom autograd functions. Create a small test case with random input data and verify that the analytical gradients match the numerical approximations.

Custom autograd functions open the door to implementing specialized behaviors and optimizing performance-critical parts of your model. By following best practices and rigorously testing your implementations, you can safely extend PyTorch's automatic differentiation capabilities to meet any advanced need. This section not only reinforces your understanding of PyTorch's dynamic computation graph but also equips you with the tools to innovate in your deep learning research and deployment.

1.4 Efficient Data Loading and Augmentation Techniques

Efficient data loading and real-time augmentation are vital for training deep learning models at scale. Delays in data processing can create bottlenecks, underutilizing powerful GPUs and slowing down training. In this section, we cover how to use PyTorch's `Dataset` and `DataLoader` classes to build efficient data pipelines. We also explore various data augmentation strategies—from basic geometric and color transforms to advanced techniques—to improve model generalization and robustness.

PyTorch Data Loading Fundamentals

The Dataset and DataLoader Classes

- **Custom Dataset:**
  PyTorch provides a base class `torch.utils.data.Dataset` to represent your dataset. By subclassing it, you can define how to load, process, and return individual samples.
- **DataLoader:**
  The `torch.utils.data.DataLoader` wraps your dataset, offering automatic batching, shuffling, and parallel data loading. Key parameters include:
    - `batch_size`: How many samples per batch.
    - `shuffle`: Randomizes the order of samples.
    - `num_workers`: Spawns multiple subprocesses to load data in parallel.
    - `pin_memory`: Locks memory during data transfer to the GPU for faster host-to-device copying.

Code Example: Custom Dataset and DataLoader

```python
python

import os
from PIL import Image
import torch
from torch.utils.data import Dataset, DataLoader
import torchvision.transforms as transforms

class CustomImageDataset(Dataset):
    def __init__(self, image_dir, transform=None):
```

```python
        self.image_dir = image_dir
        self.image_filenames =
os.listdir(image_dir)
        self.transform = transform

    def __len__(self):
        return len(self.image_filenames)

    def __getitem__(self, idx):
        img_path = os.path.join(self.image_dir,
self.image_filenames[idx])
        image = Image.open(img_path).convert("RGB")
        if self.transform:
            image = self.transform(image)
        return image

# Define common augmentation and preprocessing
transforms
transform_pipeline = transforms.Compose([
    transforms.Resize((256, 256)),
    transforms.RandomCrop(224),
    transforms.RandomHorizontalFlip(),
    transforms.ToTensor(),
    transforms.Normalize(mean=[0.485, 0.456,
0.406],
                         std=[0.229, 0.224, 0.225])
])

# Create dataset and data loader
dataset =
CustomImageDataset(image_dir="path/to/images",
transform=transform_pipeline)
data_loader = DataLoader(dataset, batch_size=32,
shuffle=True, num_workers=4, pin_memory=True)

# Example: iterate over a batch
for images in data_loader:
    print("Batch shape:", images.shape)
    break
```

In this example, a custom dataset loads images from a directory and applies a transformation pipeline that includes resizing, cropping, flipping, normalization, and conversion to a tensor. The DataLoader then efficiently batches and shuffles the data, leveraging multiple worker processes and pinned memory to reduce overhead.

Data Augmentation Techniques

Data augmentation is a powerful technique to artificially expand your dataset by applying various transformations. This not only improves generalization but also helps models learn robust features.

Common Augmentation Methods

- **Geometric Transformations:**
  - *Random Cropping, Resizing, and Flipping:*
    Easily achieved using `transforms.RandomCrop`, `transforms.Resize`, and `transforms.RandomHorizontalFlip`.
- **Color Adjustments:**
  - *Random Brightness, Contrast, Saturation:*
    Use `transforms.ColorJitter` to introduce variability in image color properties.
- **Advanced Techniques:**
  - *Mixup and CutMix:*
    Techniques that blend images and their labels to improve model robustness.
  - *RandAugment and AutoAugment:*
    Policies that automatically search for optimal augmentation strategies based on your dataset.

Example: Using Advanced Augmentation

python

```python
# Advanced augmentation pipeline using ColorJitter
and RandomRotation
advanced_transforms = transforms.Compose([
    transforms.Resize((256, 256)),
    transforms.RandomCrop(224),
    transforms.RandomHorizontalFlip(),
    transforms.ColorJitter(brightness=0.2,
contrast=0.2, saturation=0.2),
    transforms.RandomRotation(degrees=15),
```

```
    transforms.ToTensor(),
    transforms.Normalize(mean=[0.485, 0.456,
0.406],
                         std=[0.229, 0.224, 0.225])
])

# Update dataset with advanced transforms
advanced_dataset =
CustomImageDataset(image_dir="path/to/images",
transform=advanced_transforms)
advanced_loader = DataLoader(advanced_dataset,
batch_size=32, shuffle=True, num_workers=4,
pin_memory=True)
```

This pipeline introduces additional variations through color jittering and rotation. Such augmentations are especially valuable in domains where data variability is high or when you need to simulate different real-world conditions.

Best Practices and Troubleshooting

- **Optimizing DataLoader:**
  - Experiment with `num_workers` to find the optimal number for your system.
  - Use `pin_memory=True` when transferring data to GPUs.
  - Preload data into memory if the dataset is small enough to avoid disk I/O bottlenecks.
- **Augmentation Considerations:**
  - Ensure augmentations are relevant to your task; excessive or unrealistic transformations can harm performance.
  - Monitor training to see if augmentation strategies help reduce overfitting.
- **Troubleshooting Tips:**
  - If you encounter slow data loading, try increasing `num_workers` or pre-fetching data.
  - Validate that transformations are applied correctly by visualizing sample batches using `matplotlib`.

Hands-On Code Example: Visualizing Augmented Data

```python
```

```
import matplotlib.pyplot as plt

# Get a batch of augmented images
images, _ = next(iter(data_loader))   # Assuming
dataset returns (image, label); here label is
optional
images = images.cpu().numpy().transpose((0, 2, 3,
1))   # Convert to numpy array for visualization

# Denormalize images for display
mean = [0.485, 0.456, 0.406]
std = [0.229, 0.224, 0.225]
images = images * std + mean

# Display a few images
fig, axes = plt.subplots(1, 5, figsize=(15, 3))
for i in range(5):
    axes[i].imshow(images[i])
    axes[i].axis("off")
plt.show()
```

This snippet visualizes a few samples from the DataLoader, allowing you to inspect the effect of your augmentation pipeline.

Exercises

1. **Custom Dataset Challenge:**
   Create a custom dataset for a different modality (e.g., audio or text) and implement a custom data loading pipeline with appropriate transformations.
2. **Augmentation Experiment:**
   Modify the augmentation pipeline to include one advanced technique (such as RandomRotation or ColorJitter). Compare model performance (e.g., training loss and accuracy) with and without the advanced augmentation on a small dataset.
3. **DataLoader Performance Benchmark:**
   Write a script to experiment with different num_workers values. Measure the time taken to iterate through an epoch and determine the optimal setting for your hardware.
4. **Visualization Task:**
   Write a visualization script to display before-and-after augmentation

images from your dataset. This helps in verifying that your transformations are applied correctly.

This section on efficient data loading and augmentation techniques ensures that your training pipelines are robust, scalable, and optimized for performance. By leveraging these strategies, you can reduce training time and improve model generalization—key elements for building state-of-the-art deep learning solutions.

1.5 Mixed Precision and Accelerated Training

As models grow larger and more complex, the computational and memory demands during training can become significant bottlenecks. **Mixed precision training** offers an effective solution by using lower-precision (FP16) arithmetic where possible while retaining FP32 for parts of the computation that require higher precision. This not only reduces memory usage but also speeds up training, especially on modern GPUs equipped with Tensor Cores. Additionally, accelerated training techniques—such as JIT compilation and distributed training—further enhance performance. In this section, we focus on mixed precision training using PyTorch's `torch.cuda.amp` module and discuss strategies for accelerating training.

What is Mixed Precision Training?

Mixed precision training leverages both 16-bit (FP16) and 32-bit (FP32) floating point types:

- **FP16 (Half Precision):**
  Uses half the memory of FP32 and can take advantage of specialized hardware (e.g., NVIDIA Tensor Cores) to perform computations faster.
- **FP32 (Single Precision):**
  Maintains the accuracy and numerical stability for operations that are sensitive to precision.

By using FP16 where feasible (for example, in intermediate activations) and keeping critical parts like weight updates in FP32, you achieve a balance between performance and model fidelity.

PyTorch AMP: Key Components

PyTorch's Automatic Mixed Precision (AMP) simplifies integrating mixed precision into your training loop with two main components:

1. **Autocast:**
   A context manager (`torch.cuda.amp.autocast()`) that automatically casts operations to FP16 when appropriate, while keeping operations in FP32 where needed.
2. **GradScaler:**
   A utility (`torch.cuda.amp.GradScaler`) that scales the loss before backpropagation to prevent underflow in gradients. It then unscales gradients during the optimizer step and adjusts the scaling factor dynamically.

Implementing Mixed Precision Training

Below is a practical example of integrating AMP into a typical training loop. This example demonstrates how to modify your standard training code with minimal changes while leveraging the performance benefits of mixed precision.

Code Example: Training Loop with AMP

```python
import torch
from torch import nn, optim
from torch.cuda.amp import autocast, GradScaler

# Assume we have a simple model, loss function, and
data loader
model = nn.Linear(10, 1)
model.to('cuda' if torch.cuda.is_available() else
'cpu')
loss_fn = nn.MSELoss()
optimizer = optim.Adam(model.parameters(),
lr=0.001)

# Create a dummy DataLoader (replace with your
actual data)
```

```python
data = torch.randn(128, 10)  # 128 samples, 10
features
targets = torch.randn(128, 1)
dataset = torch.utils.data.TensorDataset(data,
targets)
data_loader = torch.utils.data.DataLoader(dataset,
batch_size=32, shuffle=True)

# Initialize GradScaler for AMP
scaler = GradScaler()

device = torch.device("cuda" if
torch.cuda.is_available() else "cpu")

# Training loop with AMP
num_epochs = 5
for epoch in range(num_epochs):
    model.train()
    epoch_loss = 0.0
    for batch_data, batch_targets in data_loader:
        batch_data, batch_targets =
batch_data.to(device), batch_targets.to(device)

        optimizer.zero_grad()

        # Forward pass within autocast context for
mixed precision
        with autocast():
            outputs = model(batch_data)
            loss = loss_fn(outputs, batch_targets)

        # Backward pass with gradient scaling
        scaler.scale(loss).backward()
        scaler.step(optimizer)
        scaler.update()

        epoch_loss += loss.item()

    print(f"Epoch {epoch+1}/{num_epochs}, Loss:
{epoch_loss/len(data_loader):.4f}")
```

Explanation:

- **Autocast Context:**
  Wrapping the forward pass with `with autocast():` allows PyTorch to automatically use FP16 where beneficial. This can significantly speed up operations like matrix multiplications on supported hardware.
- **Gradient Scaling:**
  The loss is scaled before calling `.backward()` to avoid issues with very small gradient values that might occur in FP16. The `GradScaler` handles scaling, unscaling, and checks for numerical issues before updating the optimizer.
- **Seamless Integration:**
  The rest of the training loop remains largely unchanged, making it straightforward to convert an existing FP32 training loop to mixed precision.

Accelerated Training Techniques Beyond AMP

While AMP is a major boost for training speed and efficiency, consider additional acceleration strategies:

- **Just-In-Time (JIT) Compilation:**
  Use `torch.jit.script` to convert your models into optimized graph representations that can run faster, especially in production environments.
- **Distributed Training:**
  Leverage PyTorch's `DistributedDataParallel` (DDP) to scale training across multiple GPUs or nodes. This is particularly beneficial when training large models or working with very large datasets.
- **Profiling and Optimization:**
  Use PyTorch's profiling tools (`torch.profiler`) to identify bottlenecks in your training loop. Optimize data loading, model architecture, or even specific operations based on the profiler's insights.

Best Practices and Troubleshooting

- **Monitor Numerical Stability:**
  Always monitor for NaN or Inf values in your loss or gradients. The

`GradScaler` is designed to help with this, but further debugging may require careful inspection of model outputs.

- **Benchmark and Compare:**
  Run side-by-side benchmarks with and without AMP to quantify the speedup and memory benefits. Use tools like `torch.cuda.synchronize()` when timing GPU operations accurately.
- **Keep Critical Operations in FP32:**
  Not all operations are suited for FP16. For example, reductions and operations that are highly sensitive to precision should remain in FP32. Trust the AMP's autocasting but also monitor your model's performance closely.
- **Combine with Other Techniques:**
  Don't rely solely on mixed precision. Combine it with data parallelism or distributed training to fully utilize hardware capabilities.

Exercises

1. **AMP Implementation Challenge:**
   Modify an existing training loop for a convolutional neural network to integrate AMP. Compare the training speed and memory usage before and after enabling mixed precision.
2. **Numerical Stability Check:**
   Implement a small experiment to test how the loss scaling mechanism of GradScaler handles very small gradient values. Try inducing an underflow scenario and observe how GradScaler adapts.
3. **Benchmarking Exercise:**
   Write a script to measure the performance of a heavy matrix multiplication operation using FP32 versus FP16. Use `torch.cuda.synchronize()` to accurately time the operations and report the speedup factor.
4. **JIT and AMP Combination:**
   Convert a simple model to its JIT-scripted version using `torch.jit.script` and run training with AMP. Evaluate any further speedup compared to using AMP alone.

Mixed precision training, enabled by AMP, is a powerful technique for accelerating deep learning workflows, reducing memory usage, and making efficient use of modern GPU hardware. Combined with other accelerated training methods such as JIT compilation and distributed training, you can significantly cut down training time while maintaining or even improving model performance. Mastering these techniques is essential for advanced practitioners looking to push the boundaries of deep learning model training.

1.6 Practical Exercise: Optimizing Training Pipelines

An optimized training pipeline is critical for reducing training time, making efficient use of hardware resources, and ensuring model reproducibility. In this exercise, you'll take a baseline training loop and apply a series of improvements—optimizing data loading, leveraging mixed precision training, and employing other advanced techniques—to build a robust, high-performance pipeline.

This exercise is designed for advanced practitioners, so expect to:

- Integrate efficient data loading using PyTorch's `DataLoader`
- Implement mixed precision training with AMP
- Utilize best practices for gradient management and performance profiling
- Incorporate strategies for model checkpointing and troubleshooting

Exercise Overview

You are provided with a baseline training script that trains a simple neural network on a synthetic dataset. Your task is to:

1. **Improve Data Loading:**
    - Use multiple workers and pin memory to minimize CPU-GPU transfer bottlenecks.
2. **Implement Mixed Precision Training:**
    - Utilize `torch.cuda.amp.autocast()` and `GradScaler` to accelerate computations while maintaining numerical stability.
3. **Optimize the Training Loop:**
    - Incorporate gradient accumulation (if necessary), checkpointing, and performance profiling to monitor improvements.
4. **Benchmark and Troubleshoot:**

o Measure the training time before and after optimizations, analyze GPU utilization, and troubleshoot any performance bottlenecks.

Baseline Code

Below is a simple baseline training loop. Your exercise is to enhance this code with the improvements listed above.

python

```python
import torch
import torch.nn as nn
import torch.optim as optim
from torch.utils.data import DataLoader,
TensorDataset
import time

# --- Baseline Setup ---
# Create a synthetic dataset (e.g., regression
task: y = 2x - 1 with noise)
torch.manual_seed(42)
X = torch.linspace(-1, 1, steps=1000).unsqueeze(1)
y = 2 * X - 1 + 0.1 * torch.randn_like(X)
dataset = TensorDataset(X, y)
baseline_loader = DataLoader(dataset,
batch_size=32, shuffle=True)

# Define a simple model
model = nn.Sequential(nn.Linear(1, 10), nn.ReLU(),
nn.Linear(10, 1))
loss_fn = nn.MSELoss()
optimizer = optim.SGD(model.parameters(), lr=0.01)

# Baseline training loop (without optimizations)
num_epochs = 5
start_time = time.time()
for epoch in range(num_epochs):
```

```python
    model.train()
    epoch_loss = 0.0
    for batch_X, batch_y in baseline_loader:
        optimizer.zero_grad()
        outputs = model(batch_X)
        loss = loss_fn(outputs, batch_y)
        loss.backward()
        optimizer.step()
        epoch_loss += loss.item()
    print(f"Epoch {epoch+1}: Loss =
{epoch_loss/len(baseline_loader):.4f}")
print("Baseline training time: {:.2f}
seconds".format(time.time() - start_time))
```

Step-by-Step Optimization

1. Improving Data Loading

- **Use multiple workers:** Increase `num_workers` in DataLoader.
- **Pin memory:** Set `pin_memory=True` to speed up host-to-device transfers.

2. Implementing Mixed Precision Training

- Wrap the forward pass in `torch.cuda.amp.autocast()`.
- Use a `GradScaler` to safely handle the backward pass.

3. Optimizing the Training Loop

- Monitor training time using `torch.cuda.synchronize()` (if using GPU).
- Optionally, integrate a checkpointing mechanism to save the best model during training.

Optimized Training Code Example

Below is an enhanced version of the training loop incorporating the improvements.

```python
python

import torch
```

```python
import torch.nn as nn
import torch.optim as optim
from torch.utils.data import DataLoader,
TensorDataset
from torch.cuda.amp import autocast, GradScaler
import time

# --- Optimized Setup ---
torch.manual_seed(42)
device = torch.device("cuda" if
torch.cuda.is_available() else "cpu")

# Create a synthetic dataset
X = torch.linspace(-1, 1, steps=1000).unsqueeze(1)
y = 2 * X - 1 + 0.1 * torch.randn_like(X)
dataset = TensorDataset(X, y)

# Optimized DataLoader: multiple workers and pinned
memory
optimized_loader = DataLoader(dataset,
batch_size=32, shuffle=True, num_workers=4,
pin_memory=True)

# Define a simple model and move it to the device
model = nn.Sequential(nn.Linear(1, 10), nn.ReLU(),
nn.Linear(10, 1))
model.to(device)

loss_fn = nn.MSELoss()
optimizer = optim.SGD(model.parameters(), lr=0.01)

# Initialize GradScaler for mixed precision
training
scaler = GradScaler()

# Optimized training loop
num_epochs = 5
start_time = time.time()

for epoch in range(num_epochs):
    model.train()
    epoch_loss = 0.0
```

```python
    for batch_X, batch_y in optimized_loader:
        # Move data to GPU if available
        batch_X, batch_y = batch_X.to(device,
non_blocking=True), batch_y.to(device,
non_blocking=True)

        optimizer.zero_grad()

        # Mixed precision forward pass
        with autocast():
            outputs = model(batch_X)
            loss = loss_fn(outputs, batch_y)

        # Backward pass with gradient scaling
        scaler.scale(loss).backward()
        scaler.step(optimizer)
        scaler.update()

        epoch_loss += loss.item()

    # Optionally: synchronize GPU to ensure
accurate timing
    if device.type == "cuda":
        torch.cuda.synchronize()

    print(f"Epoch {epoch+1}: Loss =
{epoch_loss/len(optimized_loader):.4f}")

print("Optimized training time: {:.2f}
seconds".format(time.time() - start_time))
```

Key Enhancements Explained:

- **DataLoader Improvements:**
  `num_workers=4` allows parallel data loading, and
  `pin_memory=True` accelerates the data transfer from CPU to
  GPU.
- **Mixed Precision:**
  The `autocast()` context manager and `GradScaler` enable
  mixed precision, reducing memory footprint and increasing
  throughput.

- **Device Efficiency:**
  Moving data using `to(device, non_blocking=True)` leverages pinned memory for efficient transfers, and synchronizing the GPU ensures timing accuracy.

Advanced Optimization Strategies

For further improvements, consider the following strategies:

- **Gradient Accumulation:**
  Useful when batch sizes are limited by GPU memory.
- **Model Checkpointing:**
  Save the best model during training to prevent data loss and enable later fine-tuning.
- **Profiling:**
  Utilize `torch.profiler` or similar tools to identify bottlenecks.
- **Distributed Training:**
  Scale training across multiple GPUs or nodes using `DistributedDataParallel`.

Troubleshooting and Performance Metrics

- **Benchmarking:**
  Compare training time, memory usage, and model accuracy between baseline and optimized versions.
- **Debugging Bottlenecks:**
  If the GPU remains underutilized, inspect data loading and ensure that preprocessing isn't causing delays.
- **Monitoring:**
  Use tools like `nvidia-smi` to monitor GPU memory and compute utilization during training.

Exercises

1. **Pipeline Profiling:**
   Extend the optimized training code to include profiling using

`torch.profiler`. Identify which parts of your pipeline (data loading, forward pass, backward pass) take the most time.

2. **Gradient Accumulation:**
   Modify the optimized code to perform gradient accumulation over multiple mini-batches. Analyze how this affects memory usage and training stability.

3. **Checkpointing Mechanism:**
   Integrate a checkpointing mechanism to save the model with the lowest validation loss during training. Evaluate the trade-offs between checkpointing frequency and training speed.

4. **Distributed Training:**
   If you have access to multiple GPUs, refactor the optimized training loop to use
   `torch.nn.parallel.DistributedDataParallel`.
   Benchmark the speedup compared to a single GPU.

Optimizing your training pipeline is essential for reducing training time and maximizing the utilization of your hardware resources. This exercise guides you through practical improvements—from efficient data loading and mixed precision training to advanced performance profiling. By implementing these strategies, you'll not only enhance training speed but also build a more robust and scalable deep learning workflow.

Chapter 2: Building and Optimizing CNN Architectures

2.1 Deep Dive into Advanced CNNs (ResNet, EfficientNet, ConvNeXt)

Modern deep learning has seen a surge of advanced CNN architectures that push the boundaries of accuracy and efficiency. In this section, we take a deep dive into three influential architectures:

- **ResNet** – Pioneering residual connections to mitigate vanishing gradients in very deep networks.
- **EfficientNet** – Introducing compound scaling to balance network depth, width, and resolution efficiently.
- **ConvNeXt** – Re-imagining CNN design by incorporating ideas from transformer architectures for modern vision tasks.

These architectures have transformed the way we build models for computer vision tasks, from image classification to object detection. We will explore their innovations, architectural design, and practical strategies to optimize them for real-world applications.

ResNet: Revolutionizing Deep Learning with Residual Connections

Key Concepts

- **Residual Learning:**
  ResNet introduces skip (or shortcut) connections that bypass one or more layers. This helps overcome the vanishing gradient problem, making it possible to train very deep networks.
- **Architecture Overview:**
  A typical ResNet block adds the input directly to the output of a few convolutional layers (often two), then applies a non-linear activation. This "identity mapping" ensures that even if the added layers learn sub-optimal transformations, the network can easily default to an identity function.

Practical Considerations

- **Fine-Tuning Pre-trained Models:**
  ResNet variants (e.g., ResNet-50, ResNet-101) are available pre-trained on large-scale datasets. Fine-tuning these models for specific tasks can dramatically reduce training time while maintaining high performance.
- **Optimization Strategies:**
  Use techniques such as learning rate scheduling, data augmentation, and batch normalization tuning to maximize performance.

Code Example: Loading and Fine-Tuning a ResNet Model

python

```python
import torch
import torch.nn as nn
from torchvision import models, transforms
from torch.utils.data import DataLoader, Dataset
from PIL import Image

# Load a pre-trained ResNet-50 model
resnet_model = models.resnet50(pretrained=True)
# Replace the final fully-connected layer to match
the number of classes (e.g., 10)
num_features = resnet_model.fc.in_features
resnet_model.fc = nn.Linear(num_features, 10)
resnet_model = resnet_model.to('cuda' if
torch.cuda.is_available() else 'cpu')

# Define a simple transformation pipeline
transform_pipeline = transforms.Compose([
    transforms.Resize(256),
    transforms.CenterCrop(224),
    transforms.ToTensor(),
    transforms.Normalize(mean=[0.485, 0.456,
0.406],
                         std=[0.229, 0.224, 0.225])
])

# Dummy dataset class (replace with your own)
class CustomImageDataset(Dataset):
```

```python
    def __init__(self, image_paths, transform):
        self.image_paths = image_paths
        self.transform = transform
    def __len__(self):
        return len(self.image_paths)
    def __getitem__(self, idx):
        img =
Image.open(self.image_paths[idx]).convert("RGB")
        return self.transform(img)

# Create DataLoader (assumes you have a list of
image file paths)
# image_paths = [...]  # your list of image paths
# dataset = CustomImageDataset(image_paths,
transform_pipeline)
# loader = DataLoader(dataset, batch_size=32,
shuffle=True, num_workers=4, pin_memory=True)
```

EfficientNet: Scaling Up CNNs with Compound Scaling

Key Concepts

- **Compound Scaling:**
  EfficientNet systematically scales network depth, width, and resolution using a compound coefficient. This method achieves state-of-the-art accuracy while minimizing model size and computational cost.
- **Architecture Highlights:**
  EfficientNet models, such as EfficientNet-B0 through B7, offer a spectrum of architectures optimized for various resource constraints. They utilize mobile inverted bottleneck convolution (MBConv) blocks and squeeze-and-excitation modules.

Practical Considerations

- **Resource-Conscious Training:**
  Due to its efficiency, EfficientNet is well-suited for environments with limited compute resources. Use pre-trained EfficientNet models available through libraries like TIMM for rapid prototyping.

- **Hyperparameter Tuning:**
  Fine-tune compound scaling factors when working with custom datasets to balance performance and resource usage.

Code Example: Instantiating an EfficientNet Model

```python
python

import timm

# Load a pre-trained EfficientNet-B3 model from the
TIMM library
efficientnet_model =
timm.create_model('efficientnet_b3',
pretrained=True)
# Adjust the classifier for the target number of
classes (e.g., 10)
efficientnet_model.classifier =
nn.Linear(efficientnet_model.classifier.in_features
, 10)
efficientnet_model = efficientnet_model.to('cuda'
if torch.cuda.is_available() else 'cpu')
```

ConvNeXt: Modernizing CNN Design

Key Concepts

- **Inspired by Transformers:**
  ConvNeXt revisits classic CNN design, modernizing it with design principles borrowed from vision transformers. It improves on factors like normalization, activation functions, and architectural simplicity.
- **Architecture Improvements:**
  ConvNeXt uses large kernel sizes, layer normalization, and simple residual connections. These changes lead to better performance on large-scale datasets while maintaining the computational benefits of CNNs.

Practical Considerations

- **State-of-the-Art Performance:**
  ConvNeXt achieves competitive performance on benchmark datasets.
  It is well-suited for tasks requiring high accuracy and efficiency.
- **Ease of Integration:**
  Similar to ResNet and EfficientNet, pre-trained ConvNeXt models
  are available for fine-tuning. They can serve as strong backbones for
  detection, segmentation, and classification tasks.

Code Example: Loading a ConvNeXt Model

python

```
# Load a pre-trained ConvNeXt-T model (tiny
version) from TIMM
convnext_model = timm.create_model('convnext_tiny',
pretrained=True)
# Modify the classifier to output the desired
number of classes (e.g., 10)
convnext_model.head.fc =
nn.Linear(convnext_model.head.fc.in_features, 10)
convnext_model = convnext_model.to('cuda' if
torch.cuda.is_available() else 'cpu')
```

Comparative Analysis and Best Practices

When to Choose Which Architecture?

- **ResNet:**
  Ideal for tasks requiring very deep networks with robust training due
  to residual connections. Excellent for transfer learning.
- **EfficientNet:**
  Best when resource constraints are critical. Its compound scaling
  method delivers high accuracy with lower parameter counts and
  FLOPs.
- **ConvNeXt:**
  A strong candidate for state-of-the-art performance on modern
  datasets, blending the best of CNN efficiency with transformer-
  inspired design improvements.

Optimization Strategies

- **Fine-Tuning:**
  Start with pre-trained weights and fine-tune on your target dataset. Use differential learning rates if necessary.
- **Data Augmentation and Regularization:**
  Employ advanced augmentation techniques (e.g., Mixup, CutMix) and regularization (e.g., dropout, weight decay) to boost model generalization.
- **Hyperparameter Tuning:**
  Experiment with learning rate schedules, batch sizes, and optimizer settings to fully exploit each architecture's strengths.
- **Monitoring and Debugging:**
  Utilize PyTorch's profiling tools and visualization libraries (e.g., TensorBoard) to track model performance and diagnose training bottlenecks.

Hands-On Code Exercise

1. **Experiment with Fine-Tuning:**
   Use a pre-trained ResNet-50, EfficientNet-B3, or ConvNeXt model to fine-tune on a custom image classification dataset. Compare validation accuracies, training times, and GPU utilization.
2. **Layer Visualization:**
   Extract and visualize intermediate feature maps from different layers. This helps in understanding how each architecture processes images.
3. **Model Comparison:**
   Create a script that loads all three models, feeds the same input through each, and compares their outputs. This exercise will help you appreciate the design differences in feature extraction and representation.

Exercises

1. **Build Your Own Residual Block:**
   Implement a custom residual block from scratch and integrate it into a small CNN. Compare its performance with a standard ResNet block.

2. **Compound Scaling Experiment:**
   Experiment with scaling the EfficientNet architecture manually (adjusting depth, width, and resolution) and measure the trade-offs in performance and computational cost.
3. **Analyze ConvNeXt Modifications:**
   Modify a ConvNeXt block by replacing layer normalization with batch normalization. Observe the changes in training dynamics and model performance.
4. **Performance Benchmark:**
   Write a script to measure inference times of each model (ResNet, EfficientNet, ConvNeXt) on the same hardware. Discuss how architectural differences affect latency and throughput.

This deep dive into advanced CNN architectures has covered the evolution from ResNet's residual connections, through EfficientNet's compound scaling, to ConvNeXt's modern design improvements. By understanding their core principles, practical applications, and optimization strategies, you're well-equipped to choose and fine-tune the right CNN architecture for your advanced computer vision tasks.

2.2 Transfer Learning and Custom Fine-tuning

Training deep neural networks from scratch can be computationally expensive and require vast amounts of labeled data. **Transfer learning** mitigates these challenges by leveraging models pre-trained on large datasets (e.g., ImageNet) to serve as feature extractors or starting points for new tasks. **Custom fine-tuning** involves adjusting these pre-trained models to better fit your target domain. This section will guide you through the principles behind transfer learning, demonstrate how to customize and fine-tune networks (such as ResNet, EfficientNet, or ConvNeXt), and provide practical strategies to optimize performance.

Key Concepts in Transfer Learning

What is Transfer Learning?

- **Definition:**
  Transfer learning involves using a model pre-trained on a large, generic dataset and adapting it for a specific task or domain. This

method speeds up convergence and often yields better performance when your target dataset is limited.

- **Approaches:**
  - **Feature Extraction:** Freeze the majority of the pre-trained model and use it to extract features; only the final classifier layers are retrained.
  - **Fine-Tuning:** Unfreeze part or all of the pre-trained network and retrain on the new dataset to allow for domain-specific adjustments.

Advantages of Transfer Learning

- **Reduced Training Time:**
  With pre-trained weights, you start from a learned feature space rather than random initialization.
- **Improved Generalization:**
  Pre-trained models capture robust features that often generalize well to different tasks.
- **Resource Efficiency:**
  Fine-tuning a pre-trained model is computationally less expensive than training a deep network from scratch.

Custom Fine-Tuning Strategies

Freezing and Unfreezing Layers

- **Freezing Layers:**
  Initially, you may freeze the early layers of the network, which capture general features (e.g., edges, textures). Only retrain the later layers or the classifier head.
- **Gradual Unfreezing:**
  In some scenarios, progressively unfreeze additional layers as training progresses. This allows for a smooth adaptation to the new domain while retaining useful learned features.

Differential Learning Rates

- **Different Learning Rates for Different Layers:**
  Apply lower learning rates to pre-trained layers and higher rates to newly added layers. This prevents drastic changes to already useful features while allowing the classifier to learn more quickly.

Customizing the Classifier

- **Replacing the Final Layers:**
  Most pre-trained models are designed for large-scale classification (e.g., 1000 classes on ImageNet). Replace these final layers with new fully connected layers tailored to your specific number of classes.
- **Adding Regularization:**
  Integrate dropout, batch normalization, or weight decay to reduce overfitting during fine-tuning.

Hands-On Code Example

Below is an example of fine-tuning a pre-trained ResNet-50 model for a custom 10-class classification task. The code demonstrates how to freeze early layers, replace the classifier head, apply differential learning rates, and use a learning rate scheduler.

```python
import torch
import torch.nn as nn
import torch.optim as optim
from torchvision import models, transforms
from torch.utils.data import DataLoader, Dataset
from PIL import Image
import os

# Define a custom dataset (replace with your own
image paths and labels)
class CustomImageDataset(Dataset):
    def __init__(self, image_dir, transform=None):
        self.image_dir = image_dir
        self.image_filenames =
os.listdir(image_dir)
        self.transform = transform
    def __len__(self):
        return len(self.image_filenames)
    def __getitem__(self, idx):
        img_path = os.path.join(self.image_dir,
self.image_filenames[idx])
        image = Image.open(img_path).convert("RGB")
        if self.transform:
```

```python
        image = self.transform(image)
        # Dummy label: in practice, load your label
here
        label = 0
        return image, label

# Transformation pipeline
transform_pipeline = transforms.Compose([
    transforms.Resize(256),
    transforms.CenterCrop(224),
    transforms.ToTensor(),
    transforms.Normalize(mean=[0.485, 0.456,
0.406],
                         std=[0.229, 0.224, 0.225])
])

# Instantiate dataset and dataloader
# image_dir = "path/to/images"
# dataset = CustomImageDataset(image_dir,
transform_pipeline)
# loader = DataLoader(dataset, batch_size=32,
shuffle=True, num_workers=4, pin_memory=True)

# Load a pre-trained ResNet-50 model
model = models.resnet50(pretrained=True)

# Freeze all layers except the final fully
connected layer
for param in model.parameters():
    param.requires_grad = False

# Replace the final fully connected layer to adapt
to 10 classes
num_features = model.fc.in_features
model.fc = nn.Linear(num_features, 10)

# Only parameters of the new classifier are
trainable
trainable_params = model.fc.parameters()

# Move model to device
```

```python
device = torch.device("cuda" if
torch.cuda.is_available() else "cpu")
model.to(device)

# Define loss and optimizer with differential
learning rates
loss_fn = nn.CrossEntropyLoss()
optimizer = optim.Adam(trainable_params, lr=1e-3)

# Optionally, use a learning rate scheduler
scheduler = optim.lr_scheduler.StepLR(optimizer,
step_size=7, gamma=0.1)

# Example training loop
num_epochs = 5
for epoch in range(num_epochs):
    model.train()
    running_loss = 0.0
    for images, labels in loader:  # Uncomment when
using a real DataLoader
        images, labels = images.to(device),
labels.to(device)
        optimizer.zero_grad()
        outputs = model(images)
        loss = loss_fn(outputs, labels)
        loss.backward()
        optimizer.step()
        running_loss += loss.item()

    scheduler.step()
    print(f"Epoch {epoch+1}/{num_epochs}, Loss:
{running_loss/len(loader):.4f}")

# Optionally, you can unfreeze additional layers
and fine-tune the entire model
```

Best Practices and Troubleshooting

- **Monitor Overfitting:**
  Fine-tuning can lead to overfitting, especially on small datasets. Use validation sets, early stopping, and regularization techniques.

- **Experiment with Freezing:**
  Try different configurations: freeze all layers, freeze only early layers, or unfreeze everything. Compare validation performance to determine the optimal strategy.
- **Differential Learning Rates:**
  Use optimizers that allow setting different learning rates for different parameter groups. This is essential when fine-tuning pre-trained weights.
- **Gradual Unfreezing:**
  Consider gradually unfreezing layers if initial training stagnates. This can help adapt low-level features to the new domain without destabilizing learning.
- **Checkpointing:**
  Save model checkpoints during fine-tuning to avoid losing progress and enable rollback if overfitting occurs.

Exercises

1. **Fine-Tuning Variations:**
   Experiment with different freezing strategies on a pre-trained model (e.g., freeze all layers vs. unfreeze the last two blocks). Evaluate and compare validation accuracies.
2. **Differential Learning Rates:**
   Implement an optimizer that uses a lower learning rate for pre-trained layers and a higher rate for the classifier. Observe the impact on convergence speed and accuracy.
3. **Custom Classifier Design:**
   Replace the final layer of a pre-trained EfficientNet or ConvNeXt model with a custom multi-layer classifier. Compare its performance with a single-layer classifier.
4. **Visualizing Feature Maps:**
   After fine-tuning, visualize intermediate feature maps from frozen and unfrozen layers. Analyze how fine-tuning alters the learned representations.
5. **Domain Adaptation Experiment:**
   Use a pre-trained model fine-tuned on one dataset and test it on a related domain. Explore techniques to further adapt the model, such as domain-specific data augmentation.

Transfer learning combined with custom fine-tuning is a powerful approach to rapidly develop high-performing models even when data is scarce. By leveraging pre-trained models and applying smart fine-tuning strategies, you can significantly reduce training time and improve accuracy for domain-specific tasks. Mastering these techniques is essential for advanced practitioners who aim to build state-of-the-art solutions with limited resources.

2.3 CNN Architectures for Real-world Tasks (Medical Imaging, Object Detection, Segmentation)

Real-world computer vision applications demand robust and adaptable CNN architectures that can handle unique challenges. In this section, we explore three primary application areas:

- **Medical Imaging:** Requires high sensitivity, robustness to noise, and sometimes multi-modal integration.
- **Object Detection:** Involves locating and classifying multiple objects within an image, often in real time.
- **Segmentation:** Focuses on pixel-level classification, delineating object boundaries for tasks such as autonomous driving or biomedical image analysis.

For each domain, we will discuss suitable architectures, adaptation strategies, and practical tips for fine-tuning and deployment. Hands-on code examples and exercises are provided to reinforce advanced techniques and best practices.

Medical Imaging

Key Considerations

- **Data Challenges:**
  Medical images often have high resolution, low contrast, and subtle abnormalities. Data may come from different modalities (e.g., MRI, CT, X-ray) and can be scarce due to privacy issues.
- **Architecture Choices:**

- Classification: Models like ResNet, DenseNet, and EfficientNet have been successfully used for diagnostic classification.
- Segmentation: U-Net and its variants are widely adopted due to their encoder–decoder architecture that captures fine-grained details.

Practical Strategies

- **Pre-training and Fine-tuning:**
  Leverage pre-trained models on large-scale natural image datasets and adapt them with domain-specific data.
- **Data Augmentation:**
  Use rotation, scaling, and intensity shifts to simulate variability in medical scans.
- **Attention Mechanisms:**
  Integrate attention layers to help the model focus on regions of interest (e.g., lesions, tumors).

Code Example: U-Net for Medical Image Segmentation

```python
import torch
import torch.nn as nn
import torch.nn.functional as F

class UNetBlock(nn.Module):
    def __init__(self, in_channels, out_channels):
        super(UNetBlock, self).__init__()
        self.conv1 = nn.Conv2d(in_channels, out_channels, kernel_size=3, padding=1)
        self.conv2 = nn.Conv2d(out_channels, out_channels, kernel_size=3, padding=1)
        self.relu = nn.ReLU(inplace=True)

    def forward(self, x):
        x = self.relu(self.conv1(x))
        x = self.relu(self.conv2(x))
        return x

class UNet(nn.Module):
```

```python
    def __init__(self, in_channels=1,
out_channels=1, features=[64, 128, 256, 512]):
        super(UNet, self).__init__()
        self.downs = nn.ModuleList()
        self.ups = nn.ModuleList()

        # Down-sampling path
        for feature in features:

self.downs.append(UNetBlock(in_channels, feature))
            in_channels = feature

        # Up-sampling path
        for feature in reversed(features):

self.ups.append(nn.ConvTranspose2d(feature*2,
feature, kernel_size=2, stride=2))
            self.ups.append(UNetBlock(feature*2,
feature))

        self.bottleneck = UNetBlock(features[-1],
features[-1]*2)
        self.final_conv = nn.Conv2d(features[0],
out_channels, kernel_size=1)

    def forward(self, x):
        skip_connections = []
        for down in self.downs:
            x = down(x)
            skip_connections.append(x)
            x = F.max_pool2d(x, kernel_size=2,
stride=2)

        x = self.bottleneck(x)
        skip_connections = skip_connections[::-1]

        for idx in range(0, len(self.ups), 2):
            x = self.ups[idx](x)
            skip_connection =
skip_connections[idx//2]
            if x.shape != skip_connection.shape:
```

```
                x = F.interpolate(x,
size=skip_connection.shape[2:])
            x = torch.cat((skip_connection, x),
dim=1)
            x = self.ups[idx+1](x)
        return self.final_conv(x)

# Example usage:
device = torch.device("cuda" if
torch.cuda.is_available() else "cpu")
model = UNet(in_channels=1,
out_channels=1).to(device)
dummy_input = torch.randn((1, 1, 256,
256)).to(device)
output = model(dummy_input)
print("U-Net output shape:", output.shape)
```

Object Detection

Key Considerations

- **Multi-Object Scenarios:**
  Object detection requires identifying and localizing multiple objects, which can be challenging in cluttered or dynamic scenes.
- **Popular Architectures:**
  o **Faster R-CNN:** Uses region proposal networks (RPNs) combined with CNNs for accurate detection.
  o **YOLO (You Only Look Once):** Known for real-time detection speed by treating detection as a regression problem.
  o **SSD (Single Shot MultiBox Detector):** Balances speed and accuracy by predicting object boundaries in one pass.

Practical Strategies

- **Pre-trained Models:**
  Utilize pre-trained object detection models available in libraries like Torchvision.
- **Anchor Boxes and IoU Thresholds:**
  Fine-tune anchor box sizes and Intersection over Union (IoU) thresholds to match your dataset.

- **Data Augmentation:**
  Apply random crops, flips, and photometric distortions to improve robustness.

Code Example: Fine-Tuning a Pre-trained Faster R-CNN

```python
import torchvision
from torchvision.models.detection.faster_rcnn
import FastRCNNPredictor

# Load a pre-trained Faster R-CNN model
model =
torchvision.models.detection.fasterrcnn_resnet50_fp
n(pretrained=True)

# Replace the classifier with a new one for your
dataset (e.g., 5 classes: background + 4 classes)
num_classes = 5  # example: background + 4 classes
in_features =
model.roi_heads.box_predictor.cls_score.in_features
model.roi_heads.box_predictor =
FastRCNNPredictor(in_features, num_classes)

device = torch.device("cuda" if
torch.cuda.is_available() else "cpu")
model.to(device)

# Now model is ready to be fine-tuned on your
custom dataset.
```

Segmentation

Key Considerations

- **Pixel-level Predictions:**
  Segmentation tasks require assigning a class label to every pixel, necessitating architectures that capture both local and global context.
- **Popular Architectures:**

- **Fully Convolutional Networks (FCN):** Adapt classification networks to perform pixel-wise prediction.
- **DeepLab:** Utilizes atrous convolution and conditional random fields (CRFs) to refine boundaries.
- **U-Net:** Particularly effective in medical imaging, with its encoder-decoder structure that recovers spatial resolution.

Practical Strategies

- **Loss Functions:**
  Use specialized loss functions like Dice loss, Jaccard loss, or a combination of cross-entropy and boundary-aware losses.
- **Multi-scale Feature Fusion:**
  Combine features from different layers to capture both high-level semantics and fine details.
- **Post-processing:**
  Techniques such as Conditional Random Fields (CRF) may be applied to refine segmentation outputs.

Code Example: Using DeepLabV3 for Semantic Segmentation

```python
import torchvision
import torch.nn as nn

# Load a pre-trained DeepLabV3 model with a ResNet-50 backbone
model =
torchvision.models.segmentation.deeplabv3_resnet50(
pretrained=True)
# Adjust the classifier to predict 21 classes
(e.g., for PASCAL VOC)
model.classifier[4] = nn.Conv2d(256, 21,
kernel_size=(1, 1))
model.to(device)

# Example forward pass
dummy_input = torch.randn(1, 3, 224,
224).to(device)
output = model(dummy_input)['out']
```

```
print("DeepLabV3 output shape:", output.shape)    #
Expected shape: (1, 21, H, W)
```

Best Practices and Real-world Considerations

- **Data Quality and Annotation:**
  High-quality annotations are essential, especially in medical imaging
  where small errors can be critical.
- **Evaluation Metrics:**
  - **Medical Imaging:** Use metrics like sensitivity, specificity,
    and area under the ROC curve.
  - **Object Detection:** Evaluate using mean Average Precision
    (mAP) and Intersection over Union (IoU).
  - **Segmentation:** Dice coefficient, Jaccard index, and pixel
    accuracy are commonly used.
- **Deployment Constraints:**
  Real-world applications may require models to run in real time or
  under limited computational resources. Optimize models through
  quantization, pruning, or efficient architectures.
- **Regulatory and Ethical Considerations:**
  In sensitive domains like medical imaging, ensure that models
  comply with regulatory standards and maintain patient privacy.

Exercises

1. **Medical Imaging Classification:**
   Fine-tune a pre-trained DenseNet or EfficientNet on a small medical
   image dataset (e.g., chest X-rays) and evaluate classification
   performance using ROC curves.
2. **Object Detection Fine-Tuning:**
   Using a pre-trained YOLO or Faster R-CNN model, fine-tune on a
   custom dataset (e.g., street scene images) and report mAP scores.
   Experiment with adjusting anchor boxes and IoU thresholds.
3. **Semantic Segmentation:**
   Implement a U-Net or DeepLabV3 model for a segmentation task
   (e.g., road segmentation for autonomous driving). Experiment with
   different loss functions (e.g., Dice loss vs. cross-entropy) and
   compare performance.

4. **Visualization Task:**
   Visualize feature maps or segmentation outputs from different layers of your model to understand how the network captures both local and global context.

By diving into real-world applications, this section demonstrates how advanced CNN architectures can be effectively adapted for diverse tasks—from diagnosing diseases in medical imaging to accurately detecting and segmenting objects in complex scenes. With a combination of tailored network architectures, domain-specific optimizations, and rigorous evaluation, you're equipped to develop high-performing models that translate effectively into practical solutions.

2.4 Model Interpretability (Grad-CAM, Saliency Maps)

As CNN architectures become more complex, understanding their internal decision-making process is crucial. **Model interpretability** techniques, such as **Grad-CAM** and **saliency maps**, help visualize the regions of an input image that most strongly influence the model's predictions. These visualizations not only offer insights into model behavior but also assist in diagnosing issues, validating predictions, and ensuring that models are focusing on the right features. In this section, we will explain the theory behind these methods, walk through detailed code examples, discuss best practices, and provide exercises to help you apply these techniques to your own models.

Grad-CAM (Gradient-weighted Class Activation Mapping)

Overview

Grad-CAM is a powerful technique that uses the gradients flowing into the last convolutional layer of a CNN to produce a coarse localization map. This map highlights the important regions in the image for a specific class prediction.

- **How It Works:**
  Grad-CAM computes the gradients of the target class score with

respect to the feature maps of a convolutional layer. These gradients are then global-average-pooled to obtain importance weights. The weighted sum of the feature maps, followed by a ReLU, produces the activation map highlighting discriminative regions.

- **Why It's Useful:**
  - It requires only a single backward pass.
  - It does not require architectural changes.
  - It offers class-specific explanations, making it especially useful for tasks like medical imaging or object detection.

Code Example: Grad-CAM Implementation

```python
python

import torch
import torch.nn.functional as F
import cv2
import numpy as np
import matplotlib.pyplot as plt
from torchvision import models, transforms
from PIL import Image

class GradCAM:
    def __init__(self, model, target_layer):
        self.model = model.eval()
        self.target_layer = target_layer
        self.gradients = None

        # Register hook to capture gradients from
the target layer

target_layer.register_backward_hook(self.save_gradi
ent)

    def save_gradient(self, module, grad_input,
grad_output):
        # Save the gradients coming out of the
target layer
        self.gradients = grad_output[0]

    def generate_cam(self, input_image,
target_class=None):
```

```python
        # Forward pass
        output = self.model(input_image)
        if target_class is None:
            target_class =
output.argmax(dim=1).item()

        # Zero grads
        self.model.zero_grad()

        # Compute gradient of the target class
        target = output[0, target_class]
        target.backward()

        # Get the activations from the target layer
        activations = self.target_layer.output  #
Assumes target layer saves its output via a forward
hook
        # Global Average Pooling on gradients
        weights = torch.mean(self.gradients,
dim=(2, 3), keepdim=True)

        # Compute weighted combination of forward
activation maps
        cam = torch.sum(weights * activations,
dim=1)
        cam = F.relu(cam)
        cam = cam.squeeze().cpu().detach().numpy()

        # Normalize CAM to [0, 1]
        cam -= cam.min()
        cam /= cam.max() + 1e-8
        return cam

# Example usage:
# Load a pre-trained model and set the target layer
(e.g., last conv layer of ResNet)
model = models.resnet50(pretrained=True).eval()
target_layer = model.layer4[-1]  # last block of
layer4 in ResNet50

# To capture the output of the target layer,
register a forward hook
```

```python
def save_activation(module, input, output):
    module.output = output
target_layer.register_forward_hook(save_activation)

# Preprocessing pipeline for the input image
preprocess = transforms.Compose([
    transforms.Resize((224, 224)),
    transforms.ToTensor(),
    transforms.Normalize(mean=[0.485, 0.456,
0.406],
                        std=[0.229, 0.224, 0.225])
])

# Load and preprocess an image
img =
Image.open("path_to_image.jpg").convert("RGB")
input_tensor = preprocess(img).unsqueeze(0)  # add
batch dimension

# Initialize GradCAM and generate CAM
grad_cam = GradCAM(model, target_layer)
cam = grad_cam.generate_cam(input_tensor)

# Resize CAM and overlay on the image
heatmap = cv2.resize(cam, (img.width, img.height))
heatmap = np.uint8(255 * heatmap)
heatmap = cv2.applyColorMap(heatmap,
cv2.COLORMAP_JET)
img_np = np.array(img)
overlay = cv2.addWeighted(img_np, 0.6, heatmap,
0.4, 0)

# Display the result
plt.figure(figsize=(10, 5))
plt.subplot(1, 2, 1)
plt.title("Original Image")
plt.imshow(img_np)
plt.axis("off")

plt.subplot(1, 2, 2)
plt.title("Grad-CAM")
plt.imshow(overlay)
```

```python
plt.axis("off")
plt.show()
```

Key Points:

- A backward hook captures gradients from the target convolutional layer.
- A forward hook stores the activation maps needed to compute the CAM.
- The generated heatmap is normalized and overlaid on the original image to highlight important regions.

Saliency Maps

Overview

Saliency maps provide a pixel-level explanation by computing the gradient of the output with respect to the input image. The magnitude of the gradient indicates the sensitivity of the prediction to each pixel, highlighting areas that contribute most strongly to the decision.

- **How It Works:**
  The process involves a forward pass to compute the output, followed by a backward pass to compute gradients with respect to the input pixels. The absolute values of these gradients are then aggregated (often using a maximum or sum over color channels) to produce a saliency map.
- **Why It's Useful:**
  Saliency maps offer fine-grained explanations and can be used to detect if a model is focusing on relevant details or being misled by noise.

Code Example: Saliency Map Implementation

```python
python

import torch
import torch.nn.functional as F
import matplotlib.pyplot as plt
from torchvision import models, transforms
```

```python
from PIL import Image
import numpy as np

# Load pre-trained model (e.g., VGG16)
model = models.vgg16(pretrained=True).eval()

# Preprocessing pipeline
preprocess = transforms.Compose([
    transforms.Resize((224, 224)),
    transforms.ToTensor(),
    transforms.Normalize(mean=[0.485, 0.456,
0.406],
                         std=[0.229, 0.224, 0.225])
])

# Load and preprocess an image
img =
Image.open("path_to_image.jpg").convert("RGB")
input_tensor = preprocess(img).unsqueeze(0)
input_tensor.requires_grad = True

# Forward pass
output = model(input_tensor)
# Choose the class with highest score as target
target_class = output.argmax(dim=1).item()

# Zero existing gradients
model.zero_grad()
# Backward pass: compute gradient of target class
score with respect to input image
score = output[0, target_class]
score.backward()

# Get absolute gradients and aggregate over
channels
saliency, _ =
torch.max(input_tensor.grad.data.abs(), dim=1)
saliency = saliency.squeeze().cpu().numpy()

# Normalize saliency map to [0, 1]
saliency = (saliency - saliency.min()) /
(saliency.max() - saliency.min() + 1e-8)
```

```
# Display saliency map
plt.figure(figsize=(8, 8))
plt.subplot(1, 2, 1)
plt.title("Original Image")
plt.imshow(np.array(img))
plt.axis("off")

plt.subplot(1, 2, 2)
plt.title("Saliency Map")
plt.imshow(saliency, cmap="hot")
plt.axis("off")
plt.show()
```

Key Points:

- The input tensor's `requires_grad` flag is set to `True` to compute gradients with respect to pixel values.
- The backward pass computes the gradient for the target class.
- The resulting saliency map is obtained by taking the maximum absolute gradient across the color channels and then normalizing.

Best Practices and Troubleshooting

- **Model Selection:**
  Choose the appropriate model layer for Grad-CAM. The last convolutional layer typically yields the best balance between spatial resolution and semantic meaning.
- **Normalization:**
  Always normalize the resulting maps for clear visualization.
- **Multiple Explanations:**
  Use both Grad-CAM and saliency maps to get complementary insights. Grad-CAM offers class-specific localization, while saliency maps provide fine-grained sensitivity.
- **Debugging Visualizations:**
  Verify that the heatmaps make sense by testing on images with known regions of interest. If the maps are noisy or uninterpretable, consider adjusting the layer selection or checking gradient flow.
- **Integration:**
  Combine interpretability visualizations with model debugging and

evaluation tools (e.g., TensorBoard) to track model behavior over training epochs.

Exercises

1. **Layer Selection Experiment:**
   Apply Grad-CAM on different convolutional layers of a pre-trained model and compare the resulting heatmaps. Which layer provides the most interpretable results for your application?
2. **Saliency vs. Grad-CAM Comparison:**
   For a given image and model, generate both saliency maps and Grad-CAM heatmaps. Analyze and discuss the differences in the visual explanations.
3. **Impact of Preprocessing:**
   Modify the image preprocessing steps (e.g., normalization values) and observe how they affect the interpretability visualizations.
4. **Real-World Application:**
   Use interpretability techniques on a model fine-tuned for a specific domain (e.g., medical imaging or autonomous driving). Assess whether the highlighted regions align with domain knowledge.

Model interpretability techniques like Grad-CAM and saliency maps are indispensable tools for understanding, debugging, and improving deep learning models. By visualizing which regions of an input image influence model predictions, you can gain deeper insights into model behavior, ensure that models are making decisions for the right reasons, and build trust with end users. Mastering these techniques is essential for advanced practitioners working on real-world applications.

2.5 Project: High-Performance Image Classification for Medical Diagnosis

In medical diagnosis, accurate and efficient image classification can be the key to early detection and treatment. However, medical images (such as X-rays, MRIs, or CT scans) often present unique challenges, including high resolution, subtle differences between classes, and limited labeled data. In this project, we leverage transfer learning to fine-tune a pre-trained convolutional neural network (CNN) for a binary (or multi-class) classification task—such as distinguishing between normal and abnormal findings. Our goal is to build a high-performance model that is both robust and efficient for real-world clinical applications.

2. Project Objectives

- **Leverage Pre-trained Networks:** Use a pre-trained model (e.g., ResNet-50) to exploit learned features from large-scale datasets.
- **Custom Fine-Tuning:** Replace and fine-tune the classifier head for the medical imaging task.
- **Efficient Data Pipeline:** Implement advanced data loading and augmentation to handle limited data and improve model generalization.
- **Accelerated Training:** Integrate mixed precision training to reduce memory usage and speed up the training process.
- **Model Evaluation:** Evaluate the model using relevant metrics (accuracy, sensitivity, specificity, and ROC-AUC) to ensure clinical viability.
- **Interpretability:** Optionally integrate interpretability tools (e.g., Grad-CAM) to visualize decision-making, fostering trust in model predictions.

3. Dataset and Preprocessing

For this project, assume you have a dataset of medical images organized into folders by class (e.g., "normal" and "abnormal"). We will use a custom dataset class and robust transformation pipelines to preprocess images.

Code Example: Custom Dataset and Transformations

```python
import os
from PIL import Image
import torch
from torch.utils.data import Dataset, DataLoader
import torchvision.transforms as transforms

class MedicalImageDataset(Dataset):
    def __init__(self, image_dir, transform=None):
        self.image_dir = image_dir
```

```python
        # Assume a folder structure:
image_dir/class_name/*.jpg
        self.classes =
sorted(os.listdir(image_dir))
        self.image_paths = []
        self.labels = []
        for label, class_name in
enumerate(self.classes):
            class_folder = os.path.join(image_dir,
class_name)
            for img_file in
os.listdir(class_folder):

self.image_paths.append(os.path.join(class_folder,
img_file))
                self.labels.append(label)
        self.transform = transform

    def __len__(self):
        return len(self.image_paths)

    def __getitem__(self, idx):
        img_path = self.image_paths[idx]
        image = Image.open(img_path).convert("RGB")
        if self.transform:
            image = self.transform(image)
        label = self.labels[idx]
        return image, label

# Define transformation pipeline with data
augmentation
transform_pipeline = transforms.Compose([
    transforms.Resize((256, 256)),
    transforms.RandomCrop(224),
    transforms.RandomHorizontalFlip(),
    transforms.ColorJitter(brightness=0.1,
contrast=0.1),
    transforms.ToTensor(),
    transforms.Normalize(mean=[0.485, 0.456,
0.406],
                         std=[0.229, 0.224, 0.225])
])
```

```
# Create dataset and DataLoader
image_dir = "path/to/medical_images"  # Update with
your dataset path
dataset = MedicalImageDataset(image_dir,
transform=transform_pipeline)
data_loader = DataLoader(dataset, batch_size=32,
shuffle=True, num_workers=4, pin_memory=True)
```

4. Model Architecture and Custom Fine-Tuning

We use a pre-trained ResNet-50 model from torchvision. The final fully connected layer is replaced to suit our classification task (e.g., 2 classes for binary classification). Initially, the majority of the model is frozen to leverage the robust features learned on ImageNet, and later, you may unfreeze some layers for fine-tuning.

Code Example: Model Setup

```python
python

import torch.nn as nn
import torchvision.models as models

# Load pre-trained ResNet-50 and freeze its layers
model = models.resnet50(pretrained=True)
for param in model.parameters():
    param.requires_grad = False

# Replace the classifier head for binary
classification (change num_classes as needed)
num_features = model.fc.in_features
model.fc = nn.Linear(num_features, 2)  # 2 output
classes: normal and abnormal

# Move model to device
device = torch.device("cuda" if
torch.cuda.is_available() else "cpu")
model.to(device)
```

5. Training Setup with Mixed Precision

To accelerate training and reduce GPU memory usage, we integrate PyTorch's Automatic Mixed Precision (AMP). We also employ a learning rate scheduler and differential learning rates if you later decide to unfreeze parts of the network.

Code Example: Training Loop with AMP

```python
import torch.optim as optim
from torch.cuda.amp import autocast, GradScaler

# Define loss and optimizer (only the classifier
parameters are trainable initially)
loss_fn = nn.CrossEntropyLoss()
optimizer = optim.Adam(model.fc.parameters(),
lr=1e-3)
scheduler = optim.lr_scheduler.StepLR(optimizer,
step_size=7, gamma=0.1)
scaler = GradScaler()

num_epochs = 10
for epoch in range(num_epochs):
    model.train()
    running_loss = 0.0
    correct = 0
    total = 0

    for images, labels in data_loader:
        images, labels = images.to(device,
non_blocking=True), labels.to(device,
non_blocking=True)
        optimizer.zero_grad()

        # Mixed precision forward pass
        with autocast():
            outputs = model(images)
            loss = loss_fn(outputs, labels)

        # Backward pass with gradient scaling
```

```python
        scaler.scale(loss).backward()
        scaler.step(optimizer)
        scaler.update()

        running_loss += loss.item()
        _, predicted = outputs.max(1)
        total += labels.size(0)
        correct +=
predicted.eq(labels).sum().item()

    scheduler.step()
    epoch_loss = running_loss / len(data_loader)
    accuracy = 100. * correct / total
    print(f"Epoch [{epoch+1}/{num_epochs}] Loss:
{epoch_loss:.4f} Accuracy: {accuracy:.2f}%")
```

6. Evaluation and Model Metrics

For medical diagnosis, in addition to overall accuracy, consider metrics like sensitivity (recall for the abnormal class), specificity, and ROC-AUC. These metrics ensure that the model is not only accurate but also reliable in a clinical context.

Code Example: Evaluation (Simplified)

python

```python
from sklearn.metrics import accuracy_score,
roc_auc_score, classification_report

model.eval()
all_labels = []
all_preds = []

with torch.no_grad():
    for images, labels in data_loader:
        images, labels = images.to(device),
labels.to(device)
        outputs = model(images)
        _, predicted = outputs.max(1)
        all_labels.extend(labels.cpu().numpy())
        all_preds.extend(predicted.cpu().numpy())
```

```
acc = accuracy_score(all_labels, all_preds)
print("Overall Accuracy: {:.2f}%".format(acc *
100))
print(classification_report(all_labels, all_preds,
target_names=["Normal", "Abnormal"]))
# Optionally, compute ROC-AUC if you have
probabilities for the abnormal class
```

7. Deployment Considerations and Interpretability

Once the model is trained, you may further refine it with interpretability tools such as Grad-CAM (see Section 2.4) to ensure the model is focusing on clinically relevant regions. Additionally, consider exporting the model (using TorchScript or ONNX) for deployment in clinical settings.

8. and Next Steps

This project demonstrates how to build a high-performance image classification pipeline for medical diagnosis by leveraging:

- Advanced data loading and augmentation to handle limited data.
- Transfer learning and fine-tuning of a pre-trained ResNet-50 model.
- Mixed precision training for accelerated computation.
- Evaluation metrics tailored to clinical tasks.

Next Steps:

- Experiment with unfreezing additional layers to further fine-tune the model.
- Incorporate domain-specific interpretability techniques to validate model decisions.
- Extend the project to a multi-class classification task or integrate with real-time diagnostic systems.

Exercises

1. **Experiment with Different Pre-trained Models:**
   Fine-tune an EfficientNet or ConvNeXt model on the same medical image dataset and compare performance metrics.

2. **Advanced Data Augmentation:**
   Introduce domain-specific augmentations (e.g., elastic transformations) and evaluate their impact on model generalization.
3. **Interpretability Integration:**
   Apply Grad-CAM on test images to visualize the regions influencing model decisions. Compare these visualizations with clinical annotations.
4. **Metric Analysis:**
   Compute and analyze additional metrics such as sensitivity, specificity, and ROC-AUC to assess model performance in a clinical context.

This project not only reinforces the advanced techniques discussed throughout the book but also equips you with a real-world solution applicable to critical domains like medical diagnosis. The combination of transfer learning, mixed precision training, and robust evaluation strategies ensures that you are well-prepared to deploy high-performing models in clinical environments.

2.6 Exercise: Optimizing CNNs for Edge Deployment

Deploying CNN models on edge devices—such as mobile phones, embedded systems, or IoT devices—presents unique challenges. These devices typically have limited memory, lower computational power, and strict latency requirements. The goal of this exercise is to optimize a CNN model (e.g., a fine-tuned ResNet or EfficientNet) so that it can run efficiently on an edge device without sacrificing significant accuracy.

Key optimization techniques include:

- **Quantization:** Reducing the precision of model weights and activations (e.g., FP32 to INT8) to decrease model size and increase inference speed.
- **Pruning:** Removing redundant or less important connections in the network to reduce model complexity.
- **Knowledge Distillation:** Transferring knowledge from a larger model (teacher) to a smaller, more efficient model (student).

- **Model Compression:** Combining techniques like weight sharing, low-rank approximations, and Huffman coding to further compress the model.

Objectives

- **Reduce Model Size:** Lower memory footprint to fit within edge device constraints.
- **Improve Inference Speed:** Ensure that the model delivers real-time predictions.
- **Maintain Accuracy:** Optimize without significant degradation in model performance.
- **Experiment with Tools:** Use PyTorch utilities for quantization and pruning, and optionally explore third-party libraries for knowledge distillation.

Step-by-Step Guidelines

1. Baseline Setup

Start with your pre-trained, fine-tuned CNN model (e.g., ResNet-50 fine-tuned for a specific classification task). Ensure that the model is working well on your validation data before applying optimizations.

2. Quantization

PyTorch provides post-training static quantization and quantization-aware training (QAT). In this exercise, you'll first try post-training static quantization.

Code Example: Post-Training Static Quantization

python

```
import torch
import torchvision.models as models

# Assume you have a pre-trained ResNet-50 model
fine-tuned for your task.
model = models.resnet50(pretrained=True)
# Replace the classifier if needed, and load your
fine-tuned weights.
```

```python
# model.fc = ...
model.eval()

# Define quantization configuration
model.qconfig =
torch.quantization.get_default_qconfig('fbgemm')

# Fuse Conv, BN, and ReLU layers where applicable
(required for quantization)
# This step depends on the model architecture.
fused_model =
torch.quantization.fuse_modules(model,
                    [['conv1', 'bn1', 'relu']],
inplace=False)

# Prepare the model for static quantization
quantized_model =
torch.quantization.prepare(fused_model,
inplace=False)

# Calibrate the model with a representative dataset
# Here, iterate over a few batches from your
DataLoader
calibration_loader = ...  # Replace with your
DataLoader for calibration data
with torch.no_grad():
    for batch in calibration_loader:
        images, _ = batch
        quantized_model(images)

# Convert to quantized model
quantized_model =
torch.quantization.convert(quantized_model,
inplace=False)
print("Model quantized successfully.")
```

Tips:

- Ensure proper fusion of layers before quantization.
- Use a calibration dataset that is representative of the inference data distribution.

3. Pruning

Pruning reduces model size by zeroing out less important weights. PyTorch offers structured and unstructured pruning methods.

Code Example: Unstructured Pruning

```python
python

import torch.nn.utils.prune as prune

# For example, prune 30% of weights in the first
convolutional layer
layer_to_prune = model.conv1  # adjust based on
your architecture
prune.l1_unstructured(layer_to_prune,
name="weight", amount=0.3)

# Check sparsity
sparsity = float(torch.sum(layer_to_prune.weight ==
0)) / float(layer_to_prune.weight.nelement())
print(f"Sparsity after pruning: {sparsity:.2f}")

# Optionally, remove the pruning reparameterization
to save the model
prune.remove(layer_to_prune, 'weight')
```

Tips:

- Experiment with different pruning amounts.
- Re-train or fine-tune the pruned model to recover any lost accuracy.

4. Knowledge Distillation (Optional)

Knowledge distillation transfers knowledge from a large "teacher" model to a smaller "student" model. Although optional for this exercise, it is useful when further reducing model size without losing performance.

Conceptual Steps:

- Train a student model to mimic the soft labels (predicted probabilities) from the teacher model.

- Use a combination of standard cross-entropy loss and a distillation loss (e.g., Kullback-Leibler divergence).

5. Evaluate and Benchmark

After applying quantization and pruning:

- **Evaluate Accuracy:** Ensure that accuracy does not drop significantly.
- **Measure Inference Time:** Benchmark on the target edge hardware or simulate with CPU benchmarks.
- **Analyze Model Size:** Compare file sizes before and after optimization.

Hands-On Exercise

1. **Baseline Evaluation:**
   Start with a fully functional fine-tuned CNN model and document its performance metrics (accuracy, inference time, model size).
2. **Apply Quantization:**
   Use the post-training static quantization method and re-evaluate the model. Record any drop in accuracy and the improvement in inference speed.
3. **Implement Pruning:**
   Apply unstructured pruning to one or more layers. Fine-tune the model if necessary, and compare the performance metrics with the baseline and quantized models.
4. **Combined Optimization:**
   Optionally, combine both quantization and pruning, then re-assess the overall trade-offs between size, speed, and accuracy.
5. **Report Findings:**
   Document your optimization process, including code snippets, performance metrics, and any challenges faced during deployment on edge devices.

Best Practices and Troubleshooting

- **Profiling:**
  Use PyTorch's profiler or external tools (e.g., NVIDIA TensorRT) to identify bottlenecks.

- **Iterative Optimization:**
  Optimize in steps—first quantize, then prune, and re-assess after each step.
- **Model Validation:**
  Always validate the model on a representative dataset to ensure that optimizations do not compromise clinical or application-specific requirements.
- **Edge Device Testing:**
  If possible, deploy the model on an actual edge device (or an emulator) to verify real-world performance.

Exercises

1. **Quantization Challenge:**
   Take your fine-tuned CNN model and perform post-training static quantization. Compare the accuracy and inference speed before and after quantization.
2. **Pruning Experiment:**
   Experiment with different pruning levels (e.g., 20%, 30%, 40%) on various layers of your model. Evaluate which layers are most sensitive to pruning and document the changes in accuracy and model size.
3. **Combined Optimization:**
   Combine quantization and pruning on your model and then benchmark the overall improvements. Report the trade-offs between model size reduction, inference speed improvement, and accuracy loss.
4. **Real-world Deployment Simulation:**
   Simulate an edge deployment scenario by measuring inference latency on a CPU or on a mobile device emulator. Compare these metrics against your optimized model to validate real-world performance.

Optimizing CNNs for edge deployment involves a delicate balance between reducing model size and maintaining high performance. By applying quantization and pruning techniques, you can significantly reduce the computational footprint and memory requirements of your models, making them suitable for real-world deployment on resource-constrained devices. This exercise not only reinforces best practices for model optimization but also provides practical insights into achieving efficient and reliable deep learning inference on the edge.

Chapter 3: Sequence Modeling with RNNs, LSTMs, and GRUs

Sequential data is pervasive in real-world applications—from natural language processing and speech recognition to time-series forecasting and anomaly detection. Traditional Recurrent Neural Networks (RNNs) are designed to handle such data by maintaining hidden states that capture information across time steps. However, vanilla RNNs often struggle with long-range dependencies due to vanishing and exploding gradients. To overcome these limitations, advanced architectures like **Long Short-Term Memory (LSTM)** networks and **Gated Recurrent Units (GRU)** have been developed. In this chapter, we will:

- Review the fundamentals of RNNs.
- Delve into LSTMs and GRUs, understanding their gating mechanisms.
- Compare the strengths and weaknesses of each approach.
- Provide hands-on code examples and practical exercises for real-world sequence tasks.

3.1 Advanced RNN Architectures: LSTMs, GRUs, and Attention Mechanisms

Traditional Recurrent Neural Networks (RNNs) are powerful for sequence modeling but struggle with long-range dependencies due to issues like vanishing or exploding gradients. Advanced architectures such as **Long Short-Term Memory networks (LSTMs)** and **Gated Recurrent Units (GRUs)** address these challenges with gating mechanisms that regulate information flow. Moreover, **attention mechanisms** have emerged as a transformative addition by allowing models to dynamically focus on specific parts of the input sequence during prediction. In this section, we will:

- Review the internal workings of LSTMs and GRUs.
- Introduce the core ideas behind attention mechanisms.
- Illustrate how attention can be integrated into sequence models.
- Provide hands-on code examples and best practices for applying these advanced architectures.

LSTMs and GRUs: Recap of Advanced RNN Units

LSTM Overview

LSTMs introduce memory cells and three gates—input, forget, and output—to control the flow of information. This design enables the network to retain long-term dependencies effectively. In essence:

- **Input Gate:** Decides how much new information should be stored.
- **Forget Gate:** Determines what information to discard.
- **Output Gate:** Controls what part of the cell state is exposed as the hidden state.

GRU Overview

GRUs simplify LSTMs by combining the forget and input gates into a single **update gate** and merging the cell state with the hidden state. This results in fewer parameters and often faster computation, while still capturing essential temporal dynamics:

Both LSTMs and GRUs have proven effective in tasks such as language modeling, time-series forecasting, and sentiment analysis.

to Attention Mechanisms

Attention mechanisms enhance sequence models by allowing them to focus on different parts of the input when making predictions. Rather than relying solely on the final hidden state of an encoder (which may lose detailed information over long sequences), attention dynamically computes a weighted sum of all encoder hidden states. This provides the decoder with a context vector that emphasizes relevant parts of the input.

How Attention Works

1. **Score Calculation:**
   For each decoder time step, compute a score for every encoder hidden state using a compatibility function (e.g., dot product, additive scoring).
2. **Attention Weights:**
   Normalize the scores via a softmax to obtain attention weights.

3. **Context Vector:**
   Compute a weighted sum of the encoder hidden states using these attention weights.
4. **Output Generation:**
   Use the context vector—often concatenated with the decoder's current state—to produce the output.

Code Example: Integrating Attention with an LSTM Encoder-Decoder

Below is a simplified implementation of an attention mechanism in a sequence-to-sequence model using an LSTM encoder and decoder. This example demonstrates additive attention (often called Bahdanau attention).

```python
python

import torch
import torch.nn as nn
import torch.nn.functional as F

# Define the Attention Module
class Attention(nn.Module):
    def __init__(self, encoder_hidden_dim,
decoder_hidden_dim):
        super(Attention, self).__init__()
        # Linear layers for computing attention
scores
        self.attn = nn.Linear(encoder_hidden_dim +
decoder_hidden_dim, decoder_hidden_dim)
        self.v = nn.Linear(decoder_hidden_dim, 1,
bias=False)

    def forward(self, hidden, encoder_outputs):
        # hidden: (batch_size, decoder_hidden_dim)
        # encoder_outputs: (batch_size, seq_len,
encoder_hidden_dim)
        batch_size = encoder_outputs.size(0)
        seq_len = encoder_outputs.size(1)

        # Repeat hidden state seq_len times to
concatenate with encoder outputs
```

```python
        hidden = hidden.unsqueeze(1).repeat(1,
seq_len, 1)   # (batch_size, seq_len,
decoder_hidden_dim)

        # Concatenate encoder outputs and hidden
state
        energy =
torch.tanh(self.attn(torch.cat((hidden,
encoder_outputs), dim=2)))   # (batch_size, seq_len,
decoder_hidden_dim)

        # Compute attention scores and squeeze the
last dimension
        attention = self.v(energy).squeeze(2)   #
(batch_size, seq_len)
        attention_weights = F.softmax(attention,
dim=1)   # Normalize scores

        return attention_weights

# Define the Encoder
class Encoder(nn.Module):
    def __init__(self, input_dim,
encoder_hidden_dim, num_layers=1):
        super(Encoder, self).__init__()
        self.lstm = nn.LSTM(input_dim,
encoder_hidden_dim, num_layers, batch_first=True)

    def forward(self, src):
        outputs, (hidden, cell) = self.lstm(src)
        return outputs, hidden, cell   # outputs:
(batch_size, seq_len, encoder_hidden_dim)

# Define the Decoder with Attention
class Decoder(nn.Module):
    def __init__(self, output_dim,
encoder_hidden_dim, decoder_hidden_dim,
num_layers=1):
        super(Decoder, self).__init__()
        self.attention =
Attention(encoder_hidden_dim, decoder_hidden_dim)
```

```python
        self.lstm = nn.LSTM(encoder_hidden_dim +
output_dim, decoder_hidden_dim, num_layers,
batch_first=True)
        self.fc_out = nn.Linear(encoder_hidden_dim
+ decoder_hidden_dim + output_dim, output_dim)

    def forward(self, input, hidden, cell,
encoder_outputs):
        # input: (batch_size, output_dim) -
typically the previous output or start token
embedding
        # Compute attention weights
        attn_weights = self.attention(hidden[-1],
encoder_outputs)  # (batch_size, seq_len)

        # Compute context vector as weighted sum of
encoder outputs
        context =
torch.bmm(attn_weights.unsqueeze(1),
encoder_outputs)  # (batch_size, 1,
encoder_hidden_dim)
        context = context.squeeze(1)  #
(batch_size, encoder_hidden_dim)

        # Prepare input for LSTM: concatenate
context with current input token
        lstm_input = torch.cat((input, context),
dim=1).unsqueeze(1)  # (batch_size, 1, output_dim +
encoder_hidden_dim)

        # Pass through LSTM
        output, (hidden, cell) =
self.lstm(lstm_input, (hidden, cell))
        output = output.squeeze(1)  # (batch_size,
decoder_hidden_dim)

        # Final output prediction: combine LSTM
output, context, and input token
        pred_input = torch.cat((output, context,
input), dim=1)
        prediction = self.fc_out(pred_input)  #
(batch_size, output_dim)
```

```
        return prediction, hidden, cell,
attn_weights

# Sample usage:
batch_size, seq_len, input_dim = 16, 10, 32
encoder_hidden_dim, decoder_hidden_dim, output_dim
= 64, 64, 32

# Random synthetic data
src = torch.randn(batch_size, seq_len, input_dim)
decoder_input = torch.randn(batch_size, output_dim)

# Instantiate encoder and decoder
encoder = Encoder(input_dim, encoder_hidden_dim)
encoder_outputs, hidden, cell = encoder(src)
decoder = Decoder(output_dim, encoder_hidden_dim,
decoder_hidden_dim)

# Run one decoder step
prediction, hidden, cell, attn_weights =
decoder(decoder_input, hidden, cell,
encoder_outputs)
print("Decoder prediction shape:",
prediction.shape)  # Expected: (batch_size,
output_dim)
print("Attention weights shape:",
attn_weights.shape)   # Expected: (batch_size,
seq_len)
```

Explanation:

- **Attention Module:**
  The `Attention` class computes attention scores by concatenating the decoder's last hidden state with each encoder output, transforming it through a tanh-activated linear layer, and finally projecting it to a scalar score. These scores are normalized using softmax to generate attention weights.
- **Encoder:**
  Processes the input sequence with an LSTM and returns all hidden states (for attention) along with the final hidden and cell states.
- **Decoder with Attention:**
  For each decoding step, the decoder computes attention weights,

creates a context vector (the weighted sum of encoder outputs), and concatenates it with the current input. This combined input is fed into the LSTM, and the final prediction is generated from a linear layer that integrates the LSTM output, context, and original input.

Best Practices and Troubleshooting

- **Layer Normalization:**
  Consider applying layer normalization to stabilize training, especially when using deep architectures with attention.
- **Visualization:**
  Visualize attention weights to ensure that the model focuses on relevant parts of the input. This is particularly useful for debugging and model interpretability.
- **Gradient Clipping:**
  Use gradient clipping in sequence models to mitigate exploding gradients.
- **Hyperparameter Tuning:**
  Experiment with the dimensions of the hidden states, number of layers, and type of attention (e.g., dot-product vs. additive) to find the optimal configuration.

Exercises

1. **Attention Mechanism Variations:**
   Implement an alternative attention mechanism (e.g., dot-product attention) and compare its performance with additive attention.
2. **Sequence-to-Sequence Task:**
   Build a full sequence-to-sequence model for a machine translation or text summarization task using the encoder-decoder with attention architecture.
3. **Visualization Exercise:**
   For a trained model, visualize the attention weights for a few input sequences. Analyze whether the model focuses on semantically relevant parts of the input.
4. **Comparison Experiment:**
   Train parallel models using LSTMs, GRUs, and attention-enhanced

LSTMs/GRUs on the same dataset. Compare their convergence speed, accuracy, and interpretability.

Advanced RNN architectures like LSTMs and GRUs have already pushed the envelope in sequence modeling by mitigating the shortcomings of vanilla RNNs. The addition of attention mechanisms further empowers these models by allowing them to dynamically focus on important parts of the input, significantly improving performance on tasks that require handling long sequences or capturing context-dependent relationships. Mastery of these techniques is essential for advanced practitioners aiming to build state-of-the-art sequence models.

3.2 Time-Series Forecasting with PyTorch

Time-series forecasting is critical in many real-world applications such as financial market prediction, weather forecasting, and sensor data analysis. Unlike static data, time-series data are sequential and temporal dependencies between data points must be captured for effective predictions. In this section, we explore how to use PyTorch to model and forecast time-series data. We cover data preprocessing, model selection (with LSTMs and GRUs as primary examples), and best practices for training and evaluating time-series models.

Key Concepts in Time-Series Forecasting

1. Characteristics of Time-Series Data

- **Temporal Dependency:**
  Data points are not independent; previous values influence future values.
- **Seasonality and Trend:**
  Time-series may exhibit periodic patterns (seasonality) and long-term trends.
- **Stationarity:**
  Many models assume the data have a constant mean and variance over time. Techniques such as differencing or normalization may be used to achieve stationarity.

2. Data Preparation

- **Sliding Window Approach:**
  Convert the raw sequence into input-output pairs where a fixed-length window of past observations is used to predict future values.
- **Normalization:**
  Scale the data (e.g., using MinMax or Standard scaling) to improve training stability.
- **Train-Test Split:**
  Maintain the temporal order by splitting data into training, validation, and test sets sequentially.

Modeling Time-Series with RNNs, LSTMs, and GRUs

Due to the sequential nature of time-series data, Recurrent Neural Networks (RNNs) and their advanced variants—LSTMs and GRUs—are well-suited for forecasting tasks. They can capture complex temporal dependencies and learn patterns that traditional statistical models might miss.

- **LSTMs:**
  Use memory cells and gating mechanisms to handle long-term dependencies.
- **GRUs:**
  Provide a more streamlined architecture than LSTMs, often with comparable performance and fewer parameters.

Hands-On Code Example: LSTM-Based Time-Series Forecasting

The following example demonstrates how to forecast a synthetic time-series using an LSTM. In this example, we generate a sine wave with noise, prepare the data using a sliding window approach, and build an LSTM model to predict future values.

```python
import numpy as np
import torch
import torch.nn as nn
```

```python
from torch.utils.data import DataLoader, Dataset
import matplotlib.pyplot as plt

# Set random seeds for reproducibility
np.random.seed(42)
torch.manual_seed(42)

# Generate synthetic time-series data: noisy sine
wave
time = np.arange(0, 400, 0.1)
data = np.sin(time) + 0.1 *
np.random.randn(len(time))

# Plot the generated time series
plt.figure(figsize=(10, 4))
plt.plot(time, data)
plt.title("Synthetic Time Series")
plt.xlabel("Time")
plt.ylabel("Value")
plt.show()

# Prepare data using sliding window approach
class TimeSeriesDataset(Dataset):
    def __init__(self, series, window_size):
        self.series = series
        self.window_size = window_size

    def __len__(self):
        return len(self.series) - self.window_size

    def __getitem__(self, idx):
        x = self.series[idx: idx +
self.window_size]
        y = self.series[idx + self.window_size]
        return torch.tensor(x,
dtype=torch.float32).unsqueeze(-1), torch.tensor(y,
dtype=torch.float32)

window_size = 50
dataset = TimeSeriesDataset(data, window_size)
train_size = int(0.8 * len(dataset))
test_size = len(dataset) - train_size
```

```python
train_dataset, test_dataset =
torch.utils.data.random_split(dataset, [train_size,
test_size])

batch_size = 32
train_loader = DataLoader(train_dataset,
batch_size=batch_size, shuffle=True)
test_loader = DataLoader(test_dataset,
batch_size=batch_size)

# Define the LSTM model for forecasting
class LSTMForecaster(nn.Module):
    def __init__(self, input_dim, hidden_dim,
num_layers, output_dim):
        super(LSTMForecaster, self).__init__()
        self.lstm = nn.LSTM(input_dim, hidden_dim,
num_layers, batch_first=True)
        self.fc = nn.Linear(hidden_dim, output_dim)

    def forward(self, x):
        # x: (batch_size, window_size, input_dim)
        out, _ = self.lstm(x)
        # Use the last time step's output for
prediction
        out = out[:, -1, :]
        out = self.fc(out)
        return out

input_dim = 1
hidden_dim = 64
num_layers = 2
output_dim = 1

model = LSTMForecaster(input_dim, hidden_dim,
num_layers, output_dim)
device = torch.device("cuda" if
torch.cuda.is_available() else "cpu")
model.to(device)

# Define loss and optimizer
loss_fn = nn.MSELoss()
```

```python
optimizer = torch.optim.Adam(model.parameters(),
lr=0.001)

# Training loop
num_epochs = 20
for epoch in range(num_epochs):
    model.train()
    epoch_loss = 0.0
    for x_batch, y_batch in train_loader:
        x_batch, y_batch = x_batch.to(device),
y_batch.to(device).unsqueeze(-1)
        optimizer.zero_grad()
        predictions = model(x_batch)
        loss = loss_fn(predictions, y_batch)
        loss.backward()
        optimizer.step()
        epoch_loss += loss.item() * x_batch.size(0)
    epoch_loss /= len(train_loader.dataset)
    print(f"Epoch {epoch+1}/{num_epochs}, Training
Loss: {epoch_loss:.4f}")

# Evaluate the model on test data
model.eval()
predictions_list, actual_list = [], []
with torch.no_grad():
    for x_batch, y_batch in test_loader:
        x_batch = x_batch.to(device)
        preds = model(x_batch)

predictions_list.extend(preds.cpu().numpy().flatten
())

actual_list.extend(y_batch.numpy().flatten())

# Plot predictions vs. actual values
plt.figure(figsize=(10, 4))
plt.plot(actual_list, label="Actual")
plt.plot(predictions_list, label="Predicted")
plt.title("Time-Series Forecasting on Test Data")
plt.xlabel("Sample")
plt.ylabel("Value")
plt.legend()
```

```
plt.show()
```

Best Practices and Troubleshooting

- **Data Normalization:**
  Scale your time-series data (e.g., using StandardScaler or MinMaxScaler) to accelerate training and improve stability.
- **Sequence Windowing:**
  Choose an appropriate window size. A larger window can capture more context but may also increase model complexity.
- **Overfitting Prevention:**
  Use techniques like dropout, regularization, or early stopping to prevent overfitting, especially with limited data.
- **Evaluation Metrics:**
  Beyond MSE, consider using MAE (Mean Absolute Error) or RMSE (Root Mean Squared Error) to assess performance.
- **Hyperparameter Tuning:**
  Experiment with different hidden dimensions, number of layers, learning rates, and batch sizes to find the best configuration for your dataset.
- **Gradient Clipping:**
  Apply gradient clipping (`torch.nn.utils.clip_grad_norm_`) if you observe exploding gradients during training.

Exercises

1. **Experiment with GRUs:**
   Replace the LSTM model with a GRU model and compare the training speed and forecasting performance.
2. **Window Size Variation:**
   Test different window sizes for the sliding window approach and analyze their impact on forecasting accuracy.
3. **Feature Engineering:**
   Incorporate additional features (e.g., lagged values, rolling averages) to improve the model's predictive capabilities.
4. **Real-World Data:**
   Apply the forecasting pipeline to a real-world time-series dataset (e.g., stock prices or weather data) and evaluate its performance.

5. **Quantitative Analysis:**
   Compare different evaluation metrics (MSE, MAE, RMSE) on the test set and discuss which metric better captures model performance for your task.

Time-series forecasting with deep learning models such as LSTMs and GRUs allows you to capture complex temporal dynamics that traditional statistical models may miss. By carefully preparing the data, choosing appropriate model architectures, and applying best practices during training, you can build robust forecasting models using PyTorch. The hands-on example and exercises in this section provide a solid foundation for tackling real-world forecasting challenges.

3.3 Language Modeling and Sequence Generation

Language modeling is the task of predicting the next token (word, subword, or character) in a sequence given the previous context. It is a foundational task for many applications such as text generation, translation, and speech recognition. In this section, we explore how to build language models using sequence models like LSTMs and GRUs. We also cover techniques for generating coherent and contextually relevant sequences.

Key Concepts

- **Language Modeling:**
  The goal is to compute the probability distribution over the next token given a history of previous tokens. This is typically done by maximizing the likelihood of the training text.
- **Sequence Generation:**
  Once a language model is trained, it can generate text by sampling tokens sequentially. Strategies like greedy decoding, beam search, and temperature sampling help control the randomness and diversity of the output.
- **Teacher Forcing:**
  During training, the model is often fed the true previous token as input (instead of its own prediction) to stabilize learning. This technique is known as teacher forcing.

- **Evaluation Metrics:**
  Perplexity is a common metric for language models. Lower perplexity indicates better predictive performance.

Modeling Approaches

Recurrent Neural Networks (RNNs), LSTMs, and GRUs

While vanilla RNNs provide a basic framework for sequence modeling, LSTMs and GRUs are preferred due to their ability to capture long-range dependencies. In language modeling:

- **LSTMs:**
  Use gated mechanisms (input, forget, output) to retain context over long sequences.
- **GRUs:**
  Offer a simplified architecture with similar performance but fewer parameters.

Attention Mechanisms (Optional)

For more complex tasks or longer sequences, integrating attention mechanisms can help the model focus on relevant parts of the input context. However, in this section, we focus primarily on RNN-based models for clarity.

Hands-On Code Example: LSTM Language Model

Below is a simplified character-level language model using an LSTM. The model learns to predict the next character in a sequence, and then we use it for generating text.

```python
import torch
import torch.nn as nn
import torch.nn.functional as F
import numpy as np
```

```python
# Sample text corpus (in practice, use a larger
dataset)
text = (
    "In the realm of deep learning, language models
are essential. "
    "They learn to predict the next word or
character in a sequence, "
    "enabling powerful applications like text
generation."
)

# Create vocabulary and mappings
chars = sorted(list(set(text)))
vocab_size = len(chars)
char2idx = {ch: i for i, ch in enumerate(chars)}
idx2char = {i: ch for i, ch in enumerate(chars)}

# Hyperparameters
embedding_dim = 32
hidden_dim = 128
num_layers = 2
seq_length = 30
batch_size = 16
num_epochs = 50
learning_rate = 0.003

# Prepare the dataset: Convert text to indices
data = [char2idx[ch] for ch in text]
data = torch.tensor(data, dtype=torch.long)

# Create sequences using sliding window
def create_sequences(data, seq_length):
    sequences = []
    targets = []
    for i in range(len(data) - seq_length):
        sequences.append(data[i:i+seq_length])
        targets.append(data[i+1:i+seq_length+1])
    return torch.stack(sequences),
torch.stack(targets)
```

```python
sequences, targets = create_sequences(data,
seq_length)
dataset = torch.utils.data.TensorDataset(sequences,
targets)
data_loader = torch.utils.data.DataLoader(dataset,
batch_size=batch_size, shuffle=True)

# Define the LSTM Language Model
class LSTMLanguageModel(nn.Module):
    def __init__(self, vocab_size, embedding_dim,
hidden_dim, num_layers):
        super(LSTMLanguageModel, self).__init__()
        self.embedding = nn.Embedding(vocab_size,
embedding_dim)
        self.lstm = nn.LSTM(embedding_dim,
hidden_dim, num_layers, batch_first=True)
        self.fc = nn.Linear(hidden_dim, vocab_size)

    def forward(self, x, hidden=None):
        x = self.embedding(x)  # (batch_size,
seq_length, embedding_dim)
        output, hidden = self.lstm(x, hidden)
        logits = self.fc(output)  # (batch_size,
seq_length, vocab_size)
        return logits, hidden

model = LSTMLanguageModel(vocab_size,
embedding_dim, hidden_dim, num_layers)
optimizer = torch.optim.Adam(model.parameters(),
lr=learning_rate)
loss_fn = nn.CrossEntropyLoss()

# Training loop
model.train()
for epoch in range(num_epochs):
    epoch_loss = 0.0
    hidden = None
    for x_batch, y_batch in data_loader:
        optimizer.zero_grad()
        logits, hidden = model(x_batch, hidden)
        # Detach hidden state to prevent
backpropagating through entire history
```

```python
            hidden = tuple([h.detach() for h in
hidden])
            # Reshape logits and targets for computing
loss
            loss = loss_fn(logits.view(-1, vocab_size),
y_batch.view(-1))
            loss.backward()
            optimizer.step()
            epoch_loss += loss.item()
        print(f"Epoch {epoch+1}/{num_epochs}, Loss:
{epoch_loss/len(data_loader):.4f}")

# Text Generation Function
def generate_text(model, start_text, length=100,
temperature=1.0):
    model.eval()
    input_seq = torch.tensor([char2idx[ch] for ch
in start_text], dtype=torch.long).unsqueeze(0)
    generated_text = start_text
    hidden = None
    with torch.no_grad():
        for _ in range(length):
            logits, hidden = model(input_seq,
hidden)
            # Focus on the last time step's output
            logits = logits[:, -1, :] / temperature
            probs = F.softmax(logits, dim=-1)
            next_idx = torch.multinomial(probs,
num_samples=1).item()
            generated_text += idx2char[next_idx]
            input_seq = torch.tensor([[next_idx]],
dtype=torch.long)
    return generated_text

# Generate text starting from a seed phrase
seed_text = "Language models"
generated = generate_text(model, seed_text,
length=200, temperature=0.8)
print("Generated Text:\n", generated)
```

Explanation:

- **Dataset Preparation:**
  We convert a sample text into a sequence of character indices and create sliding windows for training.
- **Model Architecture:**
  The model consists of an embedding layer, an LSTM stack, and a fully connected layer that predicts the probability distribution over the vocabulary for each time step.
- **Training:**
  The training loop uses teacher forcing by feeding in the ground truth sequence. We detach the hidden state after each batch to avoid backpropagating through the entire history.
- **Text Generation:**
  The `generate_text` function demonstrates how to generate new text by sampling from the predicted probability distribution. The temperature parameter controls the randomness of sampling.

Best Practices and Troubleshooting

- **Data Preprocessing:**
  For larger corpora, consider tokenization strategies that balance vocabulary size and contextual richness (e.g., byte-pair encoding).
- **Teacher Forcing:**
  Adjust the teacher forcing ratio during training to balance between exposure to ground truth and model predictions.
- **Temperature Sampling:**
  Experiment with different temperature values during generation. Lower temperatures make the output more deterministic, while higher temperatures introduce more randomness.
- **Evaluation Metrics:**
  Besides loss, evaluate the model using perplexity, which is a standard measure for language models.
- **Overfitting Prevention:**
  Regularization techniques such as dropout on the embeddings or LSTM layers can help improve generalization.

Exercises

1. **Model Variants:**
   Replace the LSTM with a GRU in the language model and compare the training dynamics and generated text quality.
2. **Word-Level Modeling:**
   Modify the example to build a word-level language model. Create a vocabulary of words, update the dataset preparation, and adjust the model accordingly.
3. **Attention Integration:**
   Explore adding an attention mechanism to the language model (e.g., self-attention over the sequence) to see if it improves the quality of generated text.
4. **Temperature Tuning:**
   Experiment with different temperature values during text generation. Generate samples at various temperatures and discuss how it affects creativity versus coherence.
5. **Evaluation Challenge:**
   Implement perplexity calculation on a held-out validation set and compare it to the training loss. Analyze the model's performance in terms of both metrics.

Language modeling and sequence generation are crucial tasks that underpin many natural language processing applications. By building and training a sequence model with PyTorch, you can learn to predict and generate text effectively. This section has provided both theoretical insights and practical implementations to help you understand the nuances of sequence modeling. With further experimentation—such as integrating attention or scaling to word-level models—you can extend these ideas to more complex tasks and larger datasets.

3.4 Anomaly Detection in Sequence Data

Anomaly detection involves identifying observations in a sequence that deviate significantly from the expected pattern. In time-series and sequential data, anomalies can indicate critical events such as fraud, system failures, or rare events in sensor readings. Unlike supervised tasks, anomaly detection is often unsupervised or semi-supervised because labeled anomalous data is rare. In this section, we explore how to leverage sequence models such as LSTMs, GRUs, and autoencoder architectures to detect anomalies.

Key Concepts and Approaches

- **Defining Anomalies:**
  Anomalies are data points or sequences that do not conform to the expected pattern. In sequential data, anomalies might be sudden spikes, dips, or unusual patterns in a time series.
- **Unsupervised vs. Supervised Methods:**
  - *Unsupervised Methods:* Train a model to learn the normal behavior and flag deviations (e.g., reconstruction error from an autoencoder).
  - *Supervised Methods:* Require labeled examples of normal and anomalous sequences, which can be challenging to obtain.
- **Modeling Strategies:**
  - **Reconstruction-Based Approaches:** Train an autoencoder or sequence-to-sequence model on normal data. High reconstruction error during inference signals an anomaly.
  - **Prediction-Based Approaches:** Train a model (e.g., LSTM) to predict the next value(s) in a sequence. Large prediction errors indicate deviations from the learned pattern.
  - **Hybrid Methods:** Combine reconstruction and prediction methods or incorporate probabilistic models for more robust detection.

Practical Model Example: LSTM Autoencoder for Anomaly Detection

In this example, we implement an LSTM autoencoder that learns to reconstruct normal sequences. During inference, sequences that yield a high reconstruction error are flagged as anomalies.

1. Data Preparation

We assume a univariate time-series dataset (e.g., sensor readings). The data is split into overlapping sliding windows.

```python
import numpy as np
import torch
from torch.utils.data import Dataset, DataLoader
```

```python
import matplotlib.pyplot as plt

# Generate synthetic time-series data: a sine wave
with injected anomalies
np.random.seed(42)
time = np.arange(0, 400, 0.1)
data = np.sin(time) + 0.05 *
np.random.randn(len(time))

# Inject anomalies: add spikes at random indices
anomaly_indices = np.random.choice(len(data),
size=10, replace=False)
data[anomaly_indices] += np.random.uniform(2, 3,
size=10)

plt.figure(figsize=(10, 4))
plt.plot(time, data, label="Time-Series")
plt.scatter(time[anomaly_indices],
data[anomaly_indices], color='red',
label="Anomalies")
plt.title("Synthetic Time-Series with Anomalies")
plt.xlabel("Time")
plt.ylabel("Value")
plt.legend()
plt.show()

# Create a sliding window dataset
class TimeSeriesDataset(Dataset):
    def __init__(self, series, window_size):
        self.series = series
        self.window_size = window_size

    def __len__(self):
        return len(self.series) - self.window_size

    def __getitem__(self, idx):
        x = self.series[idx: idx +
self.window_size]
        return torch.tensor(x,
dtype=torch.float32).unsqueeze(-1)

window_size = 50
```

```python
dataset = TimeSeriesDataset(data, window_size)
train_size = int(0.8 * len(dataset))
test_size = len(dataset) - train_size
train_dataset, test_dataset =
torch.utils.data.random_split(dataset, [train_size,
test_size])
batch_size = 32
train_loader = DataLoader(train_dataset,
batch_size=batch_size, shuffle=True)
test_loader = DataLoader(test_dataset,
batch_size=batch_size)
```

2. Model Architecture: LSTM Autoencoder

The autoencoder consists of an encoder LSTM that compresses the input sequence into a latent representation and a decoder LSTM that reconstructs the sequence from this representation.

python

```python
import torch.nn as nn

class LSTMAutoencoder(nn.Module):
    def __init__(self, input_dim=1, hidden_dim=64,
num_layers=1):
        super(LSTMAutoencoder, self).__init__()
        self.encoder = nn.LSTM(input_dim,
hidden_dim, num_layers, batch_first=True)
        self.decoder = nn.LSTM(hidden_dim,
hidden_dim, num_layers, batch_first=True)
        self.output_layer = nn.Linear(hidden_dim,
input_dim)

    def forward(self, x):
        # Encode
        _, (hidden, _) = self.encoder(x)
        # Repeat hidden state for each time step in
the sequence
        decoder_input = hidden.repeat(x.size(1), 1,
1).permute(1, 0, 2)
        # Decode
        decoded, _ = self.decoder(decoder_input)
```

```python
        output = self.output_layer(decoded)
        return output

device = torch.device("cuda" if
torch.cuda.is_available() else "cpu")
model = LSTMAutoencoder().to(device)
```

3. Training the Autoencoder

We train the model to minimize the reconstruction error (Mean Squared
Error).

python

```python
import torch.optim as optim

loss_fn = nn.MSELoss()
optimizer = optim.Adam(model.parameters(),
lr=0.001)
num_epochs = 20

for epoch in range(num_epochs):
    model.train()
    epoch_loss = 0.0
    for batch in train_loader:
        batch = batch.to(device)
        optimizer.zero_grad()
        reconstructed = model(batch)
        loss = loss_fn(reconstructed, batch)
        loss.backward()
        optimizer.step()
        epoch_loss += loss.item() * batch.size(0)
    epoch_loss /= len(train_loader.dataset)
    print(f"Epoch {epoch+1}/{num_epochs}, Loss:
{epoch_loss:.6f}")
```

4. Anomaly Detection Using Reconstruction Error

After training, we compute reconstruction errors on test data. Sequences with
errors above a threshold are flagged as anomalies.

python

```
model.eval()
reconstruction_errors = []
with torch.no_grad():
    for batch in test_loader:
        batch = batch.to(device)
        reconstructed = model(batch)
        error = torch.mean((batch - reconstructed)
** 2, dim=(1,2))

reconstruction_errors.extend(error.cpu().numpy())

# Visualize reconstruction errors
plt.figure(figsize=(10, 4))
plt.plot(reconstruction_errors,
label="Reconstruction Error")
plt.axhline(y=np.percentile(reconstruction_errors,
95), color='r', linestyle='--', label="95th
Percentile Threshold")
plt.title("Reconstruction Error on Test Data")
plt.xlabel("Batch Sample Index")
plt.ylabel("Error")
plt.legend()
plt.show()
```

By setting a threshold (e.g., the 95th percentile of the reconstruction errors), you can flag sequences with errors exceeding this threshold as anomalies.

Best Practices and Troubleshooting

- **Data Preprocessing:**
  Normalize or standardize your data before training to help the model learn a robust representation of normal behavior.
- **Model Capacity:**
  Adjust hidden dimensions and number of layers to balance between underfitting (missing subtle anomalies) and overfitting (memorizing the training data).
- **Threshold Selection:**
  The anomaly threshold may require tuning based on domain-specific considerations. Use validation data to set a reasonable threshold.

- **Evaluation Metrics:**
  When possible, evaluate using precision, recall, and F1-score, especially if some labeled anomalies are available.
- **Visualization:**
  Plot reconstruction error distributions and overlay detected anomalies on the time-series plot to visually assess performance.

Exercises

1. **Model Variation:**
   Replace the LSTM autoencoder with a GRU autoencoder and compare reconstruction errors on the same test data.
2. **Prediction-Based Anomaly Detection:**
   Implement an LSTM-based prediction model that forecasts the next value in the sequence. Compare prediction errors with reconstruction errors for anomaly detection.
3. **Threshold Tuning:**
   Experiment with different threshold levels (e.g., 90th, 95th, 99th percentiles) and assess how the number of detected anomalies changes.
4. **Real-World Dataset:**
   Apply your anomaly detection pipeline to a real-world time-series dataset (e.g., sensor readings from industrial equipment) and evaluate the model's performance.
5. **Hybrid Approach:**
   Combine reconstruction and prediction errors (e.g., by averaging) to develop a more robust anomaly detection score.

Anomaly detection in sequence data is a powerful tool for uncovering critical events and deviations in time-series. By leveraging deep learning models—such as LSTM autoencoders or prediction-based models—you can effectively capture the underlying patterns of normal behavior and flag unusual events. This section provided a practical walkthrough of an LSTM autoencoder for anomaly detection, complete with hands-on code, best practices, and exercises for further exploration.

3.5 Project: Financial Market Prediction Using LSTM Ensembles

Financial markets are complex systems where historical price movements, volume, and other indicators can help predict future trends. However, the inherent noise and non-stationarity of financial data make forecasting challenging. In this project, we will build an ensemble of LSTM models to capture diverse patterns in the data. Ensembles tend to offer improved robustness and accuracy compared to single models by aggregating predictions and reducing variance.

2. Project Objectives

- **Data Preparation:**
  Prepare and preprocess financial time-series data (e.g., stock prices or indices) using sliding windows, normalization, and train-test splits.
- **Model Design:**
  Build individual LSTM models that learn temporal dependencies in financial data.
- **Ensemble Learning:**
  Combine multiple LSTM models into an ensemble using techniques like averaging or weighted voting.
- **Training and Optimization:**
  Train the models using best practices such as gradient clipping, learning rate scheduling, and early stopping.
- **Evaluation:**
  Evaluate performance using metrics such as Mean Squared Error (MSE), Root Mean Squared Error (RMSE), and Mean Absolute Error (MAE).

3. Data Preparation

Assume you have a CSV file containing historical market data with columns like Date and Close price. The following example shows how to load and preprocess the data.

```python
import pandas as pd
import numpy as np
import matplotlib.pyplot as plt
```

```python
import torch
from torch.utils.data import Dataset, DataLoader
from sklearn.preprocessing import MinMaxScaler

# Load data
data = pd.read_csv("financial_data.csv")  # Replace
with your data file path
# Assume the CSV has columns 'Date' and 'Close'
data['Date'] = pd.to_datetime(data['Date'])
data = data.sort_values("Date")
prices = data['Close'].values.reshape(-1, 1)

# Normalize prices using MinMax scaling
scaler = MinMaxScaler(feature_range=(0, 1))
normalized_prices = scaler.fit_transform(prices)

# Plot the normalized time-series
plt.figure(figsize=(10, 4))
plt.plot(data['Date'], normalized_prices)
plt.title("Normalized Market Prices")
plt.xlabel("Date")
plt.ylabel("Normalized Price")
plt.show()

# Create sliding window sequences
def create_sequences(data, window_size):
    sequences = []
    targets = []
    for i in range(len(data) - window_size):
        sequences.append(data[i:i+window_size])
        targets.append(data[i+window_size])
    return np.array(sequences), np.array(targets)

window_size = 60  # e.g., using 60 days of data to
predict the next day
X, y = create_sequences(normalized_prices,
window_size)

# Split into training and testing sets (e.g., 80/20
split)
split = int(0.8 * len(X))
X_train, X_test = X[:split], X[split:]
```

```python
y_train, y_test = y[:split], y[split:]

# Convert to PyTorch tensors
X_train = torch.tensor(X_train,
dtype=torch.float32)
y_train = torch.tensor(y_train,
dtype=torch.float32)
X_test = torch.tensor(X_test, dtype=torch.float32)
y_test = torch.tensor(y_test, dtype=torch.float32)

# Create dataset and dataloaders
class FinancialDataset(Dataset):
    def __init__(self, sequences, targets):
        self.sequences = sequences
        self.targets = targets

    def __len__(self):
        return len(self.sequences)

    def __getitem__(self, idx):
        # Add an extra dimension for input feature
(channel dimension)
        return self.sequences[idx].unsqueeze(-1),
self.targets[idx]

train_dataset = FinancialDataset(X_train, y_train)
test_dataset = FinancialDataset(X_test, y_test)
batch_size = 32
train_loader = DataLoader(train_dataset,
batch_size=batch_size, shuffle=True)
test_loader = DataLoader(test_dataset,
batch_size=batch_size)
```

4. Model Architecture: Building an LSTM

Below is the definition of a simple LSTM model for time-series forecasting.

```python
python

import torch.nn as nn

class LSTMModel(nn.Module):
```

```python
    def __init__(self, input_dim, hidden_dim,
num_layers, output_dim):
        super(LSTMModel, self).__init__()
        self.lstm = nn.LSTM(input_dim, hidden_dim,
num_layers, batch_first=True)
        self.fc = nn.Linear(hidden_dim, output_dim)

    def forward(self, x):
        # x: (batch_size, window_size, input_dim)
        out, _ = self.lstm(x)
        # Use the output of the last time step
        out = out[:, -1, :]
        out = self.fc(out)
        return out

input_dim = 1
hidden_dim = 64
num_layers = 2
output_dim = 1
```

5. Ensemble Strategy

We create an ensemble of multiple LSTM models. Each model is trained independently, and during inference, their predictions are averaged.

python

```python
def create_ensemble(num_models, input_dim,
hidden_dim, num_layers, output_dim, device):
    ensemble = []
    for _ in range(num_models):
        model = LSTMModel(input_dim, hidden_dim,
num_layers, output_dim).to(device)
        ensemble.append(model)
    return ensemble

device = torch.device("cuda" if
torch.cuda.is_available() else "cpu")
num_models = 3
ensemble_models = create_ensemble(num_models,
input_dim, hidden_dim, num_layers, output_dim,
device)
```

6. Training the Ensemble

Train each model separately and store their weights. For simplicity, we use the same optimizer settings and number of epochs for all models.

```python
import torch.optim as optim

def train_model(model, train_loader, num_epochs, device):
    model.train()
    loss_fn = nn.MSELoss()
    optimizer = optim.Adam(model.parameters(), lr=0.001)
    for epoch in range(num_epochs):
        epoch_loss = 0.0
        for x_batch, y_batch in train_loader:
            x_batch, y_batch = x_batch.to(device), y_batch.to(device)
            optimizer.zero_grad()
            preds = model(x_batch)
            loss = loss_fn(preds, y_batch)
            loss.backward()
            optimizer.step()
            epoch_loss += loss.item() * x_batch.size(0)
        epoch_loss /= len(train_loader.dataset)
        print(f"Model Training Epoch {epoch+1}/{num_epochs}, Loss: {epoch_loss:.6f}")

num_epochs = 30
for idx, model in enumerate(ensemble_models):
    print(f"\nTraining model {idx+1}/{num_models}:")
    train_model(model, train_loader, num_epochs, device)
```

7. Ensemble Prediction and Evaluation

After training, aggregate the predictions from each model by averaging them. Evaluate the ensemble performance using Mean Squared Error (MSE) and plot the forecast against actual values.

```python
import torch.nn.functional as F

def ensemble_predict(ensemble, data_loader,
device):
    ensemble_preds = []
    for model in ensemble:
        model.eval()
    with torch.no_grad():
        for x_batch, _ in data_loader:
            x_batch = x_batch.to(device)
            batch_preds = []
            for model in ensemble:
                preds = model(x_batch)
                batch_preds.append(preds)
            # Average predictions from all models
in the ensemble
            avg_preds =
torch.mean(torch.stack(batch_preds), dim=0)
            ensemble_preds.append(avg_preds.cpu())
    return torch.cat(ensemble_preds, dim=0)

ensemble_predictions =
ensemble_predict(ensemble_models, test_loader,
device)

# Compute evaluation metric
from sklearn.metrics import mean_squared_error
mse = mean_squared_error(y_test.numpy(),
ensemble_predictions.numpy())
print(f"Ensemble MSE: {mse:.6f}")

# Plot actual vs. predicted values
plt.figure(figsize=(10, 4))
plt.plot(y_test.numpy(), label="Actual")
```

```
plt.plot(ensemble_predictions.numpy(),
label="Ensemble Prediction")
plt.title("Financial Market Prediction: Actual vs.
Ensemble Forecast")
plt.xlabel("Time Steps")
plt.ylabel("Normalized Price")
plt.legend()
plt.show()
```

8. Best Practices and Troubleshooting

- **Data Stationarity:**
  Financial data often exhibits non-stationarity. Consider differencing or detrending before model training.
- **Regularization:**
  Use dropout, early stopping, or L2 regularization to prevent overfitting, especially given the noisy nature of financial data.
- **Hyperparameter Tuning:**
  Experiment with different window sizes, hidden dimensions, learning rates, and number of layers to optimize forecasting performance.
- **Ensemble Diversity:**
  Ensure that ensemble models are diverse. You can achieve this by varying random seeds, architecture parameters, or even training on slightly different data splits.
- **Evaluation Metrics:**
  Besides MSE, consider MAE and RMSE. In practice, forecasting performance might also be evaluated using directional accuracy (e.g., predicting whether the market will go up or down).

9. Exercises

1. **Ensemble Variation:**
   Train ensembles with different numbers of models (e.g., 3, 5, 7) and compare their forecasting performance.
2. **Feature Engineering:**
   Incorporate additional features (e.g., trading volume, technical indicators) into the input and assess how they affect predictions.
3. **Model Diversity:**
   Experiment with ensembles that mix different architectures (e.g., combine LSTM and GRU models) and compare results.
4. **Hyperparameter Search:**
   Implement a grid or random search for hyperparameters (window

size, learning rate, hidden dimension) and analyze their impact on the ensemble's accuracy.
5. **Backtesting:**
   If you have access to historical financial data, perform backtesting of the ensemble's predictions to evaluate its practical applicability in a trading scenario.

This project demonstrated how to build and deploy an ensemble of LSTM models for financial market prediction. By leveraging the strengths of ensemble methods, you can improve forecasting robustness and accuracy in the inherently noisy financial domain. With careful data preparation, model tuning, and ensemble aggregation, these techniques offer a powerful approach for real-world market prediction.

3.6 Exercise: Building a Real-Time Chatbot with RNNs

Chatbots are an exciting application of sequence modeling, where the goal is to generate human-like responses to user inputs in real time. In this exercise, you'll build a simple chatbot using an RNN-based encoder–decoder architecture. Although production-grade chatbots are more complex and may leverage attention mechanisms or transformers, this exercise provides a hands-on to using RNNs for conversational AI.

Key objectives:

- **Data Preparation:** Process a small conversational dataset (e.g., question–response pairs) for training.
- **Model Architecture:** Implement a basic sequence-to-sequence model with an RNN encoder and decoder.
- **Training:** Train the model using teacher forcing.
- **Inference:** Build an interactive loop that accepts user input and generates responses in real time.
- **Best Practices:** Learn strategies to improve model performance and troubleshoot common issues.

1. Data Preparation

For this exercise, we use a dummy dataset of conversation pairs. In practice, you might use datasets such as the Cornell Movie Dialogs or other chat corpora. The following example demonstrates how to tokenize the text, build a vocabulary, and convert sentences to sequences of token indices.

```python
import torch
from torch.utils.data import Dataset, DataLoader
import re

# Dummy conversation pairs (question, answer)
conversation_pairs = [
    ("Hello", "Hi there!"),
    ("How are you?", "I'm good, thank you."),
    ("What's your name?", "I'm ChatBot."),
    ("Tell me a joke.", "Why did the chicken cross
the road? To get to the other side!"),
    ("Goodbye", "See you later!")
]

# Basic text preprocessing: lowercasing and
removing punctuation
def preprocess(text):
    text = text.lower()
    text = re.sub(r"[^a-zA-Z0-9\s]", "", text)
    return text

# Build vocabulary from the dataset
vocab = {"<pad>": 0, "<sos>": 1, "<eos>": 2,
"<unk>": 3}
def build_vocab(pairs):
    idx = len(vocab)
    for q, a in pairs:
        for sentence in [q, a]:
            sentence = preprocess(sentence)
            for word in sentence.split():
                if word not in vocab:
                    vocab[word] = idx
                    idx += 1

build_vocab(conversation_pairs)

# Tokenize sentences into indices
```

```python
def tokenize(sentence):
    sentence = preprocess(sentence)
    tokens = [vocab.get(word, vocab["<unk>"]) for
word in sentence.split()]
    return tokens

# Dataset class for conversation pairs
class ChatDataset(Dataset):
    def __init__(self, pairs, max_len=10):
        self.pairs = pairs
        self.max_len = max_len

    def __len__(self):
        return len(self.pairs)

    def __getitem__(self, idx):
        question, answer = self.pairs[idx]
        q_tokens = [vocab["<sos>"]] +
tokenize(question) + [vocab["<eos>"]]
        a_tokens = [vocab["<sos>"]] +
tokenize(answer) + [vocab["<eos>"]]
        # Pad sequences to max_len
        q_tokens = q_tokens + [vocab["<pad>"]] *
(self.max_len - len(q_tokens)) if len(q_tokens) <
self.max_len else q_tokens[:self.max_len]
        a_tokens = a_tokens + [vocab["<pad>"]] *
(self.max_len - len(a_tokens)) if len(a_tokens) <
self.max_len else a_tokens[:self.max_len]
        return torch.tensor(q_tokens,
dtype=torch.long), torch.tensor(a_tokens,
dtype=torch.long)

max_len = 10
dataset = ChatDataset(conversation_pairs,
max_len=max_len)
data_loader = DataLoader(dataset, batch_size=2,
shuffle=True)
```

2. Model Architecture: Encoder–Decoder with RNNs

We'll build a simple sequence-to-sequence model with:

- **Encoder:** An RNN (or LSTM) that processes the input sequence.
- **Decoder:** Another RNN that generates the response one token at a time.
- **Teacher Forcing:** During training, the decoder is provided with the actual previous token.

```python
import torch.nn as nn

class Encoder(nn.Module):
    def __init__(self, vocab_size, embedding_dim, hidden_dim, num_layers=1):
        super(Encoder, self).__init__()
        self.embedding = nn.Embedding(vocab_size, embedding_dim, padding_idx=vocab["<pad>"])
        self.rnn = nn.RNN(embedding_dim, hidden_dim, num_layers, batch_first=True)

    def forward(self, x):
        embedded = self.embedding(x)
        outputs, hidden = self.rnn(embedded)
        return hidden

class Decoder(nn.Module):
    def __init__(self, vocab_size, embedding_dim, hidden_dim, num_layers=1):
        super(Decoder, self).__init__()
        self.embedding = nn.Embedding(vocab_size, embedding_dim, padding_idx=vocab["<pad>"])
        self.rnn = nn.RNN(embedding_dim, hidden_dim, num_layers, batch_first=True)
        self.fc = nn.Linear(hidden_dim, vocab_size)

    def forward(self, x, hidden):
        embedded = self.embedding(x)
        outputs, hidden = self.rnn(embedded, hidden)
        predictions = self.fc(outputs)
        return predictions, hidden

vocab_size = len(vocab)
```

```python
embedding_dim = 50
hidden_dim = 128
num_layers = 1

encoder = Encoder(vocab_size, embedding_dim,
hidden_dim, num_layers)
decoder = Decoder(vocab_size, embedding_dim,
hidden_dim, num_layers)
```

3. Training the Chatbot

The training loop uses teacher forcing to feed the ground truth token as the next input to the decoder. The loss is computed over the entire output sequence.

python

```python
import torch.optim as optim

device = torch.device("cuda" if
torch.cuda.is_available() else "cpu")
encoder.to(device)
decoder.to(device)

loss_fn =
nn.CrossEntropyLoss(ignore_index=vocab["<pad>"])
encoder_optimizer =
optim.Adam(encoder.parameters(), lr=0.01)
decoder_optimizer =
optim.Adam(decoder.parameters(), lr=0.01)

num_epochs = 100

for epoch in range(num_epochs):
    epoch_loss = 0.0
    for q_batch, a_batch in data_loader:
        q_batch, a_batch = q_batch.to(device),
a_batch.to(device)
        encoder_optimizer.zero_grad()
        decoder_optimizer.zero_grad()
```

```
        # Encoder forward pass
        encoder_hidden = encoder(q_batch)

        # Decoder forward pass with teacher forcing
        decoder_input = a_batch[:, 0].unsqueeze(1)
# Start with <sos> token
        decoder_hidden = encoder_hidden
        loss = 0.0

        # Iterate over sequence length (excluding
the first token)
        for t in range(1, a_batch.size(1)):
            output, decoder_hidden =
decoder(decoder_input, decoder_hidden)
            # output: (batch, 1, vocab_size),
target: a_batch[:, t]
            loss += loss_fn(output.squeeze(1),
a_batch[:, t])
            # Teacher forcing: use the true token
as the next input
            decoder_input = a_batch[:,
t].unsqueeze(1)

        loss.backward()
        encoder_optimizer.step()
        decoder_optimizer.step()

        epoch_loss += loss.item() /
(a_batch.size(1) - 1)

    if (epoch + 1) % 10 == 0:
        print(f"Epoch [{epoch+1}/{num_epochs}],
Loss: {epoch_loss/len(data_loader):.4f}")
```

4. Real-Time Inference: Generating Responses

After training, the chatbot can generate responses to user inputs. During
inference, the decoder uses its own predictions as the next input.

python

```python
def generate_response(encoder, decoder, sentence,
max_len=10, temperature=1.0):
    encoder.eval()
    decoder.eval()

    # Preprocess and tokenize the input sentence
    tokens = [vocab["<sos>"]] + tokenize(sentence)
+ [vocab["<eos>"]]
    tokens = tokens + [vocab["<pad>"]] * (max_len -
len(tokens)) if len(tokens) < max_len else
tokens[:max_len]
    input_seq = torch.tensor(tokens,
dtype=torch.long).unsqueeze(0).to(device)

    # Encode the input sentence
    encoder_hidden = encoder(input_seq)

    # Initialize decoder input with <sos> token
    decoder_input =
torch.tensor([[vocab["<sos>"]]],
dtype=torch.long).to(device)
    decoder_hidden = encoder_hidden
    generated_tokens = []

    for _ in range(max_len):
        output, decoder_hidden =
decoder(decoder_input, decoder_hidden)
        # Apply temperature scaling and softmax
        output = output.squeeze(1) / temperature
        probs = torch.softmax(output, dim=-1)
        # Sample the next token
        next_token = torch.multinomial(probs,
num_samples=1).item()
        if next_token == vocab["<eos>"]:
            break
        generated_tokens.append(next_token)
        decoder_input =
torch.tensor([[next_token]],
dtype=torch.long).to(device)

    # Convert token indices back to words
```

```
    idx2word = {idx: word for word, idx in
vocab.items()}
    response = " ".join([idx2word.get(token,
"<unk>") for token in generated_tokens])
    return response

# Interactive loop for real-time conversation
while True:
    user_input = input("User: ")
    if user_input.lower() in ["exit", "quit"]:
        break
    response = generate_response(encoder, decoder,
user_input, max_len=max_len)
    print("ChatBot:", response)
```

5. Best Practices and Troubleshooting

- **Data Quality:**
  Use a diverse and rich conversational dataset to improve model performance. Data augmentation techniques can help when data is limited.
- **Teacher Forcing Ratio:**
  Experiment with varying the teacher forcing ratio during training to balance between guided learning and model autonomy.
- **Hyperparameter Tuning:**
  Adjust parameters such as hidden dimensions, learning rate, and sequence length to optimize the quality of generated responses.
- **Real-Time Performance:**
  For production-level chatbots, consider optimizing the model for latency (e.g., by quantization or model distillation) and integrating error handling for unexpected inputs.
- **Evaluation:**
  Use qualitative measures (e.g., human evaluation) and quantitative metrics (e.g., BLEU scores) to assess the coherence and relevance of the chatbot's responses.

6. Exercises

1. **Dataset Expansion:**
   Use a larger conversational dataset (e.g., Cornell Movie Dialogs) to train the chatbot. Compare the quality of responses with the dummy dataset.
2. **Model Variants:**
   Replace the basic RNNs with LSTMs or GRUs in both the encoder and decoder, and analyze any improvements in response quality.
3. **Attention Mechanism:**
   Integrate an attention mechanism in the decoder to allow the model to focus on relevant parts of the input sequence during response generation.
4. **User Interface:**
   Develop a simple graphical interface (using Flask or Streamlit) to interact with your chatbot in real time.
5. **Error Analysis:**
   Collect user feedback on generated responses, analyze common errors, and fine-tune the model or data preprocessing pipeline accordingly.

This exercise has walked you through building a basic real-time chatbot using RNN-based encoder–decoder architecture. By preparing conversational data, training the model with teacher forcing, and implementing an interactive inference loop, you've gained practical experience in applying sequence models to conversational AI. Experiment further by expanding the dataset, exploring advanced architectures, and integrating additional improvements to build a more robust chatbot.

Chapter 4: Transformers and Attention Mechanisms

4.1 Transformer Architectures: Deep Dive and Intuition

Transformers have revolutionized the field of deep learning by replacing recurrent and convolutional layers with self-attention mechanisms. Originally introduced in "Attention Is All You Need," transformers excel at modeling long-range dependencies and handling sequential data without the limitations of RNNs. This section provides a deep dive into transformer architectures, exploring their key building blocks, design choices, and practical considerations.

Key Components of the Transformer

Transformers consist of several interconnected components that work together to process input sequences in parallel:

1. Self-Attention Mechanism

- **Intuition:**
  Self-attention allows the model to weigh the relevance of each token in the input sequence relative to others. Rather than processing tokens sequentially, self-attention enables the model to capture contextual relationships across the entire sequence simultaneously.
- **Mechanics:**
  For each token, the self-attention mechanism computes queries (Q), keys (K), and values (V) using learned linear projections. Attention scores are calculated by taking the dot product between queries and keys, scaled, and then passed through a softmax to obtain weights. These weights are used to compute a weighted sum of the values, which represents the attended information for that token.

2. Multi-Head Attention

- **Intuition:**
  Instead of computing a single attention representation, transformers use multiple "heads" to attend to different aspects of the sequence. This allows the model to capture diverse patterns and relationships in parallel.

- **Mechanics:**
  Each head performs its own self-attention calculation with separate linear projections. The outputs from all heads are concatenated and projected back to the desired dimension, providing a richer representation.

3. Position-Wise Feedforward Networks

- **Intuition:**
  Following the attention layers, a fully connected feedforward network is applied to each position independently. This network adds non-linearity and further transforms the features extracted by the attention mechanism.
- **Mechanics:**
  Typically composed of two linear transformations with a ReLU activation in between, these networks help capture complex patterns beyond the linear combinations learned by attention.

4. Positional Encoding

- **Intuition:**
  Since transformers process input tokens in parallel and lack inherent sequential ordering, positional encodings are added to input embeddings to inject information about token order.
- **Mechanics:**
  Positional encodings are typically generated using sinusoidal functions or learned embeddings. They are added element-wise to the input embeddings before feeding the data into the transformer layers.

The Transformer Block

A standard transformer block combines the above components in a modular way:

1. **Multi-Head Self-Attention Layer:**
   Processes input embeddings and applies attention mechanisms with multiple heads.
2. **Add & Norm:**
   A residual connection adds the attention output to the original input, followed by layer normalization for stabilizing training.

3. **Position-Wise Feedforward Network:**
   Applies a fully connected network to each token independently.
4. **Add & Norm:**
   Another residual connection and layer normalization follow the feedforward network.

These blocks can be stacked to build deep transformer models, where each block refines the representations learned from the previous layer.

Hands-On Code Example

Below is a simplified implementation of a transformer block using PyTorch. This example illustrates the core components of self-attention, multi-head attention, and the feedforward network.

```python
import torch
import torch.nn as nn
import torch.nn.functional as F
import math

class MultiHeadSelfAttention(nn.Module):
    def __init__(self, embed_dim, num_heads):
        super(MultiHeadSelfAttention,
self).__init__()
        assert embed_dim % num_heads == 0,
"Embedding dimension must be divisible by number of
heads"
        self.embed_dim = embed_dim
        self.num_heads = num_heads
        self.head_dim = embed_dim // num_heads

        self.q_linear = nn.Linear(embed_dim,
embed_dim)
        self.k_linear = nn.Linear(embed_dim,
embed_dim)
        self.v_linear = nn.Linear(embed_dim,
embed_dim)
```

```python
        self.out_linear = nn.Linear(embed_dim,
embed_dim)

    def forward(self, x):
        batch_size, seq_length, embed_dim =
x.size()

        # Linear projections for queries, keys, and
values
        Q = self.q_linear(x)  # (batch_size,
seq_length, embed_dim)
        K = self.k_linear(x)
        V = self.v_linear(x)

        # Split into multiple heads and reshape:
(batch_size, num_heads, seq_length, head_dim)
        Q = Q.view(batch_size, seq_length,
self.num_heads, self.head_dim).transpose(1, 2)
        K = K.view(batch_size, seq_length,
self.num_heads, self.head_dim).transpose(1, 2)
        V = V.view(batch_size, seq_length,
self.num_heads, self.head_dim).transpose(1, 2)

        # Scaled dot-product attention
        scores = torch.matmul(Q, K.transpose(-2, -
1)) / math.sqrt(self.head_dim)
        attn_weights = F.softmax(scores, dim=-1)
        attn_output = torch.matmul(attn_weights, V)

        # Concatenate heads and project output
        attn_output = attn_output.transpose(1,
2).contiguous().view(batch_size, seq_length,
embed_dim)
        output = self.out_linear(attn_output)
        return output

class PositionwiseFeedForward(nn.Module):
    def __init__(self, embed_dim, ff_dim,
dropout=0.1):
        super(PositionwiseFeedForward,
self).__init__()
        self.fc1 = nn.Linear(embed_dim, ff_dim)
```

```python
        self.fc2 = nn.Linear(ff_dim, embed_dim)
        self.dropout = nn.Dropout(dropout)

    def forward(self, x):
        return
self.fc2(self.dropout(F.relu(self.fc1(x))))

class PositionalEncoding(nn.Module):
    def __init__(self, embed_dim, max_len=5000):
        super(PositionalEncoding, self).__init__()
        pe = torch.zeros(max_len, embed_dim)
        position = torch.arange(0, max_len,
dtype=torch.float).unsqueeze(1)
        div_term = torch.exp(torch.arange(0,
embed_dim, 2).float() * (-math.log(10000.0) /
embed_dim))
        pe[:, 0::2] = torch.sin(position *
div_term)
        pe[:, 1::2] = torch.cos(position *
div_term)
        pe = pe.unsqueeze(0)   # (1, max_len,
embed_dim)
        self.register_buffer('pe', pe)

    def forward(self, x):
        # x: (batch_size, seq_length, embed_dim)
        x = x + self.pe[:, :x.size(1), :]
        return x

class TransformerBlock(nn.Module):
    def __init__(self, embed_dim, num_heads,
ff_dim, dropout=0.1):
        super(TransformerBlock, self).__init__()
        self.attention =
MultiHeadSelfAttention(embed_dim, num_heads)
        self.norm1 = nn.LayerNorm(embed_dim)
        self.ff =
PositionwiseFeedForward(embed_dim, ff_dim, dropout)
        self.norm2 = nn.LayerNorm(embed_dim)
        self.dropout = nn.Dropout(dropout)

    def forward(self, x):
```

```
        # Multi-head self-attention sub-layer
        attn_output = self.attention(x)
        x = self.norm1(x +
self.dropout(attn_output))
        # Position-wise feedforward sub-layer
        ff_output = self.ff(x)
        x = self.norm2(x + self.dropout(ff_output))
        return x

# Sample usage:
batch_size, seq_length, embed_dim = 16, 50, 128
num_heads = 8
ff_dim = 256

# Create random input embeddings and add positional
encoding
x = torch.randn(batch_size, seq_length, embed_dim)
pos_enc = PositionalEncoding(embed_dim)
x = pos_enc(x)

# Pass through a transformer block
transformer_block = TransformerBlock(embed_dim,
num_heads, ff_dim)
output = transformer_block(x)
print("Transformer block output shape:",
output.shape)
```

Best Practices and Troubleshooting

- **Residual Connections and Layer Normalization:**
  Ensure proper use of residual connections and layer normalization
  after both attention and feedforward sub-layers for stable training.
- **Dropout:**
  Use dropout to prevent overfitting, especially when stacking multiple
  transformer blocks.
- **Positional Encoding:**
  Experiment with both sinusoidal and learned positional encodings to
  find the best match for your task.
- **Hyperparameter Tuning:**
  Adjust the number of attention heads, embedding dimensions, and

feedforward dimensions based on available data and computational resources.

- **Monitoring and Debugging:**
  Visualize attention weights to understand how the model focuses on different parts of the input. Use debugging tools (e.g., TensorBoard) to monitor training dynamics and detect potential issues such as vanishing gradients.

Exercises

1. **Implement Variations:**
   Modify the transformer block to experiment with different attention mechanisms (e.g., dot-product vs. additive attention) and observe their impact on performance.
2. **Stacking Transformer Blocks:**
   Build a small transformer encoder by stacking multiple transformer blocks. Train it on a synthetic sequence task (e.g., sequence classification) and analyze the effect of increasing depth.
3. **Positional Encoding Experiment:**
   Replace the sinusoidal positional encoding with learnable embeddings. Compare the performance and convergence behavior on a small benchmark task.
4. **Visualization:**
   Visualize the attention weights from the multi-head self-attention layer for sample inputs. Identify which tokens the model focuses on and discuss how this might affect downstream tasks.

This deep dive into transformer architectures provides the foundation for understanding how self-attention and multi-head mechanisms enable the parallel processing of sequences and capture complex dependencies. By exploring the inner workings of transformers and experimenting with their components, you gain both theoretical insight and practical skills crucial for cutting-edge applications. These concepts pave the way for advanced applications in natural language processing, computer vision, and beyond.

4.2 Attention Mechanisms in Practice

Attention mechanisms have transformed deep learning by allowing models to dynamically weigh the importance of different input elements. In practice, two types of attention are widely used:

- **Self-Attention:**
  Enables a model to examine all tokens within the same sequence. Each token is reweighted based on its relevance to every other token. Self-attention is the core of transformer encoders and is key to capturing long-range dependencies without recurrence.
- **Cross-Attention:**
  Used in encoder–decoder architectures, cross-attention allows the decoder to attend to encoder outputs. This mechanism lets the model focus on different parts of the input sequence (e.g., in machine translation, the source sentence) when generating each token of the output.

In this section, we explain these mechanisms, illustrate them with code examples, and discuss how to implement them in practice.

Self-Attention in Practice

Overview

In self-attention, each token in a sequence computes a weighted representation of all other tokens. The process involves:

1. **Projection:**
   The input embeddings are linearly projected into queries (Q), keys (K), and values (V).
2. **Attention Scores:**
   For each token, compute scores using the dot product between its query and all keys. These scores are scaled and passed through a softmax to generate attention weights.
3. **Context Vector:**
   The attention weights are used to compute a weighted sum of the value vectors, producing an updated representation for each token.

Code Example: Self-Attention Module

Below is a PyTorch implementation of a multi-head self-attention layer (similar to the one in Section 4.1):

```python
import torch
import torch.nn as nn
import torch.nn.functional as F
import math

class MultiHeadSelfAttention(nn.Module):
    def __init__(self, embed_dim, num_heads):
        super(MultiHeadSelfAttention,
self).__init__()
        assert embed_dim % num_heads == 0, "Embed
dimension must be divisible by number of heads."
        self.embed_dim = embed_dim
        self.num_heads = num_heads
        self.head_dim = embed_dim // num_heads

        self.q_linear = nn.Linear(embed_dim,
embed_dim)
        self.k_linear = nn.Linear(embed_dim,
embed_dim)
        self.v_linear = nn.Linear(embed_dim,
embed_dim)
        self.out_linear = nn.Linear(embed_dim,
embed_dim)

    def forward(self, x):
        batch_size, seq_length, embed_dim =
x.size()

        # Project input into queries, keys, and
values
        Q = self.q_linear(x)
        K = self.k_linear(x)
        V = self.v_linear(x)
```

```python
        # Reshape for multi-head attention:
(batch_size, num_heads, seq_length, head_dim)
        Q = Q.view(batch_size, seq_length,
self.num_heads, self.head_dim).transpose(1, 2)
        K = K.view(batch_size, seq_length,
self.num_heads, self.head_dim).transpose(1, 2)
        V = V.view(batch_size, seq_length,
self.num_heads, self.head_dim).transpose(1, 2)

        # Compute scaled dot-product attention
scores
        scores = torch.matmul(Q, K.transpose(-2, -
1)) / math.sqrt(self.head_dim)
        attn_weights = F.softmax(scores, dim=-1)
        attn_output = torch.matmul(attn_weights, V)

        # Concatenate attention heads and project
the output
        attn_output = attn_output.transpose(1,
2).contiguous().view(batch_size, seq_length,
embed_dim)
        output = self.out_linear(attn_output)
        return output

# Sample usage:
batch_size, seq_length, embed_dim = 16, 50, 128
num_heads = 8
x = torch.randn(batch_size, seq_length, embed_dim)
self_attn = MultiHeadSelfAttention(embed_dim,
num_heads)
output = self_attn(x)
print("Self-Attention output shape:", output.shape)
```

Cross-Attention in Practice

Overview

Cross-attention is key in encoder–decoder architectures. Instead of using the same input for queries, keys, and values, cross-attention uses one sequence as the source (keys and values) and another sequence as the target (queries).

This mechanism enables the decoder to focus on relevant parts of the encoder's output when generating each token.

Code Example: Cross-Attention Module

Below is an example of a multi-head cross-attention layer. Notice that the queries come from the decoder while the keys and values come from the encoder outputs.

```python
class MultiHeadCrossAttention(nn.Module):
    def __init__(self, embed_dim, num_heads):
        super(MultiHeadCrossAttention,
self).__init__()
        assert embed_dim % num_heads == 0, "Embed
dimension must be divisible by number of heads."
        self.embed_dim = embed_dim
        self.num_heads = num_heads
        self.head_dim = embed_dim // num_heads

        self.q_linear = nn.Linear(embed_dim,
embed_dim)
        self.k_linear = nn.Linear(embed_dim,
embed_dim)
        self.v_linear = nn.Linear(embed_dim,
embed_dim)
        self.out_linear = nn.Linear(embed_dim,
embed_dim)

    def forward(self, query, key, value):
        # query: (batch_size, target_seq_len,
embed_dim)
        # key, value: (batch_size, source_seq_len,
embed_dim)
        batch_size = query.size(0)

        Q = self.q_linear(query)
        K = self.k_linear(key)
        V = self.v_linear(value)

        # Reshape for multi-head attention
```

```python
        Q = Q.view(batch_size, -1, self.num_heads,
self.head_dim).transpose(1, 2)
        K = K.view(batch_size, -1, self.num_heads,
self.head_dim).transpose(1, 2)
        V = V.view(batch_size, -1, self.num_heads,
self.head_dim).transpose(1, 2)

        # Scaled dot-product attention
        scores = torch.matmul(Q, K.transpose(-2, -
1)) / math.sqrt(self.head_dim)
        attn_weights = F.softmax(scores, dim=-1)
        attn_output = torch.matmul(attn_weights, V)

        # Concatenate heads and project
        attn_output = attn_output.transpose(1,
2).contiguous().view(batch_size, -1,
self.embed_dim)
        output = self.out_linear(attn_output)
        return output, attn_weights

# Sample usage for cross-attention:
batch_size = 16
target_seq_len = 20  # length of decoder sequence
source_seq_len = 50  # length of encoder sequence
query = torch.randn(batch_size, target_seq_len,
embed_dim)
key = torch.randn(batch_size, source_seq_len,
embed_dim)
value = torch.randn(batch_size, source_seq_len,
embed_dim)
cross_attn = MultiHeadCrossAttention(embed_dim,
num_heads)
output, attn_weights = cross_attn(query, key,
value)
print("Cross-Attention output shape:",
output.shape)  # (batch_size, target_seq_len,
embed_dim)
print("Attention weights shape:",
attn_weights.shape)   # (batch_size, num_heads,
target_seq_len, source_seq_len)
```

Best Practices and Troubleshooting

- **Dimension Consistency:**
  Ensure that the dimensions of the queries, keys, and values match as required. For cross-attention, the embed dimensions for both encoder and decoder outputs should be identical.
- **Residual Connections and Normalization:**
  Use residual connections and layer normalization after attention layers to maintain stable training dynamics.
- **Dropout:**
  Incorporate dropout in attention weights and feedforward layers to prevent overfitting, especially when stacking multiple attention layers.
- **Visualization:**
  Visualize attention weights to understand which parts of the source sequence the model attends to during decoding. Tools like TensorBoard can help with this.
- **Temperature Tuning:**
  In some cases, adjusting the temperature in the softmax can help smooth the attention distribution if it becomes too peaked or too flat.

Exercises

1. **Implement Dot-Product Attention:**
   Modify the self-attention module to use dot-product attention without the additional linear projection for the compatibility function. Compare its performance with the additive version.
2. **Experiment with Cross-Attention:**
   Build a simple encoder–decoder model where the decoder uses cross-attention to attend to encoder outputs. Train the model on a small sequence-to-sequence task (e.g., machine translation or summarization) and visualize the attention weights.
3. **Attention Visualization:**
   Use a sample input sequence and visualize the attention weight matrices for both self-attention and cross-attention. Analyze which tokens receive the highest weights and discuss how this might affect the output.
4. **Layer Stacking Experiment:**
   Stack multiple attention layers (both self and cross) to form a mini-

transformer. Evaluate how increasing the number of layers impacts the model's performance on a synthetic sequence classification task.

Attention mechanisms are at the heart of modern deep learning architectures. By mastering self-attention and cross-attention, you unlock the ability to build models that can capture complex, long-range dependencies and context within sequences. This section provided practical insights and code examples for implementing these mechanisms, along with best practices and exercises to further deepen your understanding. As you experiment with these techniques, you'll gain the flexibility to design sophisticated models for a wide range of tasks, from natural language processing to computer vision.

4.3 Building Custom Transformers with PyTorch

Transformers have transformed the landscape of deep learning by enabling models to process entire sequences in parallel using self-attention mechanisms. While many pre-built transformer implementations are available, building a custom transformer from scratch offers significant flexibility. It allows you to tailor the architecture for domain-specific tasks and experiment with design choices. In this section, you'll learn how to create each component of the transformer model and assemble them into a cohesive network using PyTorch.

Key Components of a Custom Transformer

When building a transformer, you will typically implement the following components:

1. **Positional Encoding:**
   Since transformers process input sequences in parallel without recurrence, positional encodings are added to the input embeddings to provide information about token order. These can be either sinusoidal (fixed) or learnable.
2. **Multi-Head Self-Attention:**
   The self-attention mechanism computes pairwise interactions between tokens. Multi-head attention allows the model to attend to information from different representation subspaces simultaneously.

3. **Position-wise Feedforward Networks (FFN):**
   These are fully connected layers applied independently to each token. They add non-linearity and help further process the information extracted by the attention mechanism.
4. **Residual Connections and Layer Normalization:**
   To ensure stable gradients and faster convergence, residual connections and layer normalization are applied after each sub-layer.
5. **Stacking Transformer Blocks:**
   Transformer blocks, each containing multi-head attention and a feedforward network, are stacked to form deep transformer models. Depending on the task, you may implement an encoder, a decoder, or both.

Architecture Overview

A standard transformer encoder block consists of:

- **Input Embedding + Positional Encoding:**
  The raw token embeddings are enriched with positional information.
- **Multi-Head Self-Attention Sub-layer:**
  Computes attention over the entire sequence, enabling the model to capture contextual relationships.
- **Add & Norm:**
  A residual connection followed by layer normalization.
- **Feedforward Sub-layer:**
  A position-wise feedforward network that further processes each token's representation.
- **Add & Norm:**
  Another residual connection and layer normalization ensure stable signal propagation.

By stacking multiple such blocks, you can build a powerful transformer encoder tailored to your task.

Hands-On Code Example

Below is an end-to-end example of building a custom transformer encoder in PyTorch. This code includes modules for positional encoding, multi-head self-attention, a transformer block, and a final transformer encoder that can be used for tasks such as classification or sequence modeling.

```python
import torch
import torch.nn as nn
import torch.nn.functional as F
import math

# Positional Encoding Module
class PositionalEncoding(nn.Module):
    def __init__(self, embed_dim, max_len=5000):
        super(PositionalEncoding, self).__init__()
        pe = torch.zeros(max_len, embed_dim)
        position = torch.arange(0, max_len,
dtype=torch.float).unsqueeze(1)
        div_term = torch.exp(torch.arange(0,
embed_dim, 2).float() * (-math.log(10000.0) /
embed_dim))
        pe[:, 0::2] = torch.sin(position *
div_term)
        pe[:, 1::2] = torch.cos(position *
div_term)
        pe = pe.unsqueeze(0)  # shape: (1, max_len,
embed_dim)
        self.register_buffer('pe', pe)

    def forward(self, x):
        # x: (batch_size, seq_length, embed_dim)
        x = x + self.pe[:, :x.size(1)]
        return x

# Multi-Head Self-Attention Module
class MultiHeadSelfAttention(nn.Module):
    def __init__(self, embed_dim, num_heads):
        super(MultiHeadSelfAttention,
self).__init__()
        assert embed_dim % num_heads == 0, "Embed
dimension must be divisible by number of heads"
        self.embed_dim = embed_dim
        self.num_heads = num_heads
```

```python
        self.head_dim = embed_dim // num_heads

        self.q_linear = nn.Linear(embed_dim,
embed_dim)
        self.k_linear = nn.Linear(embed_dim,
embed_dim)
        self.v_linear = nn.Linear(embed_dim,
embed_dim)
        self.out_linear = nn.Linear(embed_dim,
embed_dim)

    def forward(self, x):
        batch_size, seq_length, embed_dim =
x.size()

        # Linear projections
        Q = self.q_linear(x)  # (batch_size,
seq_length, embed_dim)
        K = self.k_linear(x)
        V = self.v_linear(x)

        # Reshape into multiple heads: (batch_size,
num_heads, seq_length, head_dim)
        Q = Q.view(batch_size, seq_length,
self.num_heads, self.head_dim).transpose(1, 2)
        K = K.view(batch_size, seq_length,
self.num_heads, self.head_dim).transpose(1, 2)
        V = V.view(batch_size, seq_length,
self.num_heads, self.head_dim).transpose(1, 2)

        # Scaled dot-product attention
        scores = torch.matmul(Q, K.transpose(-2, -
1)) / math.sqrt(self.head_dim)
        attn_weights = F.softmax(scores, dim=-1)
        attn_output = torch.matmul(attn_weights, V)

        # Concatenate heads and project
        attn_output = attn_output.transpose(1,
2).contiguous().view(batch_size, seq_length,
embed_dim)
        output = self.out_linear(attn_output)
        return output
```

```python
# Position-wise Feedforward Module
class PositionwiseFeedForward(nn.Module):
    def __init__(self, embed_dim, ff_dim,
dropout=0.1):
        super(PositionwiseFeedForward,
self).__init__()
        self.fc1 = nn.Linear(embed_dim, ff_dim)
        self.fc2 = nn.Linear(ff_dim, embed_dim)
        self.dropout = nn.Dropout(dropout)

    def forward(self, x):
        return
self.fc2(self.dropout(F.relu(self.fc1(x))))

# Transformer Block: Combines Self-Attention and
Feedforward with Residuals and Layer Norm
class TransformerBlock(nn.Module):
    def __init__(self, embed_dim, num_heads,
ff_dim, dropout=0.1):
        super(TransformerBlock, self).__init__()
        self.attention =
MultiHeadSelfAttention(embed_dim, num_heads)
        self.norm1 = nn.LayerNorm(embed_dim)
        self.ffn =
PositionwiseFeedForward(embed_dim, ff_dim, dropout)
        self.norm2 = nn.LayerNorm(embed_dim)
        self.dropout = nn.Dropout(dropout)

    def forward(self, x):
        # Self-Attention sub-layer with residual
connection
        attn_output = self.attention(x)
        x = self.norm1(x +
self.dropout(attn_output))
        # Feedforward sub-layer with residual
connection
        ffn_output = self.ffn(x)
        x = self.norm2(x +
self.dropout(ffn_output))
        return x
```

```python
# Transformer Encoder: Stacks Multiple Transformer
Blocks
class TransformerEncoder(nn.Module):
    def __init__(self, num_layers, embed_dim,
num_heads, ff_dim, dropout=0.1, max_len=5000):
        super(TransformerEncoder, self).__init__()
        self.positional_encoding =
PositionalEncoding(embed_dim, max_len)
        self.layers = nn.ModuleList([
            TransformerBlock(embed_dim, num_heads,
ff_dim, dropout) for _ in range(num_layers)
        ])

    def forward(self, x):
        # x: (batch_size, seq_length, embed_dim)
        x = self.positional_encoding(x)
        for layer in self.layers:
            x = layer(x)
        return x

# Sample usage:
batch_size = 16
seq_length = 50
embed_dim = 128
num_heads = 8
ff_dim = 256
num_layers = 4

# Create random input embeddings
x = torch.randn(batch_size, seq_length, embed_dim)
# Build transformer encoder
encoder = TransformerEncoder(num_layers, embed_dim,
num_heads, ff_dim, dropout=0.1)
output = encoder(x)
print("Transformer encoder output shape:",
output.shape)
```

Best Practices and Troubleshooting

- **Residual Connections and Normalization:**
  Residual connections paired with layer normalization are crucial for

maintaining gradient flow and training stability. Ensure that these are correctly implemented.

- **Dropout Regularization:**
Apply dropout in both the attention and feedforward sub-layers to prevent overfitting, especially when stacking multiple layers.
- **Hyperparameter Tuning:**
Experiment with different numbers of layers, attention heads, and feedforward dimensions to balance performance with computational cost.
- **Visualization and Debugging:**
Use visualization tools (e.g., TensorBoard) to monitor attention weights and training dynamics. Visualizing positional encodings can also provide insight into how the model learns token order.
- **Modularity:**
Building your transformer in a modular way—as shown in the example—allows you to easily swap components (e.g., trying different attention mechanisms or positional encoding strategies).

Exercises

1. **Experiment with Positional Encodings:**
Replace the sinusoidal positional encoding with learnable positional embeddings. Compare convergence behavior and performance on a small sequence classification task.
2. **Stacking Variations:**
Vary the number of transformer blocks in your encoder. Evaluate how model depth affects training time and accuracy on a synthetic dataset.
3. **Attention Head Experiment:**
Modify the number of attention heads while keeping the embedding dimension constant. Analyze how this impacts the richness of the learned representations and downstream task performance.
4. **Custom Transformer for Classification:**
Build a complete transformer-based classifier by adding a pooling or [CLS] token mechanism after the encoder and a final classification head. Train it on a text classification dataset and report accuracy.
5. **Debugging Exercise:**
Introduce intentional bugs (e.g., mismatched dimensions) into your custom transformer and practice debugging using PyTorch's error messages and visualization tools.

Building custom transformers with PyTorch not only deepens your understanding of attention mechanisms and sequence modeling but also offers the flexibility to tailor architectures for specific tasks. This section provided a thorough walkthrough—from designing individual modules like positional encoding and multi-head attention to stacking them into a transformer encoder. With the hands-on code example and exercises, you are now equipped to experiment with and deploy custom transformer architectures in your projects.

4.4 Transformer Optimization Techniques

Optimizing transformer architectures involves not only designing the core components—like self-attention and feedforward networks—but also fine-tuning auxiliary mechanisms that improve training dynamics and model generalization. Three critical techniques in this regard are:

- **Layer Normalization:** Helps stabilize and accelerate training by normalizing inputs across features.
- **Dropouts:** Acts as a regularizer to prevent overfitting, ensuring that models generalize well to unseen data.
- **Positional Encoding:** Injects sequence order information into the model, a necessity given that transformers process tokens in parallel.

This section provides a detailed exploration of these techniques, including practical code examples, best practices, and troubleshooting tips for integrating them into your transformer models.

1. Layer Normalization

Overview

Layer normalization normalizes the inputs across the features of a layer, rather than across the batch. This technique is especially useful in transformer models, where the dynamic range of token embeddings can vary significantly across positions and layers.

- **Benefits:**

- Stabilizes training by mitigating internal covariate shift.
- Improves convergence speed.
- Works well with small batch sizes, which is common in transformer training.

Implementation

PyTorch provides a built-in `nn.LayerNorm` module. In transformer blocks, layer normalization is typically applied after the residual connections of both the attention and feedforward sub-layers.

Code Example

```python
import torch
import torch.nn as nn

# Example: Applying layer normalization to an input
tensor
embed_dim = 128
layer_norm = nn.LayerNorm(embed_dim)
x = torch.randn(16, 50, embed_dim)  # (batch_size,
seq_length, embed_dim)
normalized_x = layer_norm(x)
print("Normalized output shape:",
normalized_x.shape)
```

Best Practices

- **Placement:**
  Use layer normalization after each sub-layer and add residual connections. For example, in transformer blocks, normalize after the multi-head attention and after the feedforward network.
- **Parameter Tuning:**
  The learnable parameters (gain and bias) in layer normalization should be left to adapt naturally during training.

2. Dropouts

Overview

Dropout is a simple yet effective regularization technique that randomly zeros out a fraction of the neurons during training. This helps prevent overfitting by forcing the network to develop redundant representations and discourages reliance on any single feature.

- **Benefits:**
    - o Reduces overfitting.
    - o Encourages more robust representations.
    - o Can be applied to both the attention mechanism and the feedforward network.

Implementation

In PyTorch, dropout is implemented via `nn.Dropout`. Within transformers, dropout is used after attention weights, after the output of multi-head attention, and within feedforward networks.

Code Example

```python
import torch.nn.functional as F

# Example: Using dropout in a transformer block
snippet
dropout_rate = 0.1
dropout = nn.Dropout(dropout_rate)
x = torch.randn(16, 50, 128)
x_dropped = dropout(x)
print("Output shape after dropout:",
x_dropped.shape)
```

Best Practices

- **Dropout Rate:**
  Common dropout rates range between 0.1 and 0.3 for transformer models. Experiment with different rates to find the optimal balance between regularization and learning capacity.

- **Placement:**
  Integrate dropout after key sub-layers. In a transformer block, apply dropout after multi-head self-attention and feedforward outputs, before adding the residual connection.

---

3. Positional Encoding

Overview

Since transformers process all tokens in parallel, they lack inherent positional awareness. Positional encoding addresses this by adding information about the position of each token to its embedding. There are two common approaches:

- **Sinusoidal Positional Encoding:**
  Uses fixed sinusoidal functions to generate unique encodings for each position.
- **Learnable Positional Encoding:**
  Uses trainable parameters to learn positional representations during training.
- **Benefits:**
  - Allows the model to incorporate order information.
  - Helps capture sequential dependencies even without recurrent layers.

Implementation

The sinusoidal positional encoding is often implemented as shown in earlier sections, while learnable positional embeddings can be defined using an `nn.Embedding` layer.

Code Example: Sinusoidal Positional Encoding

```python
import math
import torch
import torch.nn as nn

class PositionalEncoding(nn.Module):
```

```python
    def __init__(self, embed_dim, max_len=5000):
        super(PositionalEncoding, self).__init__()
        pe = torch.zeros(max_len, embed_dim)
        position = torch.arange(0, max_len,
dtype=torch.float).unsqueeze(1)
        div_term = torch.exp(torch.arange(0,
embed_dim, 2).float() * (-math.log(10000.0) /
embed_dim))
        pe[:, 0::2] = torch.sin(position *
div_term)
        pe[:, 1::2] = torch.cos(position *
div_term)
        pe = pe.unsqueeze(0)  # shape: (1, max_len,
embed_dim)
        self.register_buffer('pe', pe)

    def forward(self, x):
        # x: (batch_size, seq_length, embed_dim)
        return x + self.pe[:, :x.size(1)]

# Sample usage:
embed_dim = 128
pe_module = PositionalEncoding(embed_dim)
x = torch.randn(16, 50, embed_dim)
x_with_pe = pe_module(x)
print("Input with positional encoding shape:",
x_with_pe.shape)
```

Best Practices

- **Choice of Encoding:**
  For many tasks, sinusoidal encoding works well out-of-the-box.
  However, if your data has complex positional patterns, learnable
  embeddings might yield better performance.
- **Integration:**
  Add the positional encoding to the token embeddings at the very
  beginning of the transformer model. Do not apply any further
  normalization to the sum, unless it's part of the model architecture.
- **Scaling:**
  Ensure that the positional encoding is scaled appropriately relative to
  the token embeddings.

Exercises

1. **Layer Normalization Exploration:**
   Experiment with applying layer normalization at different points within a transformer block. Compare the training stability and convergence speed with and without normalization.
2. **Dropout Tuning:**
   Test various dropout rates (e.g., 0.1, 0.2, 0.3) in a transformer model on a small dataset. Evaluate the impact on overfitting and model performance.
3. **Positional Encoding Variants:**
   Replace sinusoidal positional encoding with learnable positional embeddings. Train a transformer on a synthetic sequence classification task and compare the performance of the two approaches.
4. **Combined Optimization:**
   Build a mini transformer encoder with varying configurations of layer normalization, dropout, and positional encoding. Analyze which combination yields the best results in terms of both training speed and accuracy.
5. **Visualization:**
   Visualize the learned parameters of the layer normalization and dropout masks (if applicable) during training. Discuss how these might relate to the stability and generalization of the model.

Transformer optimization techniques such as layer normalization, dropout, and positional encoding are essential for building effective and robust models. Layer normalization ensures stable and efficient training, dropout serves as a regularizer to prevent overfitting, and positional encoding imparts necessary sequential information. By mastering these techniques and experimenting with their configurations, you can fine-tune transformer architectures to achieve state-of-the-art performance on a variety of tasks.

4.5 Project: Deploying a Transformer-based Sentiment Analyzer

Sentiment analysis is a fundamental task in natural language processing (NLP) that involves classifying text—such as reviews, tweets, or comments—into sentiment categories (e.g., positive, negative, neutral). Transformer-based models, like BERT and its variants, have achieved state-of-the-art performance on many NLP tasks, including sentiment analysis. This project focuses on leveraging a pre-trained transformer model, fine-tuning it on a sentiment analysis dataset, and deploying it as a real-time inference service.

---

2. Project Objectives

- **Leverage Pre-trained Transformers:** Use a state-of-the-art model (e.g., BERT, DistilBERT) as the base.
- **Fine-Tune for Sentiment Analysis:** Adapt the model to a sentiment dataset (e.g., SST-2, IMDB) to classify text sentiment.
- **Evaluate Performance:** Measure metrics such as accuracy, precision, recall, and F1-score.
- **Deploy as a Real-Time API:** Package the model into an API using Flask (or a similar framework) for real-time sentiment prediction.
- **Provide Interpretability (Optional):** Optionally, integrate techniques (like attention visualization) to explain model predictions.

---

3. Data Preparation

For this project, you can use a widely available sentiment analysis dataset such as SST-2 or IMDB reviews. The data should be preprocessed and tokenized to match the requirements of the pre-trained transformer model. Using Hugging Face's Transformers library simplifies this process.

Code Example: Data Loading and Tokenization

```python
from transformers import BertTokenizer
```

```python
from sklearn.model_selection import
train_test_split
import pandas as pd

# Example: Load a sentiment analysis dataset (CSV
with 'text' and 'label' columns)
data = pd.read_csv("sentiment_dataset.csv")  #
Replace with your dataset path

# Split data into training and validation sets
train_df, val_df = train_test_split(data,
test_size=0.2, random_state=42)

# Initialize the BERT tokenizer
tokenizer = BertTokenizer.from_pretrained("bert-
base-uncased")

# Tokenize the text data
def tokenize_data(df, tokenizer, max_length=128):
    return tokenizer(
        df['text'].tolist(),
        padding=True,
        truncation=True,
        max_length=max_length,
        return_tensors="pt"
    )

train_encodings = tokenize_data(train_df,
tokenizer)
val_encodings = tokenize_data(val_df, tokenizer)

# Convert labels to tensor
import torch
train_labels =
torch.tensor(train_df['label'].values)
val_labels = torch.tensor(val_df['label'].values)
```

4. Model Fine-Tuning

We will use a pre-trained BERT model with a classification head from Hugging Face's Transformers library. The model is then fine-tuned on our sentiment dataset.

Code Example: Fine-Tuning a Transformer for Sentiment Analysis

```python
from transformers import
BertForSequenceClassification, Trainer,
TrainingArguments
import numpy as np

# Load pre-trained BERT model for sequence
classification
model =
BertForSequenceClassification.from_pretrained("bert
-base-uncased", num_labels=2)

# Define a dataset class for the Trainer API
class SentimentDataset(torch.utils.data.Dataset):
    def __init__(self, encodings, labels):
        self.encodings = encodings
        self.labels = labels

    def __getitem__(self, idx):
        item = {key: val[idx] for key, val in
self.encodings.items()}
        item['labels'] = self.labels[idx]
        return item

    def __len__(self):
        return len(self.labels)

train_dataset = SentimentDataset(train_encodings,
train_labels)
val_dataset = SentimentDataset(val_encodings,
val_labels)

# Define training arguments
```

```python
training_args = TrainingArguments(
    output_dir='./results',
    num_train_epochs=3,
    per_device_train_batch_size=16,
    per_device_eval_batch_size=16,
    evaluation_strategy="epoch",
    learning_rate=2e-5,
    weight_decay=0.01,
    logging_dir='./logs',
    logging_steps=50,
)

# Create Trainer instance
trainer = Trainer(
    model=model,
    args=training_args,
    train_dataset=train_dataset,
    eval_dataset=val_dataset,
)

# Fine-tune the model
trainer.train()
```

After training, evaluate the model on the validation set:

python

```python
eval_result = trainer.evaluate()
print(f"Validation Loss:
{eval_result['eval_loss']:.4f}")
```

5. Model Deployment

Once the model is fine-tuned, the next step is to deploy it for real-time sentiment predictions. One common approach is to create a REST API using Flask.

Code Example: Deploying with Flask

1. **Save the Fine-Tuned Model**

```
python
```

```python
model.save_pretrained("./sentiment_model")
tokenizer.save_pretrained("./sentiment_model")
```

2. Create a Flask API

```
python
```

```python
from flask import Flask, request, jsonify
from transformers import
BertForSequenceClassification, BertTokenizer
import torch

app = Flask(__name__)

# Load the model and tokenizer
model =
BertForSequenceClassification.from_pretrained("./se
ntiment_model")
tokenizer =
BertTokenizer.from_pretrained("./sentiment_model")
model.eval()
device = torch.device("cuda" if
torch.cuda.is_available() else "cpu")
model.to(device)

@app.route('/predict', methods=['POST'])
def predict():
    data = request.get_json(force=True)
    text = data.get("text", "")
    if not text:
        return jsonify({"error": "No text
provided."}), 400

    # Tokenize the input text
    inputs = tokenizer(text, return_tensors="pt",
truncation=True, padding=True, max_length=128)
    inputs = {key: val.to(device) for key, val in
inputs.items()}

    # Predict sentiment
```

```
    with torch.no_grad():
        outputs = model(**inputs)
        logits = outputs.logits
        probabilities = torch.softmax(logits,
dim=1)
        prediction = torch.argmax(probabilities,
dim=1).item()

    # Map prediction to sentiment label
    sentiment = "positive" if prediction == 1 else
"negative"
    return jsonify({"sentiment": sentiment,
"probabilities":
probabilities.cpu().numpy().tolist()})

if __name__ == '__main__':
    app.run(host='0.0.0.0', port=5000)
```

Run the Flask app, and you can send POST requests to
`http://<server_ip>:5000/predict` with a JSON payload
containing the key `"text"`.

---

6. Evaluation and Metrics

When deploying a sentiment analyzer, it is essential to monitor and evaluate
the model's performance on real-world data. Use metrics such as:

- **Accuracy**
- **Precision, Recall, and F1-Score**
- **Confusion Matrix**

You may incorporate evaluation scripts or dashboards to continuously
monitor these metrics in production.

7. Exercises

1. **Dataset Expansion:**
   Fine-tune the sentiment analyzer on a larger dataset (e.g., IMDB reviews or SST-2) and compare performance metrics.
2. **Hyperparameter Tuning:**
   Experiment with different learning rates, batch sizes, and number of epochs during fine-tuning. Evaluate their impact on validation accuracy and loss.
3. **Alternative Models:**
   Replace BERT with another transformer variant (e.g., DistilBERT, RoBERTa) and analyze any differences in performance and inference speed.
4. **API Stress Test:**
   Deploy the API and perform stress tests to evaluate latency and throughput under load.
5. **Interpretability Integration:**
   Integrate an interpretability tool (e.g., attention visualization) into the API to explain why certain texts are classified as positive or negative.

This project demonstrated how to build and deploy a transformer-based sentiment analyzer using PyTorch and Hugging Face's Transformers library. By leveraging pre-trained models and fine-tuning them on a sentiment dataset, you can achieve high accuracy while minimizing training time. Deploying the model as a real-time API enables practical applications such as social media monitoring, customer feedback analysis, or any scenario requiring instant sentiment insights.

4.6 Exercise: Creating a Custom Vision Transformer (ViT) from Scratch

Vision Transformers (ViT) have emerged as a powerful alternative to convolutional neural networks for image classification tasks. Instead of using convolutions, ViTs split an image into a grid of patches, flatten them into a sequence, and then process the sequence using transformer encoders with self-attention. This exercise will help you understand and implement the key components of a ViT, including:

- **Patch Embedding:** Dividing the image into patches and embedding each patch into a fixed-dimensional vector.
- **Positional Encoding:** Adding positional information to the patch embeddings to retain spatial structure.
- **Transformer Encoder Blocks:** Stacking transformer layers to model relationships between patches.
- **Classification Head:** Aggregating the transformer outputs to produce a final classification decision.

Objectives

- **Implement Patch Embedding:** Learn to split input images into patches and project them into an embedding space.
- **Apply Positional Encoding:** Inject spatial information into the patch embeddings.
- **Build Transformer Encoder Blocks:** Assemble multi-head self-attention and feedforward layers with residual connections and layer normalization.
- **Design a Classification Head:** Use a [CLS] token or global pooling to aggregate transformer outputs and perform image classification.
- **Train and Evaluate:** Train your custom ViT on a small dataset (or synthetic data) and assess its performance.

Architecture Overview

1. **Patch Embedding:**
   - Split the image into non-overlapping patches.
   - Flatten each patch and project it using a linear layer.
2. **Positional Encoding:**
   - Add fixed or learnable positional encodings to the patch embeddings.
3. **Transformer Encoder Blocks:**
   - Each block consists of multi-head self-attention, residual connections, layer normalization, and a position-wise feedforward network.
4. **Classification Head:**
   - Prepend a learnable [CLS] token to the patch sequence, or apply global pooling to aggregate features before passing through a classifier.

Hands-On Code Example

Below is a simplified implementation of a Vision Transformer in PyTorch:

```python
python

import torch
import torch.nn as nn
import torch.nn.functional as F
import math

# 1. Patch Embedding: Split image into patches and
embed them.
class PatchEmbedding(nn.Module):
    def __init__(self, img_size, patch_size,
in_channels=3, embed_dim=768):
        super(PatchEmbedding, self).__init__()
        assert img_size % patch_size == 0, "Image
dimensions must be divisible by the patch size."
        self.num_patches = (img_size // patch_size)
** 2
        self.patch_size = patch_size
        # Flatten each patch and project it to
embed_dim
        self.proj = nn.Conv2d(in_channels,
embed_dim, kernel_size=patch_size,
stride=patch_size)

    def forward(self, x):
        # x: (batch_size, in_channels, img_size,
img_size)
        x = self.proj(x)   # (batch_size, embed_dim,
num_patches^(1/2), num_patches^(1/2))
        x = x.flatten(2)   # (batch_size, embed_dim,
num_patches)
        x = x.transpose(1, 2)   # (batch_size,
num_patches, embed_dim)
        return x

# 2. Positional Encoding: Sinusoidal encoding to
add positional info.
class PositionalEncoding(nn.Module):
```

```python
    def __init__(self, embed_dim, num_patches,
dropout=0.1):
        super(PositionalEncoding, self).__init__()
        self.dropout = nn.Dropout(dropout)
        # Learnable positional embeddings
        self.pos_embedding =
nn.Parameter(torch.zeros(1, num_patches + 1,
embed_dim))
        nn.init.trunc_normal_(self.pos_embedding,
std=0.02)

    def forward(self, x):
        # x: (batch_size, num_patches, embed_dim)
        batch_size = x.size(0)
        # Prepend the [CLS] token (will be added in
the transformer model)
        return self.dropout(x +
self.pos_embedding[:, 1:, :])

# 3. Transformer Encoder Block
class TransformerBlock(nn.Module):
    def __init__(self, embed_dim, num_heads,
ff_dim, dropout=0.1):
        super(TransformerBlock, self).__init__()
        self.attn =
nn.MultiheadAttention(embed_dim, num_heads,
dropout=dropout, batch_first=True)
        self.norm1 = nn.LayerNorm(embed_dim)
        self.ffn = nn.Sequential(
            nn.Linear(embed_dim, ff_dim),
            nn.GELU(),
            nn.Dropout(dropout),
            nn.Linear(ff_dim, embed_dim),
            nn.Dropout(dropout)
        )
        self.norm2 = nn.LayerNorm(embed_dim)

    def forward(self, x):
        # Self-attention sub-layer with residual
connection
        attn_output, _ = self.attn(x, x, x)
        x = self.norm1(x + attn_output)
```

```python
        # Feedforward sub-layer with residual
connection
        ffn_output = self.ffn(x)
        x = self.norm2(x + ffn_output)
        return x

# 4. Vision Transformer (ViT) Model
class VisionTransformer(nn.Module):
    def __init__(self, img_size=224, patch_size=16,
in_channels=3, num_classes=1000,
                 embed_dim=768, depth=12,
num_heads=12, ff_dim=3072, dropout=0.1):
        super(VisionTransformer, self).__init__()
        self.patch_embed = PatchEmbedding(img_size,
patch_size, in_channels, embed_dim)
        num_patches = self.patch_embed.num_patches

        # [CLS] token for classification
        self.cls_token =
nn.Parameter(torch.zeros(1, 1, embed_dim))
        # Positional Encoding for patches + [CLS]
token
        self.pos_embedding =
nn.Parameter(torch.zeros(1, num_patches + 1,
embed_dim))
        nn.init.trunc_normal_(self.pos_embedding,
std=0.02)
        self.dropout = nn.Dropout(dropout)

        # Stacked Transformer Encoder Blocks
        self.blocks = nn.ModuleList([
            TransformerBlock(embed_dim, num_heads,
ff_dim, dropout) for _ in range(depth)
        ])
        self.norm = nn.LayerNorm(embed_dim)

        # Classification head
        self.head = nn.Linear(embed_dim,
num_classes)
        nn.init.trunc_normal_(self.head.weight,
std=0.02)
```

```python
    def forward(self, x):
        # x: (batch_size, in_channels, img_size,
img_size)
        batch_size = x.size(0)
        x = self.patch_embed(x)  # (batch_size,
num_patches, embed_dim)

        # Prepend [CLS] token
        cls_tokens =
self.cls_token.expand(batch_size, -1, -1)  #
(batch_size, 1, embed_dim)
        x = torch.cat((cls_tokens, x), dim=1)  #
(batch_size, num_patches + 1, embed_dim)
        x = x + self.pos_embedding  # Add
positional encoding
        x = self.dropout(x)

        # Transformer Encoder Blocks
        for block in self.blocks:
            x = block(x)
        x = self.norm(x)

        # Use the [CLS] token for classification
        cls_output = x[:, 0]
        logits = self.head(cls_output)
        return logits

# Sample usage:
img_size = 224
patch_size = 16
num_classes = 10  # For example, 10 classes
vit = VisionTransformer(img_size=img_size,
patch_size=patch_size, in_channels=3,
                        num_classes=num_classes,
embed_dim=768, depth=6, num_heads=12, ff_dim=3072)

# Create a dummy image batch
dummy_images = torch.randn(8, 3, img_size,
img_size)  # (batch_size, channels, height, width)
logits = vit(dummy_images)
print("ViT logits shape:", logits.shape)  #
Expected shape: (batch_size, num_classes)
```

Best Practices and Troubleshooting

- **Patch Size Selection:**
  The patch size should balance spatial resolution and computational efficiency. Smaller patches capture finer details but increase sequence length.
- **[CLS] Token and Positional Embedding:**
  Ensure the [CLS] token is properly concatenated with patch embeddings, and that positional embeddings cover the full sequence length (patches + 1).
- **Transformer Depth and Width:**
  Experiment with different numbers of transformer blocks (depth) and attention heads (width) to suit your dataset and computational budget.
- **Regularization:**
  Use dropout and layer normalization to stabilize training and prevent overfitting.
- **Debugging:**
  Check dimensions at each stage (patch embedding, positional encoding, transformer blocks) to ensure they match expected shapes.

Exercises

1. **Patch Embedding Experiment:**
   Modify the patch size (e.g., 8, 16, 32) and evaluate its impact on classification accuracy and training time on a small image dataset.
2. **Transformer Depth Tuning:**
   Vary the number of transformer blocks (depth) and observe the effects on model performance and overfitting.
3. **Attention Head Analysis:**
   Experiment with different numbers of attention heads while keeping the embedding dimension fixed. Analyze how it affects the richness of feature representations.
4. **Positional Encoding Variants:**
   Replace sinusoidal positional encoding with learnable embeddings and compare convergence behavior.
5. **Full Pipeline Training:**
   Integrate your custom ViT into a complete training pipeline on a

public dataset (e.g., CIFAR-10 or a subset of ImageNet) and report accuracy and training curves.

Building a custom Vision Transformer from scratch provides deep insights into the workings of transformer-based architectures for image classification. Through this exercise, you have implemented key components such as patch embedding, positional encoding, transformer encoder blocks, and a classification head. Experimenting with hyperparameters like patch size, model depth, and attention heads will further refine your model for practical applications. This hands-on approach not only strengthens your understanding of ViTs but also equips you with the skills to innovate and tailor transformer architectures to your specific needs.

Chapter 5: Multimodal Deep Learning

5.1 Foundations of Multimodal Learning

Multimodal learning involves integrating and processing data from two or more modalities (e.g., images, text, audio) to improve learning performance and achieve more robust representations. Real-world applications such as visual question answering, image captioning, and sentiment analysis from multimedia data benefit from models that can effectively combine information from different sources. In this section, we explore the core principles that underpin multimodal deep learning, including data fusion strategies, representation learning, and challenges unique to multimodal data.

Key Concepts in Multimodal Learning

1. Data Modalities

- **Definition:**
  Modalities refer to the different types of data sources. For instance, images, text, and audio are common modalities. Each modality has its own structure, statistical properties, and challenges.
- **Characteristics:**
    - **Images:** Typically represented as high-dimensional pixel arrays.
    - **Text:** Sequences of words or tokens, usually processed with embeddings.
    - **Audio:** Time-series data often converted to spectrograms for deep learning applications.

2. Representation Learning

- **Modality-Specific Representations:**
  Each data modality is often processed by a dedicated network (e.g., CNNs for images, RNNs/Transformers for text) to extract features and learn a compact representation.
- **Joint Representations:**
  The goal is to fuse these modality-specific representations into a joint

representation that captures complementary information. This can be achieved through various fusion techniques.

3. Fusion Strategies

- **Early Fusion:**
  Combine raw or low-level features from different modalities at an early stage. This approach can capture inter-modal correlations early but may suffer from alignment issues if modalities have different resolutions or structures.
- **Late Fusion:**
  Process each modality independently and combine their predictions or high-level features at a later stage. Late fusion is robust to modality-specific noise but may miss fine-grained inter-modal interactions.
- **Hybrid Fusion:**
  Involves a combination of early and late fusion. For example, some intermediate representations can be fused to exploit both low-level and high-level complementarities.
- **Cross-Modal Attention:**
  Mechanisms like cross-attention allow the model to learn how much weight to assign to each modality based on the context, improving alignment and interaction between different modalities.

4. Challenges in Multimodal Learning

- **Heterogeneity:**
  Different modalities have varying structures, noise characteristics, and scales, making them challenging to integrate seamlessly.
- **Missing Data:**
  Some modalities might be missing or incomplete in real-world scenarios, so models should be robust to such situations.
- **Alignment:**
  Temporal or spatial alignment between modalities (e.g., synchronizing video frames with corresponding audio) is often required and can be complex.
- **Scalability:**
  Efficiently handling high-dimensional multimodal data and ensuring that fusion methods scale well is a significant challenge.

Practical Example: Fusion of Text and Image Features

Let's consider a simplified example that demonstrates a basic multimodal fusion strategy for a task like visual question answering (VQA). In this scenario, we extract features from an image using a CNN and from text using an embedding layer (or a simple RNN), and then combine these features using concatenation followed by a fully connected layer.

Code Example

```python
import torch
import torch.nn as nn
import torch.nn.functional as F
from torchvision import models

# Image feature extractor (pre-trained CNN)
class ImageEncoder(nn.Module):
    def __init__(self, embed_dim=256):
        super(ImageEncoder, self).__init__()
        cnn = models.resnet18(pretrained=True)
        # Remove final classification layer
        self.feature_extractor =
nn.Sequential(*list(cnn.children())[:-1])
        self.fc = nn.Linear(cnn.fc.in_features,
embed_dim)

    def forward(self, images):
        # images: (batch_size, 3, H, W)
        features = self.feature_extractor(images)
        features = features.view(features.size(0),
-1)
        features = self.fc(features)
        return features

# Text feature extractor (simple embedding and
LSTM)
class TextEncoder(nn.Module):
    def __init__(self, vocab_size, embed_dim=256,
hidden_dim=256, num_layers=1):
        super(TextEncoder, self).__init__()
```

```python
        self.embedding = nn.Embedding(vocab_size,
embed_dim)
        self.lstm = nn.LSTM(embed_dim, hidden_dim,
num_layers, batch_first=True)

    def forward(self, texts):
        # texts: (batch_size, seq_length)
        embedded = self.embedding(texts)
        _, (hidden, _) = self.lstm(embedded)
        # Use the last hidden state as the text
representation
        return hidden[-1]

# Multimodal Fusion Module for VQA
class MultimodalFusion(nn.Module):
    def __init__(self, img_embed_dim=256,
txt_embed_dim=256, output_dim=512):
        super(MultimodalFusion, self).__init__()
        self.fc = nn.Linear(img_embed_dim +
txt_embed_dim, output_dim)

    def forward(self, img_features, txt_features):
        # Concatenate along the feature dimension
        combined = torch.cat((img_features,
txt_features), dim=1)
        output = F.relu(self.fc(combined))
        return output

# Sample usage for multimodal fusion
batch_size = 8
vocab_size = 10000
seq_length = 20

# Dummy inputs
dummy_images = torch.randn(batch_size, 3, 224, 224)
dummy_texts = torch.randint(0, vocab_size,
(batch_size, seq_length))

# Instantiate modules
img_encoder = ImageEncoder(embed_dim=256)
txt_encoder = TextEncoder(vocab_size,
embed_dim=256, hidden_dim=256)
```

```
fusion_module = MultimodalFusion(img_embed_dim=256,
txt_embed_dim=256, output_dim=512)

# Forward pass
img_features = img_encoder(dummy_images)   #
(batch_size, 256)
txt_features = txt_encoder(dummy_texts)      #
(batch_size, 256)
fused_features = fusion_module(img_features,
txt_features)  # (batch_size, 512)
print("Fused features shape:",
fused_features.shape)
```

Best Practices

- **Pre-training Modalities Independently:**
  Often, it is beneficial to pre-train the image and text encoders on
  large datasets before fine-tuning them jointly on the multimodal task.
- **Experiment with Fusion Techniques:**
  Evaluate different fusion strategies (early, late, hybrid, cross-modal
  attention) to determine which works best for your specific
  application.
- **Robustness to Missing Data:**
  Consider techniques like modality dropout during training, which
  randomly masks out one modality to encourage the model to rely on
  the available modalities.
- **Alignment and Synchronization:**
  For temporal data (e.g., video and audio), ensure that the inputs are
  properly aligned. Techniques like cross-modal attention can help
  mitigate misalignment issues.

Exercises

1. **Fusion Strategy Comparison:**
   Implement at least two different fusion strategies (e.g., simple
   concatenation vs. cross-modal attention) for a multimodal
   classification task. Compare their performance on a benchmark
   dataset.

2. **Handling Missing Modalities:**
   Simulate scenarios where one modality is missing during inference (e.g., only text without images) and develop a strategy to handle this gracefully.
3. **Joint Fine-Tuning:**
   Pre-train individual encoders for images and text, then fine-tune the combined multimodal network on a dataset such as VQA or a custom multimodal dataset. Analyze performance improvements.
4. **Cross-Modal Attention Implementation:**
   Implement a cross-modal attention mechanism that allows one modality to attend to features from the other. Evaluate its impact on model performance compared to simple concatenation.
5. **Real-World Application:**
   Apply your multimodal model to a real-world task (e.g., sentiment analysis from social media posts that include both text and images) and assess its robustness and accuracy.

The foundations of multimodal learning are built on understanding how to extract, represent, and fuse diverse data modalities effectively. By integrating modality-specific encoders with robust fusion strategies, you can build models that leverage the complementary strengths of different data sources. This section has provided a theoretical overview, practical code examples, and exercises to help you master the basics of multimodal deep learning. With these foundations in place, you are well-prepared to explore advanced multimodal architectures and tackle complex, real-world tasks.

5.2 Cross-modal Architectures: Vision-Language Models

Vision-language models have emerged as a powerful paradigm for understanding and generating multimodal content. By learning a shared representation space for images and text, models such as CLIP (Contrastive Language–Image Pre-training) and ALIGN (A Large-scale ImaGe and Noisy-text embedding) have achieved state-of-the-art performance in tasks like zero-shot image classification, image-text retrieval, and visual question answering. This section explains the underlying principles of these models, focusing on cross-modal contrastive learning and the architectures that make it possible to jointly encode and align visual and linguistic information.

Key Concepts

Cross-modal Contrastive Learning

- **Objective:**
  These models learn by contrasting positive image-text pairs against a large number of negative pairs. The aim is to pull together representations of matching image-text pairs and push apart those of non-matching pairs.
- **Loss Function:**
  Typically, a contrastive loss (or InfoNCE loss) is used to maximize the cosine similarity between paired embeddings while minimizing it for unpaired samples.

Shared Representation Space

- **Dual-Encoder Architecture:**
  Both CLIP and ALIGN typically use separate encoders for images and text. The image encoder (often a Vision Transformer or CNN) and the text encoder (usually a Transformer-based language model) project inputs into the same embedding space.
- **Alignment and Retrieval:**
  Once trained, the model can perform zero-shot classification by matching image embeddings with text descriptions, or retrieve images given a textual query and vice versa.

Architectural Components

- **Image Encoder:**
  Often based on Vision Transformers (ViT) or convolutional neural networks (CNNs), it processes raw images into feature embeddings.
- **Text Encoder:**
  A Transformer-based model (similar to BERT or GPT variants) that converts text inputs into embeddings.
- **Projection Heads:**
  Linear layers that map the outputs of the encoders to a common embedding space where the contrastive loss is applied.
- **Scaling and Temperature:**
  A learnable temperature parameter is commonly used to scale the logits in the contrastive loss, improving the learning dynamics.

Model Overviews: CLIP and ALIGN

CLIP (Contrastive Language–Image Pre-training)

- **Training Data:**
  CLIP is trained on a large-scale dataset of (image, text) pairs collected from the internet. Its diversity allows it to generalize well to various downstream tasks.
- **Architecture:**
  Uses a dual-encoder setup where the image encoder (e.g., ViT or ResNet) and the text encoder (Transformer) are trained jointly using contrastive learning.
- **Zero-shot Capabilities:**
  After training, CLIP can perform zero-shot image classification by matching image embeddings with a set of text prompts describing classes.

ALIGN (A Large-scale ImaGe and Noisy-text embedding)

- **Training Approach:**
  ALIGN is trained on noisy image-text pairs from web data. Its training process also relies on contrastive learning, but with even larger datasets to achieve high-quality cross-modal alignment.
- **Architecture:**
  Similar to CLIP, ALIGN employs separate encoders for images and text and aligns them in a shared embedding space using a contrastive loss.
- **Applications:**
  The aligned representations can be used for image retrieval, text-based image generation, and other multimodal tasks.

Hands-On Code Example (Simplified)

Below is a simplified pseudocode example that demonstrates how you might set up a dual-encoder architecture for cross-modal contrastive learning using PyTorch. This example abstracts the core idea behind models like CLIP and ALIGN.

```python
```

```python
import torch
import torch.nn as nn
import torch.nn.functional as F

# Define a simple image encoder (e.g., using a
small CNN)
class SimpleImageEncoder(nn.Module):
    def __init__(self, embed_dim):
        super(SimpleImageEncoder, self).__init__()
        self.conv = nn.Sequential(
            nn.Conv2d(3, 32, kernel_size=3,
stride=2, padding=1),
            nn.ReLU(),
            nn.Conv2d(32, 64, kernel_size=3,
stride=2, padding=1),
            nn.ReLU()
        )
        self.fc = nn.Linear(64 * 56 * 56,
embed_dim)  # assuming input images are 224x224

    def forward(self, x):
        x = self.conv(x)
        x = x.view(x.size(0), -1)
        x = self.fc(x)
        return x

# Define a simple text encoder (e.g., using an
embedding layer and an RNN)
class SimpleTextEncoder(nn.Module):
    def __init__(self, vocab_size, embed_dim,
hidden_dim, num_layers=1):
        super(SimpleTextEncoder, self).__init__()
        self.embedding = nn.Embedding(vocab_size,
embed_dim)
        self.rnn = nn.GRU(embed_dim, hidden_dim,
num_layers, batch_first=True)
        self.fc = nn.Linear(hidden_dim, embed_dim)

    def forward(self, x):
        x = self.embedding(x)
        _, hidden = self.rnn(x)
        hidden = hidden[-1]
```

```python
        x = self.fc(hidden)
        return x

# Define the dual-encoder model
class CrossModalModel(nn.Module):
    def __init__(self, image_embed_dim,
text_embed_dim, common_dim):
        super(CrossModalModel, self).__init__()
        self.image_encoder =
SimpleImageEncoder(common_dim)
        self.text_encoder =
SimpleTextEncoder(vocab_size=10000, embed_dim=256,
hidden_dim=256)
        # Optionally, add normalization
        self.image_norm = nn.LayerNorm(common_dim)
        self.text_norm = nn.LayerNorm(common_dim)
        # Temperature parameter for scaling
similarities
        self.logit_scale =
nn.Parameter(torch.ones([]) * 0.07)

    def forward(self, images, texts):
        img_features = self.image_encoder(images)
        txt_features = self.text_encoder(texts)
        img_features =
self.image_norm(img_features)
        txt_features = self.text_norm(txt_features)
        # Normalize embeddings
        img_features = F.normalize(img_features,
dim=-1)
        txt_features = F.normalize(txt_features,
dim=-1)
        # Scale similarity scores
        logit_scale = self.logit_scale.exp()
        logits = logit_scale *
torch.matmul(img_features, txt_features.t())
        return logits

# Example usage:
batch_size = 8
images = torch.randn(batch_size, 3, 224, 224)
```

```
texts = torch.randint(0, 10000, (batch_size, 20))
# dummy tokenized text sequences
model = CrossModalModel(image_embed_dim=512,
text_embed_dim=512, common_dim=512)
logits = model(images, texts)
print("Logits shape:", logits.shape)  # Expected:
(batch_size, batch_size)
```

Explanation:

- **Image Encoder:**
  Processes images using a small CNN and projects the features into a common embedding space.
- **Text Encoder:**
  Processes tokenized text using an embedding layer and GRU, then projects the final hidden state.
- **Normalization and Scaling:**
  Both modalities are normalized to unit vectors. The similarity between image and text embeddings is computed using dot product and scaled by a learnable temperature parameter.
- **Contrastive Loss:**
  During training, a contrastive loss (e.g., InfoNCE) is applied to these logits to pull matching image-text pairs closer in the embedding space while pushing non-matching pairs apart.

Best Practices and Troubleshooting

- **Data Diversity:**
  Train on large, diverse datasets to ensure that the model learns robust, generalizable representations.
- **Batch Size:**
  Larger batch sizes help by providing more negative examples during contrastive learning. However, ensure your hardware can support the memory requirements.
- **Temperature Scaling:**
  The temperature parameter is crucial for controlling the smoothness of the similarity distribution. Experiment with different initial values and learning rates.

- **Encoder Quality:**
  Pre-train or fine-tune your individual encoders on modality-specific tasks before joint training to improve performance.
- **Evaluation:**
  Use retrieval metrics (e.g., recall@K) and zero-shot classification tasks to assess how well the model aligns image and text modalities.

Exercises

1. **Contrastive Loss Implementation:**
   Implement a custom contrastive loss function and train the dual-encoder model on a synthetic dataset of (image, text) pairs. Evaluate how well the model separates matching and non-matching pairs.
2. **Model Variants Comparison:**
   Replace the simple encoders with more advanced architectures (e.g., a Vision Transformer for images or a pre-trained BERT for text) and compare their performance on a multimodal retrieval task.
3. **Temperature Sensitivity:**
   Experiment with different initial values for the temperature parameter. Observe its effect on the training dynamics and final embedding alignment.
4. **Negative Sampling Strategies:**
   Investigate the impact of different negative sampling strategies (e.g., in-batch negatives vs. external negatives) on the quality of the learned representations.
5. **Zero-shot Classification:**
   Evaluate the trained model's zero-shot classification capabilities by formulating text prompts for various classes and measuring classification accuracy on an external dataset.

Vision-language models like CLIP and ALIGN demonstrate the power of cross-modal contrastive learning in aligning disparate data modalities into a unified representation space. By understanding their architectures and training strategies, you gain insights into how to build robust models for tasks such as image retrieval, zero-shot classification, and multimodal understanding. This section provided both theoretical foundations and a practical code example to guide you in developing your own cross-modal architectures. Experimentation with these models opens up a wide array of applications in multimodal AI.

5.3 Fusion Techniques for Multimodal Data

Multimodal learning requires combining information from disparate sources, each with its own unique structure and statistical properties. Fusion techniques play a crucial role in effectively integrating these diverse modalities, enabling models to capture complementary information and improve overall performance. In this section, we explore several fusion strategies:

- **Early Fusion:** Merges raw or low-level features at the input stage.
- **Late Fusion:** Combines high-level representations or predictions from modality-specific models.
- **Hybrid Fusion:** Integrates both early and late fusion approaches to leverage the strengths of each.
- **Cross-Modal Attention:** Dynamically aligns features from different modalities by letting one modality attend to another.

Each approach has its own benefits and trade-offs, and the choice often depends on the task, data characteristics, and computational constraints.

Fusion Strategies

1. Early Fusion

Overview:
Early fusion involves combining data from different modalities at the initial stage, often by concatenating raw features or low-level representations before feeding them into a joint model.

Advantages:

- Captures inter-modal interactions early in the network.
- Simple to implement with concatenation and linear transformations.

Disadvantages:

- May struggle if modalities have vastly different structures or scales.
- Requires careful normalization to avoid dominance by one modality.

Code Example:

```python
import torch
import torch.nn as nn
import torch.nn.functional as F

class EarlyFusionModel(nn.Module):
    def __init__(self, img_feature_dim,
txt_feature_dim, hidden_dim, num_classes):
        super(EarlyFusionModel, self).__init__()
        # Fusion via concatenation
        self.fc1 = nn.Linear(img_feature_dim +
txt_feature_dim, hidden_dim)
        self.fc2 = nn.Linear(hidden_dim,
num_classes)

    def forward(self, img_features, txt_features):
        # Concatenate features from both modalities
        combined = torch.cat((img_features,
txt_features), dim=1)
        x = F.relu(self.fc1(combined))
        logits = self.fc2(x)
        return logits

# Sample usage:
batch_size = 8
img_feature_dim = 256
txt_feature_dim = 256
hidden_dim = 512
num_classes = 5

# Dummy inputs for image and text features
img_features = torch.randn(batch_size,
img_feature_dim)
txt_features = torch.randn(batch_size,
txt_feature_dim)
```

```python
early_fusion_model =
EarlyFusionModel(img_feature_dim, txt_feature_dim,
hidden_dim, num_classes)
logits = early_fusion_model(img_features,
txt_features)
print("Early Fusion logits shape:", logits.shape)
```

2. Late Fusion

Overview:
Late fusion processes each modality independently, often using modality-specific models, and combines their predictions or high-level representations at a later stage.

Advantages:

- Allows for specialized feature extraction for each modality.
- Can be robust to missing or noisy modalities.

Disadvantages:

- May miss fine-grained inter-modal interactions that occur at lower levels.
- Combining predictions requires careful weighting or calibration.

Code Example:

python

```python
class LateFusionModel(nn.Module):
    def __init__(self, img_model, txt_model,
num_classes):
        super(LateFusionModel, self).__init__()
        self.img_model = img_model  # Pre-trained
image model
        self.txt_model = txt_model  # Pre-trained
text model
        # Final classifier that takes concatenated
high-level features
        self.fc = nn.Linear(self.img_model.out_dim
+ self.txt_model.out_dim, num_classes)
```

```python
    def forward(self, img_input, txt_input):
        img_features = self.img_model(img_input)  #
(batch_size, img_feature_dim)
        txt_features = self.txt_model(txt_input)  #
(batch_size, txt_feature_dim)
        combined = torch.cat((img_features,
txt_features), dim=1)
        logits = self.fc(combined)
        return logits

# Dummy image and text model definitions for late
fusion
class DummyImgModel(nn.Module):
    def __init__(self, out_dim=256):
        super(DummyImgModel, self).__init__()
        self.out_dim = out_dim
    def forward(self, x):
        return torch.randn(x.size(0), self.out_dim)

class DummyTxtModel(nn.Module):
    def __init__(self, out_dim=256):
        super(DummyTxtModel, self).__init__()
        self.out_dim = out_dim
    def forward(self, x):
        return torch.randn(x.size(0), self.out_dim)

dummy_img_model = DummyImgModel()
dummy_txt_model = DummyTxtModel()
late_fusion_model =
LateFusionModel(dummy_img_model, dummy_txt_model,
num_classes=5)

img_input = torch.randn(batch_size, 3, 224, 224)
txt_input = torch.randint(0, 10000, (batch_size,
20))
logits = late_fusion_model(img_input, txt_input)
print("Late Fusion logits shape:", logits.shape)
```

3. Hybrid Fusion

Overview:
Hybrid fusion combines aspects of early and late fusion. For instance, intermediate representations from individual modalities can be fused at multiple stages, enabling both early interaction and high-level integration.

Advantages:

- Balances the benefits of both early and late fusion.
- Can capture both low-level and high-level inter-modal relationships.

Disadvantages:

- More complex to design and tune.
- Increased computational cost due to multiple fusion points.

Code Example:

```python
class HybridFusionModel(nn.Module):
    def __init__(self, img_feature_dim,
txt_feature_dim, hidden_dim, num_classes):
        super(HybridFusionModel, self).__init__()
        # Early fusion branch
        self.early_fc = nn.Linear(img_feature_dim +
txt_feature_dim, hidden_dim)
        # Late fusion branch: process image and
text features independently
        self.img_fc = nn.Linear(img_feature_dim,
hidden_dim)
        self.txt_fc = nn.Linear(txt_feature_dim,
hidden_dim)
        # Combined classifier
        self.classifier = nn.Linear(hidden_dim * 2,
num_classes)

    def forward(self, img_features, txt_features):
        # Early fusion pathway
        early_combined = torch.cat((img_features,
txt_features), dim=1)
        early_out =
F.relu(self.early_fc(early_combined))
```

```python
        # Late fusion pathway: independent
processing
        img_out = F.relu(self.img_fc(img_features))
        txt_out = F.relu(self.txt_fc(txt_features))
        late_combined = torch.cat((img_out,
txt_out), dim=1)
        # Combine early and late fusion outputs
        fusion_output = early_out + late_combined
# simple combination strategy
        logits = self.classifier(fusion_output)
        return logits

# Sample usage with dummy features:
hybrid_model = HybridFusionModel(img_feature_dim,
txt_feature_dim, hidden_dim=512, num_classes=5)
logits = hybrid_model(img_features, txt_features)
print("Hybrid Fusion logits shape:", logits.shape)
```

4. Cross-Modal Attention

Overview:
Cross-modal attention allows one modality to dynamically attend to the other. For instance, in a vision-language task, a text query can attend to image features, refining the combined representation based on contextual relevance.

Advantages:

- Provides fine-grained alignment between modalities.
- Improves interpretability by showing which parts of one modality influence the other.

Disadvantages:

- More computationally expensive due to additional attention layers.
- Requires careful design to ensure stable training.

Code Example:

python

```python
class CrossModalAttentionFusion(nn.Module):
    def __init__(self, img_feature_dim,
txt_feature_dim, common_dim):
        super(CrossModalAttentionFusion,
self).__init__()
        self.img_proj = nn.Linear(img_feature_dim,
common_dim)
        self.txt_proj = nn.Linear(txt_feature_dim,
common_dim)
        self.attention =
nn.MultiheadAttention(common_dim, num_heads=4,
batch_first=True)
        self.fc = nn.Linear(common_dim * 2, 5)   #
for 5 classes

    def forward(self, img_features, txt_features):
        # Project features to common dimension
        img_proj =
F.relu(self.img_proj(img_features))  # (batch_size,
feature_dim)
        txt_proj =
F.relu(self.txt_proj(txt_features))
        # Expand dimensions to use
MultiheadAttention (simulate sequence length = 1)
        img_proj = img_proj.unsqueeze(1)
        txt_proj = txt_proj.unsqueeze(1)
        # Apply cross-attention: let text attend to
image features
        attn_output, _ =
self.attention(query=txt_proj, key=img_proj,
value=img_proj)
        # Remove sequence dimension
        attn_output = attn_output.squeeze(1)
        txt_proj = txt_proj.squeeze(1)
        # Concatenate and classify
        fused = torch.cat((attn_output, txt_proj),
dim=1)
        logits = self.fc(fused)
        return logits

# Sample usage with dummy features:
```

```
cross_modal_model =
CrossModalAttentionFusion(img_feature_dim,
txt_feature_dim, common_dim=256)
logits = cross_modal_model(img_features,
txt_features)
print("Cross-Modal Attention Fusion logits shape:",
logits.shape)
```

Best Practices and Troubleshooting

- **Modality Alignment:**
  Ensure that feature scales and dimensions are properly aligned before
  fusion. Normalization and projection layers can help.
- **Fusion Timing:**
  Choose the appropriate fusion stage (early vs. late) based on the task.
  Early fusion captures low-level interactions, while late fusion
  emphasizes high-level features.
- **Regularization:**
  Use dropout and layer normalization in fusion modules to prevent
  overfitting, particularly when combining high-dimensional data.
- **Experimentation:**
  Test different fusion strategies on validation data to determine which
  approach best suits your application.
- **Robustness to Missing Modalities:**
  Incorporate strategies such as modality dropout to ensure that the
  model remains effective even when one modality is missing.

Exercises

1. **Fusion Strategy Comparison:**
   Implement early, late, and hybrid fusion strategies for a multimodal
   classification task (e.g., combining image and text data). Compare
   performance metrics (accuracy, F1-score) across different fusion
   approaches.
2. **Cross-Modal Attention Analysis:**
   Build a model that uses cross-modal attention for a vision-language
   task. Visualize the attention weights to interpret how the model aligns
   information between modalities.

3. **Handling Missing Data:**
   Simulate scenarios where one modality is partially or completely missing during inference. Develop and test strategies to gracefully handle such cases.
4. **Ensemble Fusion:**
   Combine multiple fusion techniques (e.g., hybrid fusion with cross-modal attention) and evaluate the impact on model robustness and accuracy.
5. **Parameter Sensitivity:**
   Experiment with different dimensions for projected features and common embedding spaces. Analyze how these hyperparameters affect training stability and overall performance.

Fusion techniques are essential for harnessing the complementary strengths of different data modalities in multimodal learning. By exploring early, late, hybrid fusion, and cross-modal attention strategies, you can design models that effectively integrate disparate sources of information. This section provided both theoretical insights and practical examples to help you build robust multimodal fusion pipelines. Experimenting with these techniques will empower you to tackle a wide range of applications, from visual question answering to sentiment analysis in multimedia data.

5.4 Practical Implementation – Multimodal Retrieval Systems

Multimodal retrieval systems enable searching across different types of data—for example, retrieving relevant images using a text query or finding descriptive captions for an image. These systems leverage the power of deep learning to learn joint embedding spaces where data from disparate modalities are aligned based on their semantic content. This section covers the key steps involved in building such systems, including data encoding, similarity search, and evaluation metrics.

Key Components of Multimodal Retrieval

1. **Joint Embedding Space:**
   The core idea is to map different modalities (e.g., text and images) into a shared latent space where semantically similar items are close

together. Pre-trained models like CLIP have demonstrated strong performance by training on large-scale image-text pairs using contrastive learning.

2. **Encoding Modalities:**
   o **Image Encoder:** Extracts visual features from images (e.g., using a Vision Transformer or CNN).
   o **Text Encoder:** Processes textual input (e.g., using Transformer-based models) to generate corresponding embeddings.

3. **Similarity Search:**
   Once embeddings for images and text are obtained, similarity metrics—typically cosine similarity—are used to rank items. Efficient retrieval can be achieved with libraries like FAISS for large-scale datasets.

4. **Evaluation:**
   Retrieval performance is often evaluated using metrics like recall@K, mean average precision (mAP), and precision/recall curves.

Hands-On Code Example: Building a Simple Multimodal Retrieval System with CLIP

Below is a simplified example using Hugging Face's CLIP model to encode images and text, and then perform retrieval based on cosine similarity.

```python
import torch
import torch.nn.functional as F
from transformers import CLIPProcessor, CLIPModel
from PIL import Image
import numpy as np

# Load a pre-trained CLIP model and its processor
model = CLIPModel.from_pretrained("openai/clip-vit-base-patch32")
processor = CLIPProcessor.from_pretrained("openai/clip-vit-base-patch32")
```

```python
device = torch.device("cuda" if
torch.cuda.is_available() else "cpu")
model.to(device)

# Sample list of images and corresponding image
paths
image_paths = [
    "path/to/image1.jpg",
    "path/to/image2.jpg",
    "path/to/image3.jpg",
    # Add more image paths as needed
]

# Load and preprocess images
def load_images(image_paths):
    images = []
    for path in image_paths:
        image = Image.open(path).convert("RGB")
        images.append(image)
    return images

images = load_images(image_paths)

# Encode images using CLIP
image_inputs = processor(images=images,
return_tensors="pt", padding=True)
image_inputs = {k: v.to(device) for k, v in
image_inputs.items()}
with torch.no_grad():
    image_embeddings =
model.get_image_features(**image_inputs)
image_embeddings = F.normalize(image_embeddings,
dim=-1)

# Encode a text query
text_query = "A scenic view of mountains during
sunset"
text_inputs = processor(text=[text_query],
return_tensors="pt", padding=True)
text_inputs = {k: v.to(device) for k, v in
text_inputs.items()}
with torch.no_grad():
```

```
    text_embedding =
model.get_text_features(**text_inputs)
text_embedding = F.normalize(text_embedding, dim=-
1)

# Compute cosine similarities between the text
query and all images
cosine_similarities = (image_embeddings @
text_embedding.T).squeeze(1).cpu().numpy()

# Rank images by similarity
ranked_indices = np.argsort(-cosine_similarities)
print("Cosine Similarities:", cosine_similarities)
print("Ranked Image Indices:", ranked_indices)

# Display the top retrieved image path (or all
ranked indices)
print("Top retrieved image:",
image_paths[ranked_indices[0]])
```

Explanation:

- **CLIP Model:**
  The CLIP model encodes images and text into a shared embedding space. Both image and text features are normalized to unit vectors.
- **Cosine Similarity:**
  The cosine similarity between the text embedding and each image embedding is computed to rank the images.
- **Retrieval:**
  The image with the highest similarity is considered the most relevant to the text query.

Best Practices and Troubleshooting

- **Batch Processing:**
  When dealing with large datasets, process images in batches to efficiently compute embeddings.
- **Normalization:**
  Always normalize embeddings to ensure that cosine similarity is computed correctly.

- **Efficient Retrieval:**
  For large-scale retrieval, consider using FAISS or similar libraries to index embeddings and perform fast nearest neighbor searches.
- **Evaluation Metrics:**
  Evaluate retrieval performance using recall@K, precision, and mAP. This is especially important for production systems.
- **Handling Missing or Noisy Data:**
  Incorporate preprocessing steps and robust encoding methods to manage data variability.

Exercises

1. **Alternative Similarity Metrics:**
   Experiment with different similarity metrics (e.g., Euclidean distance, dot product) and compare their impact on retrieval performance.
2. **Batch Embedding:**
   Implement batch processing for encoding a larger set of images, and use FAISS to perform fast retrieval.
3. **Text Query Variations:**
   Generate multiple text queries for the same image dataset and analyze how query phrasing affects retrieval accuracy.
4. **Cross-Modal Retrieval:**
   Extend the system to support both image-to-text and text-to-image retrieval, and evaluate the performance of both.
5. **Evaluation on Benchmark Datasets:**
   Apply your multimodal retrieval system to a benchmark dataset (e.g., MSCOCO) and report standard retrieval metrics.

Multimodal retrieval systems are a powerful application of joint embedding spaces that enable seamless cross-modal search and retrieval. By encoding images and text into a unified space and employing similarity metrics, you can build systems that effectively bridge different data modalities. This section provided practical implementation details, code examples, and best practices to help you design and deploy a multimodal retrieval system. Experiment with the exercises to further refine your system and adapt it to specific real-world applications.

5.5 Project: Develop a Multimodal Image-Text Search Engine

Multimodal search engines bridge the gap between different data types by mapping them into a shared embedding space. In this project, you will build a system that allows users to search for images using text queries and, optionally, search for text descriptions given an image. We will use a pre-trained vision-language model (such as CLIP) to extract embeddings from both images and text, index the embeddings for efficient retrieval, and create a web interface to perform real-time searches.

2. Project Objectives

- **Joint Embedding Space:**
  Leverage a pre-trained CLIP model to encode images and text into a shared embedding space.
- **Efficient Retrieval:**
  Build an efficient retrieval system using FAISS to index embeddings and quickly retrieve relevant items.
- **Web Interface:**
  Develop a user-friendly interface (using Flask or Streamlit) to enable interactive multimodal search.
- **Evaluation:**
  Evaluate the system's retrieval performance using metrics such as recall@K and analyze user feedback for further improvements.

3. Data Preparation

Dataset

- **Images and Captions:**
  Use a dataset like MSCOCO, Flickr8k, or any collection where images are paired with descriptive captions.

Preprocessing

- **Text Processing:**
  Tokenize and preprocess text using the tokenizer from the CLIP model.
- **Image Processing:**
  Preprocess images (resize, center crop, normalize) as required by the CLIP image encoder.

---

4. Model Implementation

a. Load Pre-trained CLIP

Utilize Hugging Face's Transformers library to load a CLIP model, which contains both an image encoder and a text encoder.

```python
import torch
from transformers import CLIPProcessor, CLIPModel
import torch.nn.functional as F

# Load CLIP model and processor
clip_model =
CLIPModel.from_pretrained("openai/clip-vit-base-patch32")
clip_processor =
CLIPProcessor.from_pretrained("openai/clip-vit-base-patch32")
device = torch.device("cuda" if
torch.cuda.is_available() else "cpu")
clip_model.to(device)
clip_model.eval()
```

b. Extract and Normalize Embeddings

Define functions to encode images and text into normalized embeddings.

```python
```

```python
def encode_images(image_list):
    inputs = clip_processor(images=image_list,
return_tensors="pt", padding=True)
    inputs = {k: v.to(device) for k, v in
inputs.items()}
    with torch.no_grad():
        image_features =
clip_model.get_image_features(**inputs)
    return F.normalize(image_features, dim=-1)

def encode_text(text_list):
    inputs = clip_processor(text=text_list,
return_tensors="pt", padding=True)
    inputs = {k: v.to(device) for k, v in
inputs.items()}
    with torch.no_grad():
        text_features =
clip_model.get_text_features(**inputs)
    return F.normalize(text_features, dim=-1)
```

5. Indexing with FAISS

FAISS (Facebook AI Similarity Search) is a library for efficient similarity search and clustering of dense vectors. Use it to index image embeddings for fast retrieval.

```python
python

import faiss
import numpy as np

# Suppose you have a list of image file paths
image_paths = ["path/to/image1.jpg",
"path/to/image2.jpg", "path/to/image3.jpg"]
from PIL import Image

# Load images
def load_images(paths):
    return [Image.open(path).convert("RGB") for
path in paths]
```

```
images = load_images(image_paths)
image_embeddings =
encode_images(images).cpu().numpy()

# Build FAISS index
d = image_embeddings.shape[1]
index = faiss.IndexFlatIP(d)  # Inner product
(cosine similarity if vectors are normalized)
index.add(image_embeddings)
print("FAISS index size:", index.ntotal)
```

6. Retrieval Process

Perform retrieval by encoding a text query (or image query) and searching in the FAISS index.

python

```
def retrieve_images(query_text, index, image_paths,
top_k=3):
    text_embedding =
encode_text([query_text]).cpu().numpy()
    distances, indices =
index.search(text_embedding, top_k)
    # distances: similarity scores; indices:
indices of retrieved images
    return indices[0], distances[0]

# Example text query
query_text = "A beautiful sunset over the
mountains"
retrieved_indices, scores =
retrieve_images(query_text, index, image_paths,
top_k=3)
print("Retrieved indices:", retrieved_indices)
print("Similarity scores:", scores)
print("Top retrieved image path:",
image_paths[retrieved_indices[0]])
```

7. Web Interface Deployment

Create a simple API using Flask to handle incoming search requests.

```python
from flask import Flask, request, jsonify

app = Flask(__name__)

@app.route('/search', methods=['POST'])
def search():
    data = request.get_json(force=True)
    query_text = data.get("query", "")
    if not query_text:
        return jsonify({"error": "No query
provided."}), 400
    retrieved_indices, scores =
retrieve_images(query_text, index, image_paths,
top_k=5)
    # Return the corresponding image paths and
similarity scores
    results = [{"image_path": image_paths[idx],
"score": float(scores[i])}
               for i, idx in
enumerate(retrieved_indices)]
    return jsonify({"results": results})

if __name__ == '__main__':
    app.run(host="0.0.0.0", port=5000)
```

This simple Flask app listens for POST requests with a JSON payload containing a "query" key. It returns the top matched image paths along with their similarity scores.

---

8. Evaluation and Metrics

Evaluate the retrieval performance using metrics such as:

- **Recall@K:** Measures the proportion of relevant items retrieved in the top K results.
- **Precision@K:** Measures the proportion of retrieved items that are relevant.
- **Mean Average Precision (mAP):** A comprehensive measure that considers ranking quality.

For large-scale evaluations, prepare a validation set with ground-truth pairs and compute these metrics.

---

9. Best Practices and Troubleshooting

- **Batch Processing:**
  For large image datasets, process and index images in batches to manage memory efficiently.
- **Embedding Normalization:**
  Ensure all embeddings are normalized to unit length before indexing to guarantee that cosine similarity is equivalent to the inner product.
- **Index Tuning:**
  Experiment with different FAISS index types (e.g., IVF, HNSW) to improve retrieval speed on large datasets.
- **API Robustness:**
  Add error handling and logging to the Flask app to manage invalid queries and monitor performance.
- **Scalability:**
  For production systems, consider containerizing the app (using Docker) and deploying it behind a load balancer.

---

10. Exercises

1. **Dataset Expansion:**
   Use a larger public dataset (e.g., MSCOCO or Flickr30k) to build a more comprehensive retrieval system. Evaluate recall@K and precision@K.
2. **Alternative Query Modalities:**
   Extend the system to support image queries by encoding an input image and retrieving similar images from the index.

3. **Index Optimization:**
   Experiment with different FAISS index types and parameters to optimize search speed and accuracy.
4. **User Interface:**
   Develop a simple front-end interface (using Streamlit or a web framework) that allows users to input queries and view retrieved images.
5. **Performance Benchmarking:**
   Simulate high query loads and measure API response times. Investigate techniques to improve throughput and reduce latency.

Developing a multimodal image-text search engine involves integrating state-of-the-art vision-language models with efficient indexing and retrieval systems. By leveraging pre-trained models like CLIP and libraries like FAISS, you can build powerful systems that allow seamless cross-modal search. This project provided a step-by-step guide from data preparation and embedding extraction to deployment and evaluation. With further experimentation and scaling, you can adapt this system for various real-world applications such as e-commerce, digital asset management, and content recommendation.

Chapter 6: Large Language Models (LLMs): Training, Fine-tuning, and Optimization

6.1 to LLMs (GPT-family, BERT-family, LLaMA-family)

Large Language Models (LLMs) have dramatically transformed the landscape of natural language processing (NLP) by enabling a wide range of applications—from text generation and summarization to sentiment analysis and translation. In this section, we introduce three major families of LLMs:

- **GPT-family:** Autoregressive models primarily designed for text generation.
- **BERT-family:** Bidirectional encoder models optimized for understanding and classification tasks.
- **LLaMA-family:** Recent, efficient LLMs designed for both research and practical fine-tuning with competitive performance.

Understanding these families, their architectures, training methods, and target use cases is essential for leveraging LLMs in advanced applications.

GPT-Family: Autoregressive Language Models

Overview

- **Architecture:**
  GPT models are built on a decoder-only transformer architecture. They predict the next token in a sequence using autoregressive modeling, which makes them particularly well-suited for generating coherent and contextually relevant text.
- **Training Objective:**
  Trained to maximize the likelihood of the next word given previous context. A causal (uni-directional) mask ensures that predictions depend only on preceding tokens.
- **Key Characteristics:**
  - **Generative Capabilities:** Excels at tasks requiring text generation, completion, and creative writing.

- ○ **Scalability:** Models such as GPT-2, GPT-3, and GPT-4 have scaled in size, showing improved fluency and performance on a wide range of tasks.
- ○ **Applications:** Chatbots, content generation, code completion, and more.

Example Use-Case

Below is a simple example of generating text using a GPT-2 model via Hugging Face's Transformers library:

```python
from transformers import GPT2LMHeadModel, GPT2Tokenizer

# Load pre-trained GPT-2 model and tokenizer
tokenizer = GPT2Tokenizer.from_pretrained("gpt2")
model = GPT2LMHeadModel.from_pretrained("gpt2")
model.eval()

# Define a prompt
prompt = "In the future, artificial intelligence will"
input_ids = tokenizer.encode(prompt, return_tensors="pt")

# Generate text
output = model.generate(input_ids, max_length=100, num_return_sequences=1, do_sample=True, temperature=0.8)
generated_text = tokenizer.decode(output[0], skip_special_tokens=True)
print("Generated Text:\n", generated_text)
```

BERT-Family: Bidirectional Encoder Models

Overview

- **Architecture:**
  BERT models are built on a transformer encoder architecture. They

process entire sequences simultaneously, capturing context from both directions.

- **Training Objectives:**
  Trained using Masked Language Modeling (MLM) and Next Sentence Prediction (NSP). MLM involves randomly masking tokens and predicting them based on context, while NSP encourages understanding of sentence relationships.
- **Key Characteristics:**
  - **Understanding Tasks:** Ideal for tasks that require comprehension, such as text classification, question answering, and named entity recognition.
  - **Bidirectionality:** Leverages context from both left and right of a token, leading to a richer understanding of language.
  - **Applications:** Sentiment analysis, semantic similarity, information extraction, and more.

Example Use-Case

Below is a simple example of using a BERT model for text classification:

python

```python
from transformers import BertForSequenceClassification, BertTokenizer
import torch

# Load pre-trained BERT model and tokenizer
tokenizer = BertTokenizer.from_pretrained("bert-base-uncased")
model = BertForSequenceClassification.from_pretrained("bert-base-uncased", num_labels=2)
model.eval()

# Example input text
text = "I really enjoyed this movie, it was fantastic!"
inputs = tokenizer(text, return_tensors="pt", truncation=True, padding=True)

# Get classification logits
with torch.no_grad():
```

```
    outputs = model(**inputs)
logits = outputs.logits
predicted_class = torch.argmax(logits,
dim=1).item()
print("Predicted Class:", predicted_class)
```

LLaMA-Family: Efficient and Accessible LLMs

Overview

- **Architecture:**
  LLaMA models, introduced by Meta, are decoder-only transformers similar to GPT. They focus on efficiency and accessibility, offering competitive performance while requiring fewer computational resources compared to their larger counterparts.
- **Training and Performance:**
  Designed to be more efficient to fine-tune on domain-specific tasks, making them attractive for researchers and practitioners who need high-performance models without enormous hardware investments.
- **Key Characteristics:**
  - **Efficiency:** Lower resource requirements for fine-tuning and inference.
  - **Flexibility:** Capable of both generative and understanding tasks when fine-tuned appropriately.
  - **Applications:** Similar to GPT for text generation, with potential in areas where cost and computational efficiency are critical.

Example Use-Case

Although LLaMA models might not be directly available in all frameworks due to licensing, similar principles apply. For illustration, consider how you might load and use an efficient decoder-only model (conceptually similar to LLaMA) using Hugging Face's API:

```python
python

# Note: Replace "llama-model" with the actual model
identifier if available.
# from transformers import AutoModelForCausalLM,
AutoTokenizer
```

```
# tokenizer = AutoTokenizer.from_pretrained("llama-
model")
# model =
AutoModelForCausalLM.from_pretrained("llama-model")
# For demonstration, we will use GPT-2 as a proxy.
from transformers import GPT2LMHeadModel,
GPT2Tokenizer

tokenizer = GPT2Tokenizer.from_pretrained("gpt2")
model = GPT2LMHeadModel.from_pretrained("gpt2")
model.eval()

prompt = "In recent research, efficient models like
LLaMA have"
input_ids = tokenizer.encode(prompt,
return_tensors="pt")
output = model.generate(input_ids, max_length=100,
do_sample=True, temperature=0.7)
generated_text = tokenizer.decode(output[0],
skip_special_tokens=True)
print("Generated Text:\n", generated_text)
```

Best Practices and Considerations

- **Model Selection:**
  Choose the model family that best suits your task. Use GPT for
  generative tasks and BERT for understanding tasks.
- **Fine-Tuning:**
  Fine-tune models on domain-specific data to bridge the gap between
  general pre-training and specialized applications.
- **Resource Management:**
  Consider computational constraints when selecting model sizes and
  families. LLaMA models can be a great choice for efficient fine-
  tuning.
- **Evaluation Metrics:**
  Use task-appropriate metrics—perplexity for generation, accuracy
  and F1-score for classification—to assess model performance.

Exercises

1. **Model Comparison:**
   Compare the performancc of a GPT-based text generator and a BERT-based text classifier on a common dataset. Discuss the differences in architecture and training objectives.
2. **Fine-Tuning Experiment:**
   Fine-tune a pre-trained BERT model on a custom sentiment analysis dataset and evaluate its performance. Experiment with different learning rates and unfreezing strategies.
3. **Efficiency Analysis:**
   Analyze the computational efficiency of a GPT model versus a LLaMA-like model. Benchmark inference time and memory usage on a given task.
4. **Prompt Engineering:**
   Experiment with different prompts for a GPT-based model to observe how subtle changes affect generated text quality. Document your findings.
5. **Cross-Family Application:**
   Investigate scenarios where combining insights from both generative (GPT) and bidirectional (BERT) models could yield improved performance, such as in interactive dialogue systems.

This section provided an to the major families of large language models— GPT, BERT, and LLaMA. By understanding the differences in their architectures, training objectives, and practical applications, you can make informed decisions when selecting and fine-tuning LLMs for your projects. With hands-on code examples and exercises, you're equipped to explore further the vast potential of LLMs and adapt them to a variety of advanced NLP tasks.

6.2 Efficient Fine-tuning Techniques (LoRA, QLoRA, PEFT)

Fine-tuning large language models like GPT, BERT, or LLaMA on domain-specific tasks can be challenging due to their enormous number of parameters and the significant computational resources required. Efficient fine-tuning techniques address these challenges by introducing lightweight, trainable modules while keeping the majority of the model's parameters frozen. This approach drastically reduces the memory footprint and training time while maintaining or even improving performance on downstream tasks.

In this section, we focus on three prominent techniques:

- **LoRA (Low-Rank Adaptation):**
  Injects trainable low-rank matrices into certain layers (typically attention and feedforward layers) of a pre-trained model. This reduces the number of parameters that need updating during fine-tuning.
- **QLoRA:**
  Builds on LoRA by incorporating quantization (e.g., 4-bit quantization) to further compress the model and reduce computational requirements, making fine-tuning even more efficient.
- **PEFT (Parameter Efficient Fine Tuning):**
  A broader framework that encompasses LoRA, adapters, and other techniques to achieve efficient fine-tuning by updating only a small subset of parameters.

---

1. LoRA: Low-Rank Adaptation

Overview

LoRA fine-tunes LLMs by injecting low-rank trainable matrices into specific weight matrices (e.g., in attention layers) while keeping the original weights frozen. Instead of updating the full weight matrix W, LoRA learns a pair of low-rank matrices A and B such that the update is given by $\Delta W = BA$. This approach drastically reduces the number of trainable parameters.

Benefits

- **Parameter Efficiency:**
  Only a small fraction of parameters are updated during fine-tuning.
- **Reduced Memory and Compute:**
  Lower training and inference costs.
- **Simplicity:**
  Easy to integrate into existing pre-trained models.

Code Example: Using LoRA with Hugging Face's PEFT Library

Below is an illustrative example using the Hugging Face PEFT library (make sure to install it via `pip install peft`):

```python
from transformers import AutoModelForCausalLM,
AutoTokenizer
from peft import get_peft_model, LoraConfig,
TaskType

# Load a pre-trained model (e.g., GPT-2)
model_name = "gpt2"
model =
AutoModelForCausalLM.from_pretrained(model_name)
tokenizer =
AutoTokenizer.from_pretrained(model_name)

# Define LoRA configuration
lora_config = LoraConfig(
    task_type=TaskType.CAUSAL_LM,  # Suitable for
language modeling
    inference_mode=False,
    r=8,             # Rank of the low-rank matrices
    lora_alpha=16, # Scaling factor
    lora_dropout=0.1
)

# Integrate LoRA into the model
peft_model = get_peft_model(model, lora_config)
peft_model.print_trainable_parameters()

# Now, you can fine-tune `peft_model` on your
domain-specific dataset.
```

2. QLoRA: Quantized LoRA

Overview

QLoRA extends LoRA by quantizing the base model (often to 4-bit precision) before applying LoRA. Quantization significantly reduces the model's memory footprint and computational cost without sacrificing performance, enabling efficient fine-tuning even on hardware with limited resources.

Benefits

- **Further Compression:**
  Lower precision representation reduces storage and memory usage.
- **Cost Efficiency:**
  Enables fine-tuning on less powerful hardware.
- **Synergy with LoRA:**
  Combines parameter efficiency with quantization benefits.

Implementation Considerations

While the full implementation of QLoRA might require specialized libraries (such as bitsandbytes), the core idea is to quantize the pre-trained model and then apply the LoRA adapters on top of the quantized model. Check the latest documentation and repositories from the community for detailed integration steps.

3. PEFT: Parameter Efficient Fine Tuning

Overview

PEFT is an umbrella framework that includes various techniques (such as LoRA, adapters, prefix-tuning, and prompt-tuning) to fine-tune large models efficiently. The goal of PEFT is to update only a small subset of parameters while keeping the majority of the model frozen, thereby reducing the computational and storage burden.

Benefits

- **Flexibility:**
  Offers multiple strategies under one framework.
- **Scalability:**
  Can be applied to models of any size.
- **Ease of Use:**
  Integrates with popular libraries and pipelines for seamless fine-tuning.

Code Example

The LoRA example provided above is a part of the broader PEFT framework. Other PEFT methods can be accessed via similar APIs in the PEFT library.

Best Practices and Troubleshooting

- **Hyperparameter Tuning:**
  Experiment with the rank rrr, dropout rate, and scaling factor lora_alphalora_alphalora_alpha. These parameters can significantly influence performance.
- **Layer Selection:**
  Determine which layers benefit most from adaptation. Common choices are attention layers and intermediate feedforward layers.
- **Monitoring:**
  Use tools like TensorBoard to monitor training loss and evaluate the contribution of the fine-tuned parameters.
- **Resource Management:**
  When using quantization (QLoRA), validate that model performance remains stable and that the reduced precision does not hurt downstream task performance.
- **Integration Testing:**
  Test the fine-tuned model on a small validation set to ensure that the adaptation is effective before scaling up.

Exercises

1. **LoRA Hyperparameter Search:**
   Fine-tune a pre-trained GPT-2 model on a small dataset using LoRA. Experiment with different values of rrr (e.g., 4, 8, 16) and lora_alphalora_alphalora_alpha (e.g., 8, 16, 32) to analyze their impact on performance and training time.
2. **Compare Fine-Tuning Techniques:**
   Implement both LoRA and another PEFT method (such as adapters) on the same task. Compare metrics such as accuracy, training loss, and number of trainable parameters.
3. **Quantization Experiment:**
   Apply 4-bit quantization to a pre-trained model (using libraries like bitsandbytes) and then fine-tune with LoRA (QLoRA). Evaluate the

trade-off between reduced resource usage and any potential performance degradation.

4. **Layer Unfreezing:**
Experiment with unfreezing additional layers in combination with LoRA. Analyze whether a hybrid approach (partial full fine-tuning plus LoRA) yields better results.

5. **Real-world Task:**
Choose a domain-specific task (e.g., customer support response generation or domain-specific summarization) and fine-tune a large language model using one or more PEFT techniques. Report performance improvements and resource savings compared to full fine-tuning.

Efficient fine-tuning techniques such as LoRA, QLoRA, and the broader PEFT framework represent a paradigm shift in adapting large language models to specialized tasks. By updating only a small subset of parameters and leveraging low-rank adaptations and quantization, these methods enable significant reductions in training cost and memory usage while maintaining high performance. Experimenting with these techniques provides valuable insights into scalable model adaptation, empowering you to deploy LLMs in resource-constrained environments.

6.3 Quantization and Model Compression for LLMs

Large language models (LLMs) such as GPT, BERT, and LLaMA achieve state-of-the-art performance across a wide range of natural language processing tasks. However, their massive sizes lead to high computational costs and memory usage, making deployment on resource-constrained devices challenging. Quantization and model compression techniques address these issues by reducing model precision and size while aiming to retain performance. This section covers the fundamentals of quantization and compression, explains popular methods, and illustrates how to apply these techniques to LLMs.

Key Concepts

1. Quantization

- **Definition:**
  Quantization involves reducing the numerical precision of model parameters and activations (e.g., from 32-bit floating point to 8-bit integers or even 4-bit) to reduce memory usage and accelerate inference.
- **Types of Quantization:**
  - **Post-Training Quantization (PTQ):**
    Converts a pre-trained model to lower precision without further training. Simple but might incur a slight accuracy drop.
  - **Quantization-Aware Training (QAT):**
    Simulates lower precision during training so that the model learns to be robust to quantization effects, typically resulting in better performance than PTQ.
  - **Dynamic Quantization:**
    Quantizes weights ahead of time and dynamically quantizes activations during inference.
- **Benefits:**
  - Significant reduction in model size and memory bandwidth.
  - Faster inference due to lower-precision arithmetic.
  - Enables deployment on devices with limited hardware resources.

2. Model Compression

- **Techniques:**
  - **Pruning:**
    Removes redundant or less important weights from the model, reducing its size and computation.
  - **Knowledge Distillation:**
    Transfers knowledge from a large "teacher" model to a smaller "student" model, aiming to mimic the teacher's performance.
  - **Weight Sharing and Low-Rank Factorization:**
    Groups similar weights or approximates weight matrices with lower-rank representations to further compress the model.
  - **Parameter Efficient Fine Tuning (PEFT):**
    Updates only a small subset of parameters (e.g., via LoRA) during fine-tuning while keeping most of the model fixed.
- **Benefits:**
  - Reduced model complexity and size.
  - Lower inference latency and energy consumption.

- o Easier deployment in production environments with hardware constraints.

Hands-On Code Example: Post-Training Dynamic Quantization with PyTorch

Below is a simplified example of applying dynamic quantization to a pre-trained transformer model (e.g., a GPT-2 variant) using PyTorch's built-in utilities. Dynamic quantization is particularly useful for reducing inference latency on CPU.

```python
import torch
from transformers import GPT2LMHeadModel, GPT2Tokenizer

# Load a pre-trained GPT-2 model and tokenizer
model_name = "gpt2"
model = GPT2LMHeadModel.from_pretrained(model_name)
tokenizer = GPT2Tokenizer.from_pretrained(model_name)
model.eval()

# Move model to CPU for quantization (dynamic
quantization works on CPU)
model.to("cpu")

# Apply dynamic quantization on the model's linear
layers
quantized_model =
torch.quantization.quantize_dynamic(
    model, {torch.nn.Linear}, dtype=torch.qint8
)

# Check model size before and after quantization
import os

def get_size_of_model(model, filename="temp.p"):
    torch.save(model.state_dict(), filename)
```

```
    size = os.path.getsize(filename) / 1e6   # size
in MB
    os.remove(filename)
    return size

original_size = get_size_of_model(model)
quantized_size = get_size_of_model(quantized_model)
print(f"Original Model Size: {original_size:.2f}
MB")
print(f"Quantized Model Size: {quantized_size:.2f}
MB")

# Test the quantized model for text generation
prompt = "In a world where technology"
input_ids = tokenizer.encode(prompt,
return_tensors="pt")
output = quantized_model.generate(input_ids,
max_length=50, do_sample=True, temperature=0.7)
generated_text = tokenizer.decode(output[0],
skip_special_tokens=True)
print("Generated Text:\n", generated_text)
```

Explanation:

- The model is loaded and moved to CPU.
- Dynamic quantization is applied to all `Linear` layers using `torch.quantization.quantize_dynamic`.
- The code measures the model size before and after quantization to illustrate compression benefits.
- Finally, the quantized model is used to generate text, demonstrating that performance remains effective.

Best Practices and Troubleshooting

- **Choosing the Right Quantization Method:**
    o For inference on CPU, dynamic quantization is often the easiest to implement.

- o For GPU or edge devices, consider QAT or PTQ based on performance trade-offs.
- **Balancing Compression and Accuracy:**
  - o Evaluate the impact of quantization on downstream task performance. In some cases, slight accuracy loss is acceptable for significant resource savings.
- **Combining Techniques:**
  - o Consider combining quantization with other compression methods such as pruning or knowledge distillation for additional gains.
- **Monitoring Performance:**
  - o Use evaluation metrics (e.g., perplexity for language models, accuracy for classification) to ensure that compressed models meet your application's requirements.
- **Hardware Considerations:**
  - o Test quantized models on the target hardware to verify improvements in latency and memory usage, as behavior may vary across devices.

Exercises

1. **Experiment with QAT:**
   Fine-tune a transformer model using quantization-aware training and compare its performance and model size to a dynamically quantized model.
2. **Pruning Integration:**
   Implement structured pruning on a large language model and evaluate the trade-offs between pruning levels, model performance, and inference speed.
3. **Knowledge Distillation:**
   Train a smaller "student" model to mimic the outputs of a large teacher model. Compare the student model's performance to the original and analyze the resource savings.
4. **Combined Compression:**
   Combine dynamic quantization and pruning on a pre-trained model. Measure the combined effect on model size and inference latency.
5. **Real-World Deployment:**
   Deploy a quantized model on an edge device or mobile phone and benchmark its performance against the full-precision version under real-world conditions.

Quantization and model compression are powerful techniques for making large language models more efficient, enabling faster inference and reduced memory usage without a significant drop in performance. By leveraging methods like dynamic quantization, quantization-aware training, pruning, and knowledge distillation, practitioners can deploy LLMs in resource-constrained environments. Experimentation and careful tuning are key to finding the right balance between efficiency and accuracy. This section has provided both theoretical insights and practical code examples to help you get started with quantizing and compressing your LLMs.

6.4 Deployment and Inference Strategies for LLMs

Deploying large language models (LLMs) in real-world applications requires careful planning to ensure that they are efficient, scalable, and responsive under production loads. This section outlines key strategies for converting and optimizing models for inference, integrating them into serving pipelines, and deploying them using modern frameworks and containerization techniques. The goal is to provide practical guidance that balances performance, cost, and reliability.

Key Strategies for Efficient Inference

1. **Model Conversion and Optimization:**
   - **TorchScript/ONNX Conversion:**
     Convert PyTorch models to TorchScript or ONNX formats to optimize runtime performance and enable compatibility with various inference engines.
   - **Quantization and Pruning:**
     Use quantization (e.g., dynamic quantization, QAT) and pruning to reduce model size and computational load.
   - **Batching and Caching:**
     Process multiple requests in a batch and use caching strategies to reuse intermediate computations where possible.
2. **Serving Frameworks:**

- o **FastAPI or Flask:**
  Use modern web frameworks like FastAPI or Flask to expose model predictions as RESTful APIs.
- o **Inference Servers:**
  Tools like NVIDIA Triton Inference Server or TorchServe can be used to manage multiple models, scale dynamically, and handle high-throughput requests.
- o **Containerization:**
  Deploy models using Docker to create isolated, reproducible, and scalable environments.

3. **Latency and Throughput Optimization:**
   - o **Asynchronous Processing:**
     Use asynchronous request handling and GPU batching to maximize throughput.
   - o **Hardware Acceleration:**
     Leverage GPUs, TPUs, or specialized inference accelerators to reduce latency.
   - o **Load Balancing:**
     Use load balancers to distribute inference requests across multiple instances, ensuring reliability and responsiveness.

Deployment Pipeline Example

Below is an end-to-end example demonstrating how to:

- Convert a pre-trained LLM (e.g., GPT-2) to TorchScript.
- Serve the model with a FastAPI application for real-time inference.

Step 1: Model Conversion with TorchScript

```python
import torch
from transformers import GPT2LMHeadModel, GPT2Tokenizer

# Load pre-trained GPT-2 model and tokenizer
model_name = "gpt2"
model = GPT2LMHeadModel.from_pretrained(model_name)
model.eval()
```

```python
# Convert the model to TorchScript for optimized
inference
scripted_model = torch.jit.script(model)
scripted_model.save("gpt2_scripted.pt")
print("Model successfully converted to TorchScript
and saved.")
```

Step 2: Building an Inference API with FastAPI

Create a simple API to serve model predictions.

python

```python
# Save this as app.py
from fastapi import FastAPI, HTTPException
from pydantic import BaseModel
import torch
from transformers import GPT2Tokenizer
import uvicorn

app = FastAPI(title="LLM Inference API")

# Load the TorchScript model and tokenizer
device = torch.device("cuda" if
torch.cuda.is_available() else "cpu")
model = torch.jit.load("gpt2_scripted.pt",
map_location=device)
model.eval()
tokenizer = GPT2Tokenizer.from_pretrained("gpt2")

class InferenceRequest(BaseModel):
    prompt: str
    max_length: int = 50
    temperature: float = 0.7

@app.post("/generate")
async def generate_text(request: InferenceRequest):
    if not request.prompt:
        raise HTTPException(status_code=400,
detail="Prompt cannot be empty.")
```

```python
    # Tokenize input prompt
    input_ids = tokenizer.encode(request.prompt,
return_tensors="pt").to(device)
    # Generate text using the TorchScript model
    with torch.no_grad():
        outputs = model.generate(
            input_ids,
            max_length=request.max_length,
            do_sample=True,
            temperature=request.temperature
        )
    generated_text = tokenizer.decode(outputs[0],
skip_special_tokens=True)
    return {"generated_text": generated_text}


if __name__ == "__main__":
    uvicorn.run(app, host="0.0.0.0", port=8000)
```

Run the FastAPI application with:

```bash
```

```bash
uvicorn app:app --reload
```

Now, you can send a POST request to
http://localhost:8000/generate with a JSON payload:

```json
```

```json
{
  "prompt": "In the future, artificial intelligence
will",
  "max_length": 100,
  "temperature": 0.8
}
```

Best Practices and Troubleshooting

- **Monitoring and Logging:**
  Integrate logging (e.g., using Python's logging module or external
  tools like Prometheus) to monitor API usage, latency, and errors.

- **Scaling:**
  Use container orchestration tools like Kubernetes to scale the number of API replicas based on load.
- **Latency Reduction:**
  Profile the inference pipeline to identify bottlenecks. Use batch processing for simultaneous requests when possible.
- **Hardware Considerations:**
  Test your deployment on target hardware (e.g., GPUs, CPUs) and optimize configuration (e.g., number of worker threads, GPU memory allocation) accordingly.
- **Fallback Mechanisms:**
  Implement error handling and fallback strategies to ensure that the API remains responsive even under heavy load or during failures.

Exercises

1. **Experiment with Model Conversion:**
   Convert a different LLM (e.g., BERT or a domain-specific model) to TorchScript and measure the impact on inference latency.
2. **Batch Inference Testing:**
   Modify the FastAPI endpoint to accept a batch of prompts and compare throughput with single-prompt inference.
3. **Deploy with Docker:**
   Containerize your FastAPI application using Docker. Write a Dockerfile and deploy your containerized app to a cloud service.
4. **Load Testing:**
   Use tools such as Apache JMeter or Locust to simulate high request loads and evaluate the API's performance and scalability.
5. **Integration with Front-End:**
   Build a simple web interface (using Streamlit or a JavaScript framework) that interacts with your API, allowing users to input prompts and view generated text in real time.

Deploying and serving large language models requires a combination of model optimization, efficient inference techniques, and robust API design. By converting models to optimized formats (e.g., TorchScript), leveraging serving frameworks like FastAPI, and employing best practices for scaling and monitoring, you can effectively deploy LLMs in production environments. This section provided a practical roadmap—from model conversion to API deployment—empowering you to build scalable and efficient inference systems for LLMs.

6.5 Project: Custom Domain Chatbot with Fine-tuned LLM

Chatbots are widely used in customer support, healthcare, finance, and other specialized domains. While general-purpose language models can generate fluent text, adapting them to a specific domain (e.g., legal, medical, technical) often requires fine-tuning on domain-specific conversational data. In this project, you will:

- Gather and preprocess domain-specific conversation data.
- Fine-tune a pre-trained large language model (LLM) to serve as a custom domain chatbot.
- Implement an interactive interface for real-time conversation.
- Evaluate the chatbot using qualitative and quantitative metrics.

This approach leverages efficient fine-tuning techniques (e.g., PEFT methods) to minimize training overhead while adapting the model to specialized language and context.

---

2. Project Objectives

- **Data Collection & Preparation:**
  Assemble a dataset of domain-specific conversational exchanges. Preprocess the text (cleaning, tokenization, etc.) to create a suitable training corpus.
- **Model Fine-Tuning:**
  Load a pre-trained LLM (such as GPT-2, GPT-3, or LLaMA) and fine-tune it on the custom conversation dataset. Consider using efficient fine-tuning techniques like LoRA or PEFT to reduce resource requirements.
- **Interactive Chat Interface:**
  Build a real-time chatbot interface using a web framework (e.g., FastAPI or Flask) or a command-line interface.
- **Evaluation and Iteration:**
  Evaluate the chatbot's responses with both automatic metrics (if

applicable) and human feedback. Iterate on data and fine-tuning scttings to improve performance.

- **Deployment:**
  Package the fine-tuned model into an API or application for real-world usage.

---

3. Data Preparation

a. Collecting Domain-specific Data

For a custom domain chatbot, you might use:

- Transcripts of customer support interactions.
- Domain-specific FAQs and chat logs.
- Synthetic conversation pairs generated by experts.

b. Preprocessing

Key preprocessing steps include:

- Lowercasing, removing extraneous punctuation, and normalizing text.
- Tokenizing text using the tokenizer associated with your chosen LLM.
- Creating conversation pairs (input-response) and optionally formatting with special tokens (e.g., <sos> for start, <eos> for end).

Code Example: Data Preprocessing

```python
python

import pandas as pd
import re

# Load your domain-specific conversation data (CSV
with 'input' and 'response' columns)
data = pd.read_csv("domain_chat_data.csv")

# Basic preprocessing function
```

```
def preprocess(text):
    text = text.lower().strip()
    text = re.sub(r"[^a-z0-9\s\.,!?']", "", text)
    return text

data["input"] = data["input"].apply(preprocess)
data["response"] =
data["response"].apply(preprocess)

# Optionally, save the preprocessed data
data.to_csv("preprocessed_domain_chat_data.csv",
index=False)
```

---

4. Model Fine-Tuning

a. Loading a Pre-trained LLM

We will use a pre-trained model (e.g., GPT-2) from Hugging Face. Fine-tuning can be done with the Trainer API or a custom training loop. Consider applying efficient fine-tuning techniques (e.g., LoRA) to update only a small fraction of parameters.

b. Fine-Tuning Setup

Below is a simplified fine-tuning example using Hugging Face's Trainer API. Ensure your conversation data is formatted as prompt-response pairs concatenated into a single text sequence.

Code Example: Fine-Tuning with Trainer

```python
from transformers import GPT2LMHeadModel,
GPT2Tokenizer, TextDataset,
DataCollatorForLanguageModeling, Trainer,
TrainingArguments

# Load pre-trained GPT-2 model and tokenizer
model_name = "gpt2"
tokenizer =
GPT2Tokenizer.from_pretrained(model_name)
```

```python
model = GPT2LMHeadModel.from_pretrained(model_name)

# Optionally, resize token embeddings if you add
new special tokens
special_tokens = {"additional_special_tokens":
["<sos>", "<eos>"]}
tokenizer.add_special_tokens(special_tokens)
model.resize_token_embeddings(len(tokenizer))

# Prepare the dataset for language modeling fine-
tuning
# Assume 'domain_chat.txt' contains concatenated
conversation pairs separated by newlines.
train_dataset = TextDataset(
    tokenizer=tokenizer,
    file_path="domain_chat.txt",  # Your
preprocessed conversation data file
    block_size=128,
)

data_collator = DataCollatorForLanguageModeling(
    tokenizer=tokenizer, mlm=False,  # GPT-2 uses
causal LM, so mlm is False
)

training_args = TrainingArguments(
    output_dir="./custom_domain_chatbot",
    overwrite_output_dir=True,
    num_train_epochs=3,
    per_device_train_batch_size=4,
    save_steps=500,
    save_total_limit=2,
    prediction_loss_only=True,
)

trainer = Trainer(
    model=model,
    args=training_args,
    data_collator=data_collator,
    train_dataset=train_dataset,
)
```

```python
# Fine-tune the model
trainer.train()
model.save_pretrained("./custom_domain_chatbot")
tokenizer.save_pretrained("./custom_domain_chatbot"
)
```

Tip:
If you wish to integrate efficient fine-tuning (e.g., LoRA), refer to the PEFT library as shown in Section 6.2 before starting fine-tuning.

---

5. Building an Interactive Chat Interface

After fine-tuning, create an interface for real-time conversation. Below is an example using FastAPI.

Code Example: Chatbot API with FastAPI

```python
from fastapi import FastAPI, HTTPException
from pydantic import BaseModel
import torch
from transformers import GPT2LMHeadModel,
GPT2Tokenizer
import uvicorn

app = FastAPI(title="Custom Domain Chatbot API")

# Load the fine-tuned model and tokenizer
model_path = "./custom_domain_chatbot"
tokenizer =
GPT2Tokenizer.from_pretrained(model_path)
model = GPT2LMHeadModel.from_pretrained(model_path)
device = torch.device("cuda" if
torch.cuda.is_available() else "cpu")
model.to(device)
model.eval()

class ChatRequest(BaseModel):
    prompt: str
```

```python
        max_length: int = 100
        temperature: float = 0.7

@app.post("/chat")
async def chat(request: ChatRequest):
    if not request.prompt:
        raise HTTPException(status_code=400,
detail="Prompt is required.")
    input_ids = tokenizer.encode(request.prompt,
return_tensors="pt").to(device)
    with torch.no_grad():
        outputs = model.generate(
            input_ids,
            max_length=request.max_length,
            do_sample=True,
            temperature=request.temperature,
            pad_token_id=tokenizer.eos_token_id,
        )
    response_text = tokenizer.decode(outputs[0],
skip_special_tokens=True)
    return {"response": response_text}

if __name__ == "__main__":
    uvicorn.run(app, host="0.0.0.0", port=8000)
```

Run the API with:

bash

```bash
uvicorn app:app --reload
```

You can then send a POST request to `http://localhost:8000/chat`
with a JSON payload such as:

json

```json
{
  "prompt": "Hello, how can I help you with your
legal query?",
  "max_length": 100,
  "temperature": 0.7
}
```

6. Evaluation and Metrics

Evaluate the chatbot by:

- **Human Evaluation:**
  Collect feedback from domain experts on the relevance and accuracy of responses.
- **Automatic Metrics:**
  Compute perplexity, BLEU score (if using reference responses), or semantic similarity scores.
- **User Interaction Logs:**
  Analyze conversation logs to identify common issues or improvements.

7. Best Practices and Troubleshooting

- **Data Quality:**
  High-quality, domain-specific conversational data is crucial. Ensure data is diverse and representative.
- **Efficient Fine-Tuning:**
  Use techniques like LoRA to update only a subset of parameters, preserving general language understanding while adapting to domain specifics.
- **Prompt Engineering:**
  Experiment with different prompt formulations during inference to guide the chatbot's responses effectively.
- **Monitoring and Iteration:**
  Continuously monitor chatbot interactions, collect user feedback, and iterate on data and model fine-tuning.
- **Deployment:**
  Ensure the deployed model is optimized for low latency and efficient resource usage, possibly by integrating quantization or model distillation techniques.

8. Exercises

1. **Dataset Expansion:**
   Gather a larger dataset of domain-specific conversations and fine-tune the model. Compare response quality before and after data expansion.
2. **Prompt Engineering Exploration:**
   Experiment with different prompt styles and structures during inference. Document how subtle changes affect the chatbot's responses.
3. **Alternative Fine-Tuning Techniques:**
   Fine-tune the model using both full fine-tuning and efficient fine-tuning (e.g., LoRA). Compare performance metrics and resource usage.
4. **User Interface Enhancement:**
   Develop a simple web-based interface (using Streamlit or a JavaScript framework) that allows users to interact with your chatbot in real time.
5. **Error Analysis:**
   Analyze common failure modes in the chatbot's responses (e.g., off-topic replies or misinterpretations). Propose and test solutions to address these issues.

This project has guided you through building a custom domain chatbot by fine-tuning a large language model on specialized conversational data. By carefully preparing the data, efficiently fine-tuning the model, and developing an interactive API, you have created a system capable of providing domain-specific responses in real time. Continuous evaluation and iteration, combined with best practices in deployment, will further enhance your chatbot's performance and user satisfaction.

6.6 Exercise: Deploying a Question-Answering Service using Hugging Face Transformers

Question-answering systems are a core application of natural language processing that allow users to obtain answers to questions based on a given context. Hugging Face offers several state-of-the-art pre-trained models fine-tuned on QA datasets such as SQuAD. In this exercise, you will:

- Load a pre-trained question-answering model and its tokenizer.

- Build an inference pipeline to process user-provided context and questions.
- Deploy the QA model as a RESTful API using FastAPI.
- Evaluate the service and optimize it for real-time usage.

This exercise provides a hands-on approach to deploying large language models in production, ensuring low latency and efficient resource usage.

Objectives

- **Load and Test a Pre-trained QA Model:**
  Use Hugging Face Transformers to load a QA model (e.g., BERT fine-tuned on SQuAD) and test its performance on sample inputs.
- **Build an Inference Pipeline:**
  Create a pipeline that accepts a context passage and a question, then outputs an answer.
- **Deploy as a REST API:**
  Use FastAPI to serve the QA model, enabling real-time question answering through HTTP requests.
- **Optimize for Inference:**
  Incorporate best practices such as batch processing, asynchronous handling, and error management to improve the robustness of the service.

Hands-On Code Example

1. Model Loading and Testing

Below is an example of how to load a pre-trained question-answering model using Hugging Face Transformers and test it with a simple prompt.

```python
from transformers import pipeline

# Load the question-answering pipeline with a pre-
trained model
qa_pipeline = pipeline(
```

```python
    "question-answering",
    model="bert-large-uncased-whole-word-masking-
finetuned-squad",
    tokenizer="bert-large-uncased-whole-word-
masking-finetuned-squad"
)

# Define a sample context and question
context = (
    "Hugging Face is a technology company that
specializes in natural language processing. "
    "It provides tools and models that help
developers and researchers build state-of-the-art
NLP systems."
)
question = "What does Hugging Face specialize in?"

# Get the answer
result = qa_pipeline(question=question,
context=context)
print("Answer:", result['answer'])
```

2. Building the FastAPI Inference Service

Next, we integrate the QA pipeline into a FastAPI application to expose it as a RESTful service.

python

```python
# Save this code as app.py
from fastapi import FastAPI, HTTPException
from pydantic import BaseModel
import uvicorn
from transformers import pipeline

app = FastAPI(title="Question Answering Service")

# Load the QA pipeline once at startup
qa_pipeline = pipeline(
    "question-answering",
    model="bert-large-uncased-whole-word-masking-
finetuned-squad",
```

```python
    tokenizer="bert-large-uncased-whole-word-masking-finetuned-squad"
)

class QARequest(BaseModel):
    context: str
    question: str

@app.post("/answer")
async def answer_question(request: QARequest):
    if not request.context or not request.question:
        raise HTTPException(status_code=400, detail="Both context and question are required.")

    try:
        result = qa_pipeline(question=request.question, context=request.context)
        return {"answer": result['answer'], "score": result['score']}
    except Exception as e:
        raise HTTPException(status_code=500, detail=str(e))

if __name__ == "__main__":
    uvicorn.run(app, host="0.0.0.0", port=8000)
```

To run the API, execute:

```bash
uvicorn app:app --reload
```

Now, you can send a POST request to
`http://localhost:8000/answer` with a JSON payload:

```json
{
  "context": "Hugging Face is a technology company
that specializes in natural language processing. It
```

```
provides tools and models that help developers
build state-of-the-art NLP systems.",
  "question": "What does Hugging Face specialize
in?"
}
```

The API will respond with the answer and confidence score.

Best Practices and Troubleshooting

- **Efficient Model Loading:**
  Load the model only once when the API starts to avoid reloading for each request.
- **Error Handling:**
  Implement proper error handling in your API to manage cases where the context or question is missing or the model fails to generate an answer.
- **Performance Optimization:**
  For high-traffic applications, consider using asynchronous request handling, model quantization, or deploying on GPU-backed instances if available.
- **Batching:**
  If your application can accumulate multiple requests, consider processing them in batches to improve throughput.
- **Monitoring:**
  Use logging and monitoring tools (e.g., Prometheus, Grafana) to track API performance and model response times.

Exercises

1. **Alternative Models:**
   Replace the QA model with another transformer (e.g., RoBERTa or DistilBERT fine-tuned on SQuAD) and compare the quality and latency of the answers.
2. **Error Simulation:**
   Modify the API to simulate different error scenarios (e.g., missing context or question) and implement robust error handling to return meaningful error messages.

3. **Batch Processing:**
   Extend the API to accept a batch of questions for a given context and return all answers simultaneously. Measure any improvements in throughput.
4. **Load Testing:**
   Use a tool like Locust or Apache JMeter to simulate multiple concurrent requests and evaluate the scalability of your deployed QA service.
5. **Advanced Logging:**
   Integrate a logging mechanism that records each request, response time, and any errors. Analyze the logs to identify potential bottlenecks or failure points.

Deploying a question-answering service using Hugging Face Transformers demonstrates how to bring cutting-edge NLP models into production. This exercise provided a complete roadmap—from loading a pre-trained model and building an inference pipeline to deploying it as a RESTful API with FastAPI. By following the provided best practices and experimenting with the exercises, you'll be well-prepared to deploy efficient and robust LLM-based applications in real-world environments.

Chapter 7: Generative Models – GANs, VAEs, and Diffusion Models

Generative models are a cornerstone of modern deep learning, enabling the synthesis of realistic images, audio, and text. They learn the underlying data distribution to generate new samples that resemble the training data. In this chapter, we delve into three popular classes of generative models:

- **Generative Adversarial Networks (GANs):**
  GANs consist of two networks—a generator that produces fake samples and a discriminator that attempts to distinguish between real and fake samples. Through adversarial training, the generator learns to create increasingly realistic data.
- **Variational Autoencoders (VAEs):**
  VAEs are probabilistic models that learn a latent space representing the input data. They combine an encoder, which maps inputs to a latent distribution, and a decoder, which reconstructs data from latent variables using the reparameterization trick.
- **Diffusion Models:**
  Diffusion models are a newer class of generative models that generate samples by iteratively denoising data starting from pure noise. They have demonstrated state-of-the-art performance in high-fidelity image synthesis.

Each of these models offers unique advantages and trade-offs. GANs are renowned for generating sharp, realistic images, while VAEs provide a principled probabilistic framework with smooth latent spaces. Diffusion models, on the other hand, are emerging as a powerful alternative, particularly for high-resolution synthesis.

7.1 Advanced GAN Architectures

Generative Adversarial Networks (GANs) have revolutionized image synthesis and manipulation by pitting a generator network against a discriminator in an adversarial game. While early GANs demonstrated impressive results, advanced architectures such as DCGAN, CycleGAN, and StyleGAN have significantly improved the quality, stability, and versatility of generated images. This section provides an in-depth look at these three architectures:

- **DCGAN (Deep Convolutional GAN):**
  Introduced convolutional structures into GANs, resulting in more stable training and higher-quality image synthesis.
- **CycleGAN:**
  Enables unpaired image-to-image translation, allowing models to learn mappings between two domains without one-to-one correspondence.
- **StyleGAN:**
  Focuses on high-resolution, photorealistic image synthesis and introduces innovative style-based generator architecture with adaptive instance normalization (AdaIN) for fine-grained control over image attributes.

DCGAN: Deep Convolutional GAN

Overview

DCGANs leverage deep convolutional neural networks in both the generator and discriminator, eliminating fully connected layers for image synthesis tasks. They utilize techniques such as batch normalization, ReLU activations in the generator, and LeakyReLU in the discriminator. These design choices help stabilize training and produce higher-quality images.

Key Components

- **Generator:**
  Uses transposed convolutions to upscale noise vectors into images. Batch normalization and ReLU activations help maintain stable gradients.
- **Discriminator:**
  A convolutional neural network that classifies images as real or fake. LeakyReLU activations help in propagating gradients for negative inputs.

Code Snippet: Simplified DCGAN Generator

```python
```

```python
import torch
import torch.nn as nn

class DCGANGenerator(nn.Module):
    def __init__(self, latent_dim, channels_img,
features_g):
        super(DCGANGenerator, self).__init__()
        self.gen = nn.Sequential(
            # Input: N x latent_dim x 1 x 1
            nn.ConvTranspose2d(latent_dim,
features_g * 16, kernel_size=4, stride=1,
padding=0, bias=False),
            nn.BatchNorm2d(features_g * 16),
            nn.ReLU(True),
            # State: N x (features_g*16) x 4 x 4
            nn.ConvTranspose2d(features_g * 16,
features_g * 8, kernel_size=4, stride=2, padding=1,
bias=False),
            nn.BatchNorm2d(features_g * 8),
            nn.ReLU(True),
            # State: N x (features_g*8) x 8 x 8
            nn.ConvTranspose2d(features_g * 8,
features_g * 4, kernel_size=4, stride=2, padding=1,
bias=False),
            nn.BatchNorm2d(features_g * 4),
            nn.ReLU(True),
            # State: N x (features_g*4) x 16 x 16
            nn.ConvTranspose2d(features_g * 4,
features_g * 2, kernel_size=4, stride=2, padding=1,
bias=False),
            nn.BatchNorm2d(features_g * 2),
            nn.ReLU(True),
            # State: N x (features_g*2) x 32 x 32
            nn.ConvTranspose2d(features_g * 2,
channels_img, kernel_size=4, stride=2, padding=1,
bias=False),
            nn.Tanh()
            # Output: N x channels_img x 64 x 64
        )

    def forward(self, x):
```

```
        return self.gen(x)

# Example usage:
latent_dim = 100
channels_img = 3
features_g = 64
generator = DCGANGenerator(latent_dim,
channels_img, features_g)
noise = torch.randn(8, latent_dim, 1, 1)
fake_images = generator(noise)
print("DCGAN Generator output shape:",
fake_images.shape)
```

CycleGAN: Unpaired Image-to-Image Translation

Overview

CycleGAN addresses the challenge of unpaired image-to-image translation by learning mappings between two domains (e.g., horses to zebras) without requiring one-to-one correspondence between images. The key innovation is the **cycle consistency loss**, which ensures that a translation from one domain to another and back results in the original image.

Key Components

- **Generators:**
  Two generators learn mappings $G: X \rightarrow Y$ and $F: Y \rightarrow F: Y \rightarrow X$.
- **Discriminators:**
  Two discriminators DX and DY evaluate the authenticity of images in domains X and Y, respectively.
- **Cycle Consistency Loss:**
  Enforces $F(G(x)) \approx x$ and $G(F(y)) \approx y$, ensuring meaningful translations.

Example Pseudocode

python

```
# Pseudocode for cycle consistency loss:
# Given image x from domain X:
fake_y = G(x)
```

```
reconstructed_x = F(fake_y)
cycle_loss_x = L1Loss(reconstructed_x, x)
```

Note: Full CycleGAN implementations require sophisticated network designs (often using ResNet blocks) and multiple loss components. Detailed code implementations can be found in popular repositories.

StyleGAN: High-Resolution and Controllable Image Synthesis

Overview

StyleGAN introduces a style-based generator architecture that separates high-level attributes (styles) from stochastic variation, enabling unprecedented control over generated images. Innovations include:

- **Adaptive Instance Normalization (AdaIN):**
  Injects style information into the generator at each layer, allowing control over image attributes.
- **Progressive Growing:**
  Originally used to stabilize training by gradually increasing image resolution, though later versions (StyleGAN2, StyleGAN3) have refined the approach.
- **Noise Injection:**
  Adds stochastic variation to fine details, resulting in high-fidelity and diverse images.

Key Components

- **Mapping Network:**
  Transforms a latent vector zzz into an intermediate latent space www that controls style.
- **Synthesis Network:**
  Generates images from www using AdaIN layers and noise injection.
- **Style Mixing:**
  Allows multiple styles to be combined, providing fine-grained control over image features.

Example Outline

```
python
```

```
# Pseudocode for StyleGAN generator:
# 1. Mapping Network: z -> w
# 2. Synthesis Network:
#    For each layer:
#       - Apply AdaIN using w
#       - Inject noise
#       - Upsample progressively
# 3. Generate final image from the synthesis
network
```

Note: StyleGAN implementations are complex. For practical applications, refer to open-source implementations (e.g., NVIDIA's official StyleGAN repositories).

Best Practices and Troubleshooting

- **Training Stability:**
  GAN training is notoriously unstable. Techniques such as label smoothing, gradient penalty, and careful hyperparameter tuning are critical.
- **Mode Collapse:**
  Monitor for mode collapse, where the generator produces limited varieties of images. Diversification techniques and modifications to the loss function can help.
- **CycleGAN Specifics:**
  Ensure that cycle consistency losses are well-balanced with adversarial losses. Overweighting the cycle loss can lead to blurry outputs.
- **StyleGAN Nuances:**
  Experiment with the latent space and style mixing to achieve desired image attributes. Fine-tuning noise injection levels can affect image diversity and realism.

Exercises

1. **DCGAN Experiment:**
   Train a DCGAN on a simple dataset (e.g., CIFAR-10 or MNIST) and visualize the progression of generated images over epochs.
2. **CycleGAN Implementation:**
   Implement a CycleGAN for a small unpaired dataset (e.g., translating between summer and winter landscapes). Evaluate the quality of the translations using cycle consistency loss.
3. **StyleGAN Exploration:**
   Study a pre-trained StyleGAN model and experiment with style mixing and noise injection. Visualize how changes in the intermediate latent vector www affect generated image attributes.
4. **Loss Function Analysis:**
   Compare different adversarial loss functions (e.g., vanilla GAN loss vs. Wasserstein loss) in DCGAN training and analyze their impact on training stability.
5. **Hybrid Models:**
   Experiment with combining elements from different GAN architectures (e.g., using CycleGAN's cycle consistency loss in a StyleGAN framework) and report on the challenges and benefits.

Advanced GAN architectures such as DCGAN, CycleGAN, and StyleGAN have significantly advanced the field of generative modeling. Each architecture offers unique strengths: DCGAN for stable image synthesis using convolutional structures, CycleGAN for unpaired image translation, and StyleGAN for high-resolution, controllable image generation. By understanding their underlying principles, training strategies, and potential pitfalls, you are well-equipped to implement and innovate upon these models. Experimentation through hands-on exercises will further solidify your grasp of advanced GAN techniques, paving the way for cutting-edge applications in image synthesis and beyond.

7.2 Variational Autoencoders (VAEs)

Variational Autoencoders (VAEs) are probabilistic generative models that learn to encode input data into a latent space and then reconstruct the data from this latent representation. Unlike traditional autoencoders, VAEs impose a probabilistic structure on the latent space, enabling smooth interpolation and meaningful sampling. They achieve this by optimizing a loss function that combines a reconstruction loss with a regularization term based on the Kullback-Leibler (KL) divergence, ensuring that the latent space approximates a prior distribution (usually Gaussian).

Theoretical Foundations

1. Encoder and Decoder Networks

- **Encoder (Inference Model):**
  Maps an input x to a latent distribution q(z|x), typically modeled as a Gaussian distribution with parameters μ (mean) and σ\sigmaσ (standard deviation). This is achieved using neural networks that output μ\muμ and log⁡σ2\log \sigma^2logσ2.
- **Decoder (Generative Model):**
  Generates a reconstruction x^\hat{x}x^ from a latent variable zzz sampled from q(z|x)q(z|x)q(z|x). The decoder learns to approximate the data likelihood p(x|z)p(x|z)p(x|z).

2. The Reparameterization Trick

Since sampling from q(z|x) is a stochastic operation, backpropagation through the sampling process is not straightforward. The reparameterization trick solves this by expressing the sample as:

Implementation: A Simple VAE on MNIST

Below is an implementation of a VAE for the MNIST dataset using PyTorch.

Code Example

```python
import torch
import torch.nn as nn
import torch.optim as optim
from torchvision import datasets, transforms
from torch.utils.data import DataLoader
```

```python
# Define the VAE model
class VAE(nn.Module):
    def __init__(self, img_dim=784, hidden_dim=400,
latent_dim=20):
        super(VAE, self).__init__()
        # Encoder layers
        self.fc1 = nn.Linear(img_dim, hidden_dim)
        self.fc_mu = nn.Linear(hidden_dim,
latent_dim)
        self.fc_logvar = nn.Linear(hidden_dim,
latent_dim)

        # Decoder layers
        self.fc3 = nn.Linear(latent_dim,
hidden_dim)
        self.fc4 = nn.Linear(hidden_dim, img_dim)

    def encode(self, x):
        h = torch.relu(self.fc1(x))
        mu = self.fc_mu(h)
        logvar = self.fc_logvar(h)
        return mu, logvar

    def reparameterize(self, mu, logvar):
        std = torch.exp(0.5 * logvar)
        eps = torch.randn_like(std)
        return mu + eps * std

    def decode(self, z):
        h = torch.relu(self.fc3(z))
        x_recon = torch.sigmoid(self.fc4(h))
        return x_recon

    def forward(self, x):
        mu, logvar = self.encode(x.view(-1, 784))
        z = self.reparameterize(mu, logvar)
        x_recon = self.decode(z)
        return x_recon, mu, logvar

# Loss function: Reconstruction loss + KL
divergence
```

```python
def vae_loss(recon_x, x, mu, logvar):
    BCE =
nn.functional.binary_cross_entropy(recon_x,
x.view(-1, 784), reduction='sum')
    KLD = -0.5 * torch.sum(1 + logvar - mu.pow(2) -
logvar.exp())
    return BCE + KLD

# Data loading and preprocessing for MNIST
transform = transforms.ToTensor()
mnist_dataset = datasets.MNIST(root='./data',
train=True, transform=transform, download=True)
dataloader = DataLoader(mnist_dataset,
batch_size=128, shuffle=True)

# Initialize the VAE and optimizer
vae = VAE(img_dim=784, hidden_dim=400,
latent_dim=20)
optimizer = optim.Adam(vae.parameters(), lr=1e-3)

# Training loop
num_epochs = 10
vae.train()
for epoch in range(num_epochs):
    total_loss = 0
    for batch_idx, (data, _) in
enumerate(dataloader):
        optimizer.zero_grad()
        recon_batch, mu, logvar = vae(data)
        loss = vae_loss(recon_batch, data, mu,
logvar)
        loss.backward()
        total_loss += loss.item()
        optimizer.step()
    avg_loss = total_loss / len(mnist_dataset)
    print(f"Epoch {epoch+1}, Average Loss:
{avg_loss:.4f}")

# Example: Generate new samples from the trained
VAE
vae.eval()
with torch.no_grad():
```

```
    z = torch.randn(64, 20)  # 64 samples from
standard normal
    generated = vae.decode(z).view(-1, 1, 28, 28)
    # (Here, you can visualize the generated images
using matplotlib or similar libraries)
```

Best Practices and Troubleshooting

- **Balancing Loss Terms:**
  Carefully balance the reconstruction loss and KL divergence. If KL
  loss dominates, the latent space may collapse; if reconstruction loss
  dominates, the latent space may not be well-regularized.
- **Latent Space Exploration:**
  Visualize the latent space using techniques like t-SNE or PCA to
  ensure that similar images are clustered together.
- **Architectural Tuning:**
  Experiment with different values for hidden and latent dimensions to
  find a balance between reconstruction quality and meaningful latent
  representations.
- **Training Stability:**
  Monitor training losses closely. If the model fails to converge,
  consider techniques like learning rate adjustments or gradient
  clipping.
- **Regularization:**
  Incorporate dropout in the encoder and decoder if overfitting is
  observed.

Exercises

1. **Latent Space Visualization:**
   Train the VAE on MNIST and visualize the latent space using t-SNE.
   Analyze how well the latent variables cluster according to digit
   classes.
2. **Loss Function Experiment:**
   Compare using Binary Cross-Entropy (BCE) versus Mean Squared
   Error (MSE) for the reconstruction loss. Which one produces better
   reconstructions for MNIST?
3. **Conditional VAE:**
   Extend the VAE to a conditional VAE (CVAE) by conditioning the

encoder and decoder on digit labels. Evaluate if conditioning improves the quality of generated samples.

4. **Hyperparameter Tuning:**
Experiment with different latent dimensions (e.g., 10, 20, 50) and observe the effects on reconstruction quality and latent space organization.

5. **Reconstruction Quality:**
Implement an evaluation pipeline that computes the reconstruction error on a test set and compare the performance of your VAE with a standard autoencoder.

Variational Autoencoders provide a powerful framework for learning probabilistic latent representations and generating new data samples. By combining an encoder that maps data to a latent space with a decoder that reconstructs the data, VAEs enable smooth interpolations and creative generation while enforcing a well-structured latent space. Through this section, you have explored both the theory behind VAEs and a practical implementation example, preparing you to experiment further with generative models in your projects.

7.3 Diffusion Models for Image Generation

Diffusion models have recently emerged as a breakthrough in generative modeling, achieving state-of-the-art results in high-fidelity image synthesis. Unlike GANs and VAEs, diffusion models generate images through a gradual denoising process that starts from pure noise and iteratively refines the sample until a realistic image is produced. These models are based on the idea of reversing a forward diffusion process, where noise is systematically added to the data. The reverse process, learned through training, removes the noise step by step.

Theoretical Foundations

1. The Forward Diffusion Process

- **Concept:**
In the forward process, noise is gradually added to an image over a

series of time steps. At each step t, the image becomes increasingly noisy until it converges to a nearly isotropic Gaussian distribution.
- **Mathematical Formulation:**
  Given an image x_0 and a predefined noise schedule β_t, the forward process produces noisy images

2. The Reverse Diffusion Process

- **Concept:**
  The reverse process aims to invert the forward diffusion by learning a model $p_\theta(x_{t-1} | x_t)$ that gradually removes noise from x_T to recover x_0. This process is typically parameterized using a neural network.
- **Training Objective:**
  The model is trained to predict either the noise added at each step or the denoised image itself. The loss function commonly combines the mean squared error (MSE) between the predicted noise and the true noise with other regularization terms:

3. Score Matching and Denoising

Some diffusion models also utilize score matching, where the model learns the gradient of the log-probability density function (the "score") of the data. This score is used to iteratively update the noisy image toward regions of higher data likelihood.

Implementation Outline

Implementing a full diffusion model involves several components:

- **Noise Scheduler:**
  Define a schedule $\{\beta_t\}$ that controls how noise is added at each time step.
- **Neural Network (often a U-Net):**
  A denoising network that predicts the noise component (or the denoised image) given a noisy input and the current timestep t.
- **Training Loop:**
  For each batch of images, sample a random timestep, add noise according to the schedule, predict the noise with the network, and compute the loss.

Below is a simplified pseudocode outline of a diffusion model training loop:

```python
import torch
import torch.nn as nn
import torch.nn.functional as F
import numpy as np

# Example noise schedule (linear for simplicity)
T = 1000   # total timesteps
beta = torch.linspace(0.0001, 0.02, T)   # noise
variance at each timestep

# A simplified U-Net-like model for denoising
(placeholder)
class DenoiseNet(nn.Module):
    def __init__(self, in_channels, out_channels):
        super(DenoiseNet, self).__init__()
        self.conv1 = nn.Conv2d(in_channels, 64, 3,
padding=1)
        self.conv2 = nn.Conv2d(64, out_channels, 3,
padding=1)

    def forward(self, x, t):
        # t can be embedded and concatenated if
needed; here, we ignore it for simplicity
        x = F.relu(self.conv1(x))
        x = self.conv2(x)
        return x

# Instantiate the model
model = DenoiseNet(in_channels=3, out_channels=3)
optimizer = torch.optim.Adam(model.parameters(),
lr=1e-4)

# Training loop pseudocode
num_epochs = 10
for epoch in range(num_epochs):
    for images in dataloader:   # Assume images are
of shape (batch_size, 3, H, W)
        batch_size = images.size(0)
```

```
        # Randomly sample timesteps for each image
in the batch
        t = torch.randint(0, T, (batch_size,))

        # Add noise to images based on t
        noise = torch.randn_like(images)
        beta_t = beta[t].view(-1, 1, 1, 1)
        noisy_images = torch.sqrt(1 - beta_t) *
images + torch.sqrt(beta_t) * noise

        # Predict the noise component with the
model
        predicted_noise = model(noisy_images, t)

        # Compute loss as the MSE between the
predicted and true noise
        loss = F.mse_loss(predicted_noise, noise)

        optimizer.zero_grad()
        loss.backward()
        optimizer.step()

    print(f"Epoch {epoch+1}/{num_epochs} - Loss:
{loss.item():.4f}")
```

Note: This code is a simplified outline meant for educational purposes. Full implementations typically involve additional complexities, such as time-step embeddings, improved U-Net architectures, and more sophisticated noise schedules.

Best Practices and Troubleshooting

- **Noise Schedule Tuning:**
  Experiment with different noise schedules (e.g., cosine schedule) to optimize the trade-off between sample quality and training stability.
- **Model Architecture:**
  Use powerful architectures like U-Net for the denoising network to capture both global and local image features effectively.

- **Loss Balancing:**
  Monitor the balance between reconstruction loss (predicting noise) and any additional regularization losses. Adjust learning rates and weighting factors as needed.
- **Visualization:**
  Regularly visualize intermediate denoised outputs during the reverse diffusion process to qualitatively assess model performance.
- **Computational Resources:**
  Diffusion models can be computationally intensive; ensure that you have adequate GPU resources and consider using mixed precision training to reduce memory usage.

Exercises

1. **Noise Schedule Experiment:**
   Implement and compare at least two different noise schedules (e.g., linear vs. cosine). Evaluate their impact on the quality of generated images.
2. **U-Net vs. Simple CNN:**
   Replace the simple DenoiseNet with a U-Net architecture and assess improvements in the denoising performance.
3. **Reverse Process Visualization:**
   Implement the reverse diffusion process to generate images starting from pure noise. Visualize the image at various timesteps to understand how the model refines the image.
4. **Training Stability:**
   Experiment with different learning rates and batch sizes to analyze their effects on training stability and convergence.
5. **Quantitative Evaluation:**
   Compute metrics such as the Fréchet Inception Distance (FID) to quantitatively evaluate the quality of images generated by your diffusion model.

Diffusion models represent a powerful and increasingly popular approach to generative modeling, particularly in high-quality image synthesis. By gradually removing noise from a random initialization through a learned reverse diffusion process, these models can produce impressive results that rival or surpass those of GANs and VAEs. Through this section, you have gained an understanding of the theoretical underpinnings of diffusion models, seen a simplified implementation outline, and reviewed best practices and exercises to further your exploration. With continued experimentation and refinement, diffusion models offer exciting possibilities for advancing generative tasks in various domains.

7.4 Conditional Generative Models for Real-World Applications

Conditional generative models enhance traditional generative frameworks by leveraging auxiliary information to guide the data synthesis process. Instead of generating data blindly, these models use external signals—such as class labels, text prompts, or other context—to influence the output. This controlled generation is essential for a wide range of real-world applications, including:

- **Image-to-Image Translation:** Converting images from one domain to another (e.g., summer to winter landscapes, or sketches to photographs).
- **Text-to-Image Synthesis:** Generating images based on textual descriptions.
- **Style Transfer and Data Augmentation:** Creating images with specific artistic styles or augmenting datasets with labeled synthetic data.

In this section, we cover:

- **Conditioning Mechanisms:** How to inject external information into generative models.
- **Conditional Architectures:** An overview of popular methods such as Conditional GANs (cGANs), Conditional VAEs (CVAEs), and conditional diffusion models.
- **Practical Implementation:** Code examples demonstrating conditioning using concatenation, conditional normalization, and embedding layers.
- **Best Practices and Exercises:** Tips and challenges to help you design and implement robust conditional generative models.

Key Concepts and Conditioning Mechanisms

1. Conditioning Mechanisms

- **Concatenation:**
  One of the simplest approaches is to concatenate a condition vector (e.g., a one-hot encoded label or text embedding) with the noise vector (or an intermediate feature vector) that is fed into the generator. This method injects the condition directly into the generation process.
- **Conditional Normalization:**
  Techniques such as Conditional Batch Normalization or Adaptive Instance Normalization (AdaIN) dynamically modulate the normalization parameters (scale and bias) based on the conditioning information. This allows the model to adjust feature statistics according to the condition.
- **Learnable Embeddings:**
  When conditions are categorical or textual, you can embed these inputs into dense vectors using embedding layers. These embeddings can then be combined with the generator's input or intermediate representations.

2. Conditional Architectures

- **Conditional GANs (cGANs):**
  In cGANs, both the generator and discriminator receive the condition as an additional input. The generator learns to produce images that conform to the provided condition, while the discriminator not only distinguishes between real and fake images but also checks if the generated image matches the condition.
- **Conditional VAEs (CVAEs):**
  CVAEs extend the VAE framework by conditioning both the encoder and decoder on external information. This conditioning helps the latent space to capture both the underlying data distribution and the specific attributes dictated by the condition.
- **Conditional Diffusion Models:**
  These models incorporate conditions into the denoising process, allowing the reverse diffusion process to be guided by external signals. For example, a text prompt might steer the denoising process to generate images that match the description.

Practical Implementation Example: Conditional GAN for Image Generation

Below is a simplified implementation of a Conditional GAN (cGAN) using PyTorch. In this example, we condition the generation process on class labels for a dataset like MNIST.

Code Example: Conditional GAN (cGAN)

```python
import torch
import torch.nn as nn
import torch.optim as optim
from torchvision import datasets, transforms
from torch.utils.data import DataLoader

# Hyperparameters
latent_dim = 100
num_classes = 10
img_shape = (1, 28, 28)
batch_size = 64
lr = 0.0002

# Generator network with conditional input
class ConditionalGenerator(nn.Module):
    def __init__(self, latent_dim, num_classes, img_shape):
        super(ConditionalGenerator, self).__init__()
        self.img_shape = img_shape
        self.label_emb = nn.Embedding(num_classes, num_classes)

        self.model = nn.Sequential(
            nn.Linear(latent_dim + num_classes, 128),
            nn.ReLU(inplace=True),
            nn.Linear(128, 256),
            nn.BatchNorm1d(256, 0.8),
            nn.ReLU(inplace=True),
            nn.Linear(256, 512),
```

```python
            nn.BatchNorm1d(512, 0.8),
            nn.ReLU(inplace=True),
            nn.Linear(512,
int(torch.prod(torch.tensor(img_shape)))),
            nn.Tanh()
        )

    def forward(self, noise, labels):
        label_input = self.label_emb(labels)
        gen_input = torch.cat((noise, label_input),
-1)
        img = self.model(gen_input)
        img = img.view(img.size(0),
*self.img_shape)
        return img

# Discriminator network with conditional input
class ConditionalDiscriminator(nn.Module):
    def __init__(self, num_classes, img_shape):
        super(ConditionalDiscriminator,
self).__init__()
        self.label_emb = nn.Embedding(num_classes,
num_classes)

        self.model = nn.Sequential(
            nn.Linear(num_classes +
int(torch.prod(torch.tensor(img_shape))), 512),
            nn.LeakyReLU(0.2, inplace=True),
            nn.Linear(512, 256),
            nn.LeakyReLU(0.2, inplace=True),
            nn.Linear(256, 1),
            nn.Sigmoid()
        )

    def forward(self, img, labels):
        img_flat = img.view(img.size(0), -1)
        label_input = self.label_emb(labels)
        d_in = torch.cat((img_flat, label_input), -
1)
        validity = self.model(d_in)
        return validity
```

```python
# Initialize models
generator = ConditionalGenerator(latent_dim,
num_classes, img_shape)
discriminator =
ConditionalDiscriminator(num_classes, img_shape)

adversarial_loss = nn.BCELoss()
optimizer_G = optim.Adam(generator.parameters(),
lr=lr, betas=(0.5, 0.999))
optimizer_D =
optim.Adam(discriminator.parameters(), lr=lr,
betas=(0.5, 0.999))

# Data loading (MNIST)
transform = transforms.Compose([
    transforms.ToTensor(),
    transforms.Normalize([0.5], [0.5])
])
mnist = datasets.MNIST(root='./data', train=True,
transform=transform, download=True)
dataloader = DataLoader(mnist,
batch_size=batch_size, shuffle=True)

# Training loop
for epoch in range(20):
    for i, (imgs, labels) in enumerate(dataloader):
        batch_size = imgs.size(0)
        valid = torch.ones(batch_size, 1)
        fake = torch.zeros(batch_size, 1)

        # Train Generator
        optimizer_G.zero_grad()
        noise = torch.randn(batch_size, latent_dim)
        gen_labels = labels  # Using the same
labels for conditioning
        gen_imgs = generator(noise, gen_labels)
        g_loss =
adversarial_loss(discriminator(gen_imgs,
gen_labels), valid)
        g_loss.backward()
        optimizer_G.step()
```

```
        # Train Discriminator
        optimizer_D.zero_grad()
        real_loss =
adversarial_loss(discriminator(imgs, labels),
valid)
        fake_loss =
adversarial_loss(discriminator(gen_imgs.detach(),
gen_labels), fake)
        d_loss = (real_loss + fake_loss) / 2
        d_loss.backward()
        optimizer_D.step()

    print(f"Epoch [{epoch+1}/20] | D Loss:
{d_loss.item():.4f} | G Loss: {g_loss.item():.4f}")
```

Best Practices and Troubleshooting

- **Condition Embedding:**
  Ensure that the condition (e.g., label) is properly embedded and concatenated with the input noise vector or image features.
- **Loss Balancing:**
  Monitor the generator and discriminator losses closely to avoid scenarios where one network overpowers the other.
- **Regularization:**
  Techniques such as label smoothing or dropout can help stabilize training.
- **Data Preparation:**
  Ensure that your dataset is well-balanced across conditions to prevent bias in the generative process.

Exercises

1. **Alternative Conditioning:**
   Experiment with conditioning mechanisms beyond concatenation—for example, using conditional normalization layers (e.g., Conditional BatchNorm).
2. **Architecture Variations:**
   Modify the generator and discriminator architectures (e.g., adding

more layers or using different activation functions) and evaluate their impact on generated image quality.

3. **Conditional Generation Evaluation:**
   Design quantitative metrics to evaluate how well the generated images correspond to the conditioning labels.

4. **Domain-Specific Conditional GAN:**
   Apply a conditional GAN to a domain-specific dataset (e.g., generating fashion images conditioned on clothing type) and analyze the results.

5. **Experiment with Loss Functions:**
   Implement alternative loss functions such as Wasserstein GAN loss with gradient penalty and compare training stability and output quality.

Conditional generative models extend the capabilities of traditional generative models by allowing controlled synthesis based on external conditions. This project demonstrated how to build a conditional GAN that leverages label information to guide the generation process, making it suitable for various real-world applications such as image-to-image translation and text-to-image synthesis. By experimenting with different conditioning mechanisms, architectures, and loss functions, you can further refine these models to meet domain-specific requirements.

7.5 Project: Building a GAN-based Art Generator

Art generation using GANs opens up exciting possibilities for creative applications—from producing unique digital artworks to assisting human artists in exploring novel visual styles. In this project, you'll build a GAN that learns to generate art-style images. Unlike standard GANs that target natural images, an art generator often emphasizes stylistic diversity and imaginative outputs. We will leverage a GAN framework (in this case, an advanced variant inspired by DCGAN) and incorporate design choices to stabilize training and enhance creative quality.

2. Project Objectives

- **Dataset Preparation:**
  Collect and preprocess an art dataset (e.g., paintings, sketches, or digital art). Apply necessary transformations such as resizing, normalization, and data augmentation.
- **Model Architecture:**
  Design a generator network capable of synthesizing high-quality art images from random noise. Implement a discriminator network to distinguish between real art and generated images.
- **Training Strategy:**
  Train the GAN using adversarial loss functions. Monitor both generator and discriminator losses to maintain a balance and prevent issues like mode collapse.
- **Enhancements for Artistic Diversity:**
  Explore techniques such as style mixing, noise injection, or latent space interpolation to boost the creativity and diversity of generated artworks.
- **Evaluation and Visualization:**
  Regularly visualize generated art samples, evaluate their quality using qualitative assessments, and consider metrics like Inception Score (IS) or Fréchet Inception Distance (FID) for quantitative evaluation.

---

3. Dataset and Preprocessing

For an art generator, you might use datasets like WikiArt, Kaggle art collections, or curated digital art images. Preprocessing steps include:

- **Resizing:**
  Standardize images to a fixed resolution (e.g., 64×64 or 128×128).
- **Normalization:**
  Scale pixel values to a range of $[-1,1][-1, 1][-1,1]$ to suit the Tanh output activation of the generator.
- **Data Augmentation:**
  Optionally apply random rotations, flips, or color jitter to increase dataset diversity.

Example: Data Preprocessing with PyTorch

```python
python

import torchvision.transforms as transforms
from torchvision.datasets import ImageFolder
from torch.utils.data import DataLoader

transform = transforms.Compose([
    transforms.Resize((64, 64)),
    transforms.CenterCrop(64),
    transforms.ToTensor(),
    transforms.Normalize([0.5]*3, [0.5]*3)  # For
3-channel images, scale to [-1, 1]
])

# Assuming art images are organized in folders by
style or category
dataset = ImageFolder(root='path/to/art_dataset',
transform=transform)
dataloader = DataLoader(dataset, batch_size=64,
shuffle=True, num_workers=4)
```

4. Model Architecture

We will implement a GAN with two main components:

Generator

- **Objective:**
  Transform a random noise vector into an art-style image.
- **Architecture:**
  Use a series of transposed convolutional layers (ConvTranspose2d)
  with batch normalization and ReLU activations. The final layer uses
  a Tanh activation.

Discriminator

- **Objective:**
  Distinguish real art images from fake ones.

- **Architecture:**
  Use convolutional layers with LeakyReLU activations and batch normalization. The final output is a probability indicating whether the image is real or fake.

Code Example: GAN Architecture

```python
python

import torch
import torch.nn as nn
import torch.nn.functional as F

# Generator network for art image synthesis
class ArtGenerator(nn.Module):
    def __init__(self, latent_dim, channels_img,
features_gen):
        super(ArtGenerator, self).__init__()
        self.gen = nn.Sequential(
            # Input: N x latent_dim x 1 x 1
            nn.ConvTranspose2d(latent_dim,
features_gen * 8, kernel_size=4, stride=1,
padding=0, bias=False),
            nn.BatchNorm2d(features_gen * 8),
            nn.ReLU(True),
            # State: N x (features_gen*8) x 4 x 4
            nn.ConvTranspose2d(features_gen * 8,
features_gen * 4, kernel_size=4, stride=2,
padding=1, bias=False),
            nn.BatchNorm2d(features_gen * 4),
            nn.ReLU(True),
            # State: N x (features_gen*4) x 8 x 8
            nn.ConvTranspose2d(features_gen * 4,
features_gen * 2, kernel_size=4, stride=2,
padding=1, bias=False),
            nn.BatchNorm2d(features_gen * 2),
            nn.ReLU(True),
            # State: N x (features_gen*2) x 16 x 16
            nn.ConvTranspose2d(features_gen * 2,
features_gen, kernel_size=4, stride=2, padding=1,
bias=False),
            nn.BatchNorm2d(features_gen),
```

```python
            nn.ReLU(True),
            # State: N x features_gen x 32 x 32
            nn.ConvTranspose2d(features_gen,
channels_img, kernel_size=4, stride=2, padding=1,
bias=False),
            nn.Tanh()  # Output scaled to [-1, 1]
        )

    def forward(self, x):
        return self.gen(x)

# Discriminator network for art image evaluation
class ArtDiscriminator(nn.Module):
    def __init__(self, channels_img,
features_disc):
        super(ArtDiscriminator, self).__init__()
        self.disc = nn.Sequential(
            # Input: N x channels_img x 64 x 64
            nn.Conv2d(channels_img, features_disc,
kernel_size=4, stride=2, padding=1),
            nn.LeakyReLU(0.2, inplace=True),
            # State: N x features_disc x 32 x 32
            nn.Conv2d(features_disc, features_disc
* 2, kernel_size=4, stride=2, padding=1),
            nn.BatchNorm2d(features_disc * 2),
            nn.LeakyReLU(0.2, inplace=True),
            # State: N x (features_disc*2) x 16 x
16
            nn.Conv2d(features_disc * 2,
features_disc * 4, kernel_size=4, stride=2,
padding=1),
            nn.BatchNorm2d(features_disc * 4),
            nn.LeakyReLU(0.2, inplace=True),
            # State: N x (features_disc*4) x 8 x 8
            nn.Conv2d(features_disc * 4,
features_disc * 8, kernel_size=4, stride=2,
padding=1),
            nn.BatchNorm2d(features_disc * 8),
            nn.LeakyReLU(0.2, inplace=True),
            # State: N x (features_disc*8) x 4 x 4
            nn.Conv2d(features_disc * 8, 1,
kernel_size=4, stride=1, padding=0),
```

```python
            nn.Sigmoid()   # Output probability
        )

    def forward(self, x):
        return self.disc(x)

# Hyperparameters and model initialization
latent_dim = 100
channels_img = 3  # For RGB art images
features_gen = 64
features_disc = 64

generator = ArtGenerator(latent_dim, channels_img,
features_gen)
discriminator = ArtDiscriminator(channels_img,
features_disc)
```

5. Training Strategy

Train the GAN by alternating between training the generator and discriminator. Monitor losses carefully to ensure neither network overwhelms the other.

Training Loop Outline

1. **Generator Training:**
   - Sample random noise.
   - Generate fake images.
   - Compute loss against the discriminator's prediction of these images as real.
2. **Discriminator Training:**
   - Compute loss on real images.
   - Compute loss on fake images (generated by the generator).
   - Update the discriminator based on the average loss.

Example Training Loop Snippet

python

```python
import torch.optim as optim
```

```python
adversarial_loss = nn.BCELoss()
optimizer_G = optim.Adam(generator.parameters(),
lr=0.0002, betas=(0.5, 0.999))
optimizer_D =
optim.Adam(discriminator.parameters(), lr=0.0002,
betas=(0.5, 0.999))

# Training loop
num_epochs = 50
for epoch in range(num_epochs):
    for i, (real_images, _) in
enumerate(dataloader):
        batch_size = real_images.size(0)
        valid = torch.ones(batch_size, 1)
        fake = torch.zeros(batch_size, 1)

        # Train Generator
        optimizer_G.zero_grad()
        noise = torch.randn(batch_size, latent_dim,
1, 1)
        generated_images = generator(noise)
        g_loss =
adversarial_loss(discriminator(generated_images),
valid)
        g_loss.backward()
        optimizer_G.step()

        # Train Discriminator
        optimizer_D.zero_grad()
        real_loss =
adversarial_loss(discriminator(real_images), valid)
        fake_loss =
adversarial_loss(discriminator(generated_images.det
ach()), fake)
        d_loss = (real_loss + fake_loss) / 2
        d_loss.backward()
        optimizer_D.step()

    print(f"Epoch [{epoch+1}/{num_epochs}] | D
Loss: {d_loss.item():.4f} | G Loss:
{g_loss.item():.4f}")
```

6. Enhancements for Artistic Diversity

- **Style Mixing:**
  Introduce variations by mixing latent vectors from different sources to generate new styles.
- **Noise Injection:**
  Vary the random noise input during training and inference to promote diversity.
- **Latent Space Interpolation:**
  Interpolate between two latent vectors to explore smooth transitions between different art styles.

7. Best Practices and Troubleshooting

- **Monitor for Mode Collapse:**
  Ensure that the generator produces diverse outputs and isn't stuck generating similar images.
- **Balanced Training:**
  Adjust learning rates and training iterations so that the discriminator and generator improve in tandem.
- **Regular Visualization:**
  Frequently save and visualize generated images during training to track progress and spot issues early.
- **Hyperparameter Tuning:**
  Experiment with different architectural hyperparameters, such as the number of convolutional filters and latent dimension size, to optimize output quality.
- **Data Quality:**
  Use a diverse and high-quality art dataset to help the GAN learn varied styles and features.

8. Exercises

1. **Dataset Exploration:**
   Experiment with different art datasets (e.g., digital art, classical paintings, modern sketches) and analyze how the GAN adapts to various styles.

2. **Loss Function Variants:**
   Compare the performance of vanilla GAN loss versus alternative loss functions (e.g., Wasserstein loss) on the quality of generated art.
3. **Latent Space Manipulation:**
   Visualize and manipulate the latent space by interpolating between random noise vectors. Observe how gradual changes in the latent space influence the generated art.
4. **Advanced Architectures:**
   Extend your GAN by incorporating architectural improvements such as spectral normalization, attention layers, or residual blocks to enhance image quality.
5. **User Feedback Integration:**
   Develop a simple interface that displays generated art and allows users to provide feedback. Use this feedback to iteratively improve the model's performance.

Building a GAN-based art generator combines the creative potential of generative adversarial networks with the artistic diversity found in real-world art datasets. Through this project, you have learned to prepare data, design a GAN architecture, and implement training strategies tailored for artistic image synthesis. Experimenting with style mixing, latent space interpolation, and various loss functions can further enhance the creativity and quality of your generated art. With continuous iteration and user feedback, you can refine the model to produce truly unique and compelling artworks.

7.6 Exercise: Implement a Diffusion Model for High-Resolution Image Generation

Diffusion models have recently emerged as a state-of-the-art approach for high-quality image synthesis. Unlike GANs or VAEs, diffusion models generate images by starting from pure noise and iteratively denoising the image over a series of timesteps. This reverse diffusion process, when learned properly, can produce remarkably detailed and realistic high-resolution images.

In this exercise, you will:

- Understand the forward and reverse diffusion processes.
- Implement a simplified diffusion model architecture using PyTorch.

- Set up a training loop that gradually learns to remove noise from images.
- Discuss best practices and challenges in scaling diffusion models for high-resolution generation.

Key Concepts

1. Forward Diffusion Process

- **Purpose:** Gradually add noise to an image until it becomes almost pure Gaussian noise.
- **Noise Schedule:**
  A common choice is a linear schedule, although cosine schedules are also popular.

2. Reverse Diffusion Process

- **Purpose:** Learn to reverse the forward process by iteratively denoising to recover.
- **Modeling:**
  A neural network (often a U-Net) is trained to predict the noise (or directly the denoised image) given and the current timestep t.
- **Loss Function:**
  Typically, mean squared error (MSE) is used between the predicted noise and the actual noise added:

3. High-Resolution Challenges

- **Computational Cost:**
  High-resolution images increase memory and computation requirements significantly.
- **Model Capacity:**
  Architectures like U-Net are commonly used due to their ability to capture both global and local features.
- **Training Stability:**
  Carefully tuning the noise schedule, learning rate, and network architecture is crucial to prevent instability.

Implementation Outline

Below is a simplified implementation that demonstrates the core elements of a diffusion model for high-resolution image generation. This example uses a U-Net-like architecture for denoising and a linear noise schedule.

Code Example

```python
import torch
import torch.nn as nn
import torch.nn.functional as F
import math
from torch.utils.data import DataLoader, Dataset
import torchvision.transforms as transforms
from torchvision.datasets import ImageFolder


# --- Noise Schedule ---
T = 1000  # Total diffusion steps
beta = torch.linspace(0.0001, 0.02, T)   # Linear
schedule
alpha = 1.0 - beta
alpha_bar = torch.cumprod(alpha, dim=0)   #
Cumulative product for each timestep

# --- U-Net-like Denoising Model ---
class SimpleUNet(nn.Module):
    def __init__(self, in_channels=3,
out_channels=3, features=64):
        super(SimpleUNet, self).__init__()
        # Encoder
        self.enc1 = nn.Sequential(
            nn.Conv2d(in_channels, features,
kernel_size=3, padding=1),
            nn.ReLU(inplace=True)
        )
        self.enc2 = nn.Sequential(
            nn.Conv2d(features, features * 2,
kernel_size=3, stride=2, padding=1),
            nn.ReLU(inplace=True)
        )
```

```python
        # Bottleneck
        self.bottleneck = nn.Sequential(
            nn.Conv2d(features * 2, features * 4,
kernel_size=3, padding=1),
            nn.ReLU(inplace=True)
        )
        # Decoder
        self.dec2 = nn.Sequential(
            nn.ConvTranspose2d(features * 4,
features * 2, kernel_size=3, stride=2, padding=1,
output_padding=1),
            nn.ReLU(inplace=True)
        )
        self.dec1 = nn.Sequential(
            nn.Conv2d(features * 2, out_channels,
kernel_size=3, padding=1)
        )

    def forward(self, x, t):
        # Here, t can be used for time-step
conditioning (e.g., via embedding), omitted for
simplicity
        e1 = self.enc1(x)
        e2 = self.enc2(e1)
        b = self.bottleneck(e2)
        d2 = self.dec2(b)
        out = self.dec1(d2)
        return out

# --- Dataset Preparation ---
# For high-resolution, assume images are 256x256.
transform = transforms.Compose([
    transforms.Resize((256, 256)),
    transforms.ToTensor(),
    transforms.Normalize([0.5]*3, [0.5]*3)
])
# Use an image folder dataset of high-resolution
images (e.g., a subset of ImageNet or a custom
dataset)
dataset =
ImageFolder(root='path/to/high_res_dataset',
transform=transform)
```

```python
dataloader = DataLoader(dataset, batch_size=8,
shuffle=True, num_workers=4)

# --- Training Setup ---
device = torch.device("cuda" if
torch.cuda.is_available() else "cpu")
model = SimpleUNet(in_channels=3, out_channels=3,
features=64).to(device)
optimizer = torch.optim.Adam(model.parameters(),
lr=1e-4)

def diffusion_loss(x0, t, model, beta, alpha_bar):
    batch_size = x0.size(0)
    noise = torch.randn_like(x0)
    # Get alpha_bar_t for each sample in the batch,
shape: (batch_size, 1, 1, 1)
    alpha_bar_t = alpha_bar[t].view(batch_size, 1,
1, 1).to(device)
    # Forward diffusion: add noise to the image
    x_t = torch.sqrt(alpha_bar_t) * x0 +
torch.sqrt(1 - alpha_bar_t) * noise
    # Predict noise using the model
    predicted_noise = model(x_t, t)
    # Loss: MSE between actual noise and predicted
noise
    return F.mse_loss(predicted_noise, noise)

num_epochs = 20
model.train()
for epoch in range(num_epochs):
    total_loss = 0
    for batch_idx, (images, _) in
enumerate(dataloader):
        images = images.to(device)
        batch_size = images.size(0)
        # Sample a random timestep for each image
in the batch
        t = torch.randint(0, T, (batch_size,))
        loss = diffusion_loss(images, t, model,
beta, alpha_bar)
        optimizer.zero_grad()
        loss.backward()
```

```python
        optimizer.step()
        total_loss += loss.item()
    avg_loss = total_loss / len(dataloader)
    print(f"Epoch {epoch+1}/{num_epochs} - Average
Loss: {avg_loss:.4f}")

# --- Inference: Reverse Diffusion Process
(Simplified) ---
def sample_image(model, T, beta, alpha_bar, device,
img_size=(3, 256, 256)):
    model.eval()
    # Start from pure noise
    x = torch.randn(1, *img_size).to(device)
    with torch.no_grad():
        for t in reversed(range(T)):
            t_tensor = torch.full((1,), t,
dtype=torch.long).to(device)
            # Predict noise at timestep t
            predicted_noise = model(x, t_tensor)
            # Remove noise based on the diffusion
formula (simplified)
            alpha_bar_t = alpha_bar[t]
            x = (x - torch.sqrt(1 - alpha_bar_t) *
predicted_noise) / torch.sqrt(alpha_bar_t)
    return x

# Generate a sample image
sample = sample_image(model, T, beta, alpha_bar,
device)
# Denormalize image to [0,1] for visualization
sample = (sample + 1) / 2.0
# Convert tensor to PIL image if needed for display
(omitted here)
print("Generated sample image tensor shape:",
sample.shape)
```

Best Practices and Troubleshooting

- **Noise Schedule Tuning:**
  Experiment with different noise schedules (e.g., cosine) to optimize image quality and training convergence.

- **Time Conditioning:**
  Consider embedding the timestep t (using learnable or sinusoidal embeddings) and integrating it into your model for better conditioning.
- **Model Architecture:**
  For high-resolution images, a full U-Net architecture with skip connections can capture both local and global features more effectively.
- **Computational Resources:**
  Diffusion models are computationally intensive. Use mixed precision training and, if possible, multiple GPUs to speed up training.
- **Visualization:**
  Regularly visualize intermediate outputs during the reverse diffusion process to ensure that noise is being effectively removed.
- **Stability:**
  Monitor losses and consider gradient clipping if training becomes unstable.

Exercises

1. **Noise Schedule Experiment:**
   Implement a cosine noise schedule and compare its performance with the linear schedule in terms of sample quality and training stability.
2. **U-Net Integration:**
   Replace the simple CNN-based denoising model with a more sophisticated U-Net architecture. Evaluate improvements in the quality of the generated high-resolution images.
3. **Time Embedding:**
   Integrate a learnable time embedding into the model so that the network explicitly conditions on the current timestep t. Experiment with different embedding dimensions.
4. **Reverse Process Analysis:**
   Visualize and save generated images at various timesteps during the reverse diffusion process to understand the denoising progression.
5. **Quantitative Metrics:**
   Compute quantitative metrics (e.g., FID score) on a validation set to evaluate the quality of generated images. Analyze how changes in hyperparameters affect these metrics.

Diffusion models offer a promising pathway for generating high-resolution images by progressively refining random noise into detailed, realistic outputs. This exercise provided a hands-on to implementing a diffusion model using a simplified U-Net-like architecture, along with an outline of the forward and reverse processes and best practices for scaling to high-resolution generation. Continued experimentation with noise schedules, time embeddings, and advanced network architectures can further improve performance and sample quality.

Chapter 8: Advanced Model Deployment Strategies

8.1 TorchScript and Model Serialization

Deploying deep learning models in production often requires models to be optimized for speed, portability, and scalability. TorchScript is a powerful tool in PyTorch that converts dynamic PyTorch models into static, optimized representations. By serializing models with TorchScript, you can:

- **Improve Inference Efficiency:** Optimize runtime performance with ahead-of-time (AOT) compilation.
- **Enhance Portability:** Deploy models independently of Python, making it easier to integrate with production systems written in other languages.
- **Facilitate Deployment:** Serialize models into files that can be loaded by various serving frameworks.

This section provides an in-depth look at TorchScript, detailing how to convert and serialize models, and discusses best practices for integrating serialized models into your deployment pipeline.

Key Concepts

1. What is TorchScript?

TorchScript is an intermediate representation (IR) of a PyTorch model that enables it to run independently from Python. It allows you to transform your PyTorch code into a statically analyzable and optimizable format. There are two main approaches to converting a PyTorch model to TorchScript:

- **Tracing:**
  Uses a sample input to record the operations performed by the model. It is simple to use but may not capture dynamic control flows.
- **Scripting:**
  Converts the model by analyzing its source code, supporting dynamic control flows. This method is more flexible but may require minor code modifications to adhere to TorchScript's constraints.

2. Benefits of Using TorchScript

- **Optimized Execution:**
  TorchScript can leverage optimizations such as kernel fusion and parallelism to speed up inference.
- **Platform Independence:**
  The serialized model can be deployed in C++ environments and integrated into production systems without a Python dependency.
- **Ease of Deployment:**
  Serialized TorchScript models are saved as files, making it easier to version control and distribute across different systems.

3. Model Serialization

Serialization refers to the process of saving a model's state (and sometimes its code) to a file, which can be later loaded for inference or further training. TorchScript provides a seamless way to serialize models, ensuring that both the model's architecture and its learned parameters are preserved.

Converting and Serializing a Model with TorchScript

1. Tracing vs. Scripting

- **Tracing Example:**
  Use `torch.jit.trace` with a sample input to capture the operations of the model.
- **Scripting Example:**
  Use `torch.jit.script` to compile the model, supporting models with dynamic behavior.

Code Example: Tracing a Simple Model

```python
import torch
import torch.nn as nn

# Define a simple model
class SimpleModel(nn.Module):
    def __init__(self, input_dim, output_dim):
```

```python
        super(SimpleModel, self).__init__()
        self.fc = nn.Linear(input_dim, output_dim)

    def forward(self, x):
        return torch.relu(self.fc(x))

model = SimpleModel(input_dim=10, output_dim=5)
model.eval()  # Set the model to evaluation mode

# Create a sample input tensor
sample_input = torch.randn(1, 10)

# Trace the model
traced_model = torch.jit.trace(model, sample_input)
traced_model.save("simple_model_traced.pt")
print("Traced model saved as
'simple_model_traced.pt'.")
```

Code Example: Scripting a Model

```python
python

import torch
import torch.nn as nn

# Define a model with dynamic control flow
class DynamicModel(nn.Module):
    def __init__(self):
        super(DynamicModel, self).__init__()
        self.fc = nn.Linear(10, 10)

    def forward(self, x):
        # Dynamic behavior: use a loop based on
input values
        for _ in range(int(x.sum().item()) % 3 +
1):
            x = torch.relu(self.fc(x))
        return x

model = DynamicModel()
model.eval()
```

```
# Script the model (supports dynamic control flow)
scripted_model = torch.jit.script(model)
scripted_model.save("dynamic_model_scripted.pt")
print("Scripted model saved as
'dynamic_model_scripted.pt'.")
```

Loading and Using Serialized Models

Once serialized, TorchScript models can be loaded in Python or C++ for inference.

Code Example: Loading a Serialized Model in Python

```python
python

# Load the traced model
loaded_model =
torch.jit.load("simple_model_traced.pt")
loaded_model.eval()

# Perform inference
input_tensor = torch.randn(1, 10)
output = loaded_model(input_tensor)
print("Model output:", output)
```

Best Practices and Troubleshooting

- **Choosing the Right Method:**
  - Use **tracing** for models with static control flow.
  - Use **scripting** for models with dynamic behaviors (loops, conditionals).
- **Sample Input:**
  When tracing, ensure that the sample input is representative of the variety of inputs the model will encounter in production.
- **Model Modifications:**
  TorchScript imposes some restrictions (e.g., no arbitrary Python objects). Adjust your model code if necessary to comply with TorchScript requirements.
- **Debugging:**
  Use torch.jit.trace warnings and errors to identify parts of

the model that may not be traceable. Scripting might be more robust in these cases.
- **Version Compatibility:**
  Ensure compatibility between the PyTorch version used for model conversion and the deployment environment.
- **Deployment Testing:**
  Test the serialized model in an environment similar to production (e.g., C++ runtime if deploying in C++) to catch potential integration issues.

Exercises

1. **Model Comparison:**
   Trace and script the same model with both static and dynamic behaviors. Compare the performance and output consistency between the traced and scripted versions.
2. **Complex Model Serialization:**
   Serialize a more complex model (e.g., a Transformer-based model) using both tracing and scripting. Identify challenges and propose solutions to make the model TorchScript-compatible.
3. **Integration Testing:**
   Deploy a serialized TorchScript model in a simple C++ application using PyTorch C++ API (libtorch). Evaluate the performance differences between the Python and C++ environments.
4. **Performance Benchmarking:**
   Measure and compare inference latency and throughput of a serialized model versus its full PyTorch (dynamic) counterpart on a fixed dataset.
5. **Troubleshooting:**
   Intentionally introduce a dynamic control flow bug in a model and attempt to trace it. Use the error messages to guide modifications needed for successful serialization.

TorchScript and model serialization are essential tools for transitioning PyTorch models from research to production. By converting models into an optimized, static representation, you can achieve improved inference performance, better portability, and seamless deployment across various platforms. Experimenting with both tracing and scripting methods—and understanding their respective trade-offs—will empower you to deploy robust, efficient models in real-world applications.

8.2 Model Deployment with TorchServe

Deploying machine learning models in production requires a robust, scalable, and efficient serving solution. TorchServe is an open-source model serving framework designed specifically for PyTorch models. It enables you to package, deploy, and manage models easily with features such as RESTful APIs, batch processing, logging, and model versioning. TorchServe converts your model into a serialized format, typically a model archive (.mar file), and provides a production-ready server that can handle high-throughput inference requests.

Key Components of TorchServe

1. **Model Archive (.mar file):**
   A model archive bundles the model's state dictionary, model definition, and any additional assets (e.g., tokenizer files) into a single file. This file is created using the `torch-model-archiver` tool.
2. **Model Handler:**
   The handler defines how the model processes input data and produces output. TorchServe provides default handlers for common tasks (e.g., image classification, text generation), but you can also implement custom handlers.
3. **Configuration Files:**
   TorchServe uses configuration files (e.g., `config.properties`) to manage server settings, such as batch size, logging, and inference timeout.
4. **Management and Inference APIs:**
   TorchServe exposes REST APIs for model management (register, unregister, scale) and inference, allowing you to integrate model serving into your production workflow.

Steps for Deploying a Model with TorchServe

1. Prepare Your Model for Serialization

Before creating a model archive, ensure that your PyTorch model is in evaluation mode and that any necessary pre- or post-processing code is encapsulated within your model or handler.

```python
import torch
import torch.nn as nn

# Example: Define a simple model for demonstration
class SimpleModel(nn.Module):
    def __init__(self, input_dim, output_dim):
        super(SimpleModel, self).__init__()
        self.fc = nn.Linear(input_dim, output_dim)

    def forward(self, x):
        return self.fc(x)

model = SimpleModel(input_dim=10, output_dim=2)
model.eval()  # Set the model to evaluation mode
torch.save(model.state_dict(), "simple_model.pth")
```

2. Create a Model Archive (.mar)

Use the `torch-model-archiver` command-line tool to package your model. You need to provide a serialized model file, a model definition file, and a handler file (or use a default handler).

```bash
torch-model-archiver --model-name simple_model \
    --version 1.0 \
    --serialized-file simple_model.pth \
    --handler image_classifier \
    --export-path model_store \
    --extra-files "simple_model.py,
index_to_name.json"
```

In this command:

- `--model-name`: Name of the model.
- `--version`: Model version.
- `--serialized-file`: Path to the saved model state dictionary.
- `--handler`: Specifies the handler (e.g., a default handler such as `image_classifier` or a custom handler).
- `--export-path`: Directory where the .mar file will be stored.
- `--extra-files`: Additional files required by the model (e.g., the model definition script or a JSON mapping file).

3. Start TorchServe

Launch TorchServe using the model archive you created. You can start TorchServe with a command like:

bash

```
torchserve --start --ncs --model-store model_store
--models my_simple_model=simple_model.mar
```

Flags used:

- `--start`: Starts the TorchServe server.
- `--ncs`: No config snapshot; useful during development.
- `--model-store`: Directory containing your model archives.
- `--models`: A mapping of model names to archive files.

4. Inference via REST API

Once TorchServe is running, you can send inference requests to the server using tools like `curl` or Postman.

bash

```
curl -X POST
http://127.0.0.1:8080/predictions/my_simple_model -
T sample_input.json
```

Where `sample_input.json` contains your input data in the format expected by your model handler.

Best Practices and Troubleshooting

- **Handler Customization:**
  If the default handlers do not meet your needs, implement a custom handler by subclassing `BaseHandler` and overriding methods such as `preprocess`, `inference`, and `postprocess`.
- **Testing Locally:**
  Before deploying to production, test your model archive and API locally using TorchServe's management API and `curl` requests.
- **Logging and Monitoring:**
  Configure logging to capture request/response logs and monitor performance. Tools like Prometheus and Grafana can be integrated for real-time monitoring.
- **Batch Processing:**
  Configure batch sizes and timeouts in the `config.properties` file to optimize throughput without compromising latency.
- **Version Control:**
  Maintain version control for your model archives and configuration files to facilitate smooth updates and rollbacks.
- **Resource Management:**
  Optimize model inference by utilizing GPUs where available, and consider using quantized or pruned models to reduce latency.

Exercises

1. **Model Archive Creation:**
   Create a model archive for a more complex model (e.g., a Transformer-based classifier) using a custom handler. Test the archive locally using TorchServe.
2. **Custom Handler Development:**
   Develop and test a custom handler that includes additional preprocessing (e.g., image resizing, normalization) and postprocessing steps (e.g., converting model outputs to human-readable labels).
3. **Load Testing:**
   Simulate high-concurrency inference requests using Apache JMeter

or Locust. Monitor TorchServe's performance and adjust batch size and worker settings accordingly.

4. **Integration with a Web App:**
   Build a simple web application (using Flask or Streamlit) that sends requests to the TorchServe API and displays the model's predictions.

5. **Quantization and Compression:**
   Experiment with deploying a quantized version of your model. Compare inference speed and accuracy between the full-precision and quantized models.

TorchServe provides a robust framework for deploying PyTorch models in production environments. By converting your model into a serialized format and leveraging TorchServe's scalable serving capabilities, you can achieve efficient and reliable inference. Following best practices such as custom handler development, logging, monitoring, and resource optimization will ensure a smooth deployment process. Experiment with the provided exercises to deepen your understanding and further refine your deployment strategy.

8.3 Building Scalable APIs with FastAPI and PyTorch

As deep learning models transition from research to production, it becomes crucial to expose them as robust and scalable APIs. FastAPI is a modern, high-performance web framework for building APIs with Python that leverages asynchronous programming for enhanced throughput. In this section, we cover how to integrate PyTorch models into a FastAPI application, optimize the API for efficient inference, and deploy it for high-concurrency environments.

Key Concepts

1. **FastAPI Overview:**
   - **Asynchronous Capabilities:**
     FastAPI uses asynchronous programming to handle multiple requests concurrently, reducing latency and improving throughput.

- o **Automatic Documentation:**
  FastAPI automatically generates interactive API documentation using Swagger UI.
- o **Type Hints and Validation:**
  Type hints and Pydantic models are used for automatic input validation and serialization.
2. **Integrating PyTorch with FastAPI:**
   - o **Model Loading:**
     Load the PyTorch model once during application startup to avoid repeated initialization overhead.
   - o **Inference Pipeline:**
     Create an inference pipeline that preprocesses inputs, performs predictions, and post-processes outputs.
   - o **Asynchronous Processing:**
     Use asynchronous endpoints to process requests concurrently.
3. **Scalability and Deployment:**
   - o **Batch Processing:**
     Implement batching strategies to handle multiple inference requests simultaneously.
   - o **Containerization:**
     Deploy the API using Docker to ensure consistency and scalability in production environments.
   - o **Monitoring and Logging:**
     Integrate logging and monitoring tools to track API performance and troubleshoot issues.

Hands-On Code Example

Step 1: Create the FastAPI Application

The following example demonstrates how to build a scalable FastAPI application that serves a PyTorch model for inference. In this example, we use a simple PyTorch model for demonstration, but the same principles apply to larger models.

```python
from fastapi import FastAPI, HTTPException
from pydantic import BaseModel
import uvicorn
```

```python
import torch
import torch.nn as nn
import torch.nn.functional as F

# Define a simple PyTorch model for demonstration
class SimpleModel(nn.Module):
    def __init__(self, input_dim, output_dim):
        super(SimpleModel, self).__init__()
        self.fc = nn.Linear(input_dim, output_dim)

    def forward(self, x):
        return F.relu(self.fc(x))

# Initialize model, load weights, and set
evaluation mode
model = SimpleModel(input_dim=10, output_dim=2)
model.load_state_dict(torch.load("simple_model.pth"
, map_location=torch.device("cpu")))
model.eval()

# FastAPI input schema using Pydantic
class InferenceRequest(BaseModel):
    features: list  # Expect a list of 10 numerical
features

# Create FastAPI app
app = FastAPI(title="Scalable PyTorch Inference
API")

@app.post("/predict")
async def predict(request: InferenceRequest):
    # Validate input length
    if len(request.features) != 10:
        raise HTTPException(status_code=400,
detail="Input must contain 10 features.")

    # Convert input list to a tensor
    input_tensor = torch.tensor([request.features],
dtype=torch.float32)

    # Perform inference
    with torch.no_grad():
```

```python
        output = model(input_tensor)
    prediction = output.argmax(dim=1).item()

    return {"prediction": prediction, "raw_output":
output.tolist()}

if __name__ == "__main__":
    # Run FastAPI app with Uvicorn
    uvicorn.run(app, host="0.0.0.0", port=8000)
```

Step 2: Deploying and Scaling the API

- **Dockerize the Application:**

Create a `Dockerfile` to containerize the FastAPI app for consistent deployment.

```dockerfile
dockerfile

# Use an official Python runtime as a parent image
FROM python:3.9-slim

# Set working directory in the container
WORKDIR /app

# Copy the requirements file and install
dependencies
COPY requirements.txt .
RUN pip install --no-cache-dir -r requirements.txt

# Copy the rest of the application code
COPY . .

# Expose port 8000 for the FastAPI app
EXPOSE 8000

# Command to run the application with Uvicorn
CMD ["uvicorn", "app:app", "--host", "0.0.0.0", "--
port", "8000"]
```

- **requirements.txt:**

```plaintext

fastapi
uvicorn
torch
pydantic
```

- **Deploying with Docker:**

Build and run the Docker container.

```bash

docker build -t pytorch-fastapi-api .
docker run -p 8000:8000 pytorch-fastapi-api
```

- **Scaling:**
  Use container orchestration tools like Kubernetes or Docker Swarm
  to scale the application horizontally, handling increased load and
  ensuring high availability.

Best Practices and Troubleshooting

- **Model Initialization:**
  Load your model once at startup to avoid reloading it for every
  request. This reduces latency significantly.
- **Asynchronous Endpoints:**
  Leverage FastAPI's asynchronous capabilities by defining async
  endpoints. If your model inference is blocking, consider offloading it
  to a thread pool.
- **Batch Inference:**
  Implement batch processing if your API needs to handle multiple
  requests simultaneously, which can be achieved by aggregating
  inputs and running them together through the model.
- **Monitoring:**
  Integrate logging (e.g., using Python's logging module) and
  monitoring solutions (e.g., Prometheus) to keep track of API
  performance, latency, and errors.

- **Testing:**
  Thoroughly test the API locally using tools like Postman or curl before deploying to production.
- **Load Balancing:**
  Use load balancers to distribute incoming requests across multiple instances of your API for better scalability and reliability.

Exercises

1. **Batch Processing Implementation:**
   Modify the API endpoint to accept a batch of feature vectors and process them together to improve throughput. Compare the performance with single-request processing.
2. **Asynchronous Inference:**
   Explore using Python's `concurrent.futures.ThreadPoolExecutor` to offload model inference to a separate thread. Measure improvements in latency when handling multiple concurrent requests.
3. **Performance Benchmarking:**
   Use tools such as Apache JMeter or Locust to simulate high load on your API. Monitor the response times and resource usage, and adjust configurations accordingly.
4. **Logging and Monitoring Integration:**
   Integrate a logging mechanism that records request details, processing times, and errors. Set up a basic monitoring dashboard to track API performance over time.
5. **Deployment Simulation:**
   Deploy the containerized API on a cloud service (e.g., AWS, GCP, or Azure) and evaluate its performance under real-world network conditions.

Building scalable APIs with FastAPI and PyTorch provides a robust foundation for deploying deep learning models in production. By leveraging FastAPI's asynchronous capabilities, efficient model loading, and best practices in deployment and monitoring, you can create APIs that handle high throughput with low latency. This section equipped you with practical code examples, Docker deployment strategies, and troubleshooting tips to ensure your model serving solution is both scalable and efficient. Experiment with the exercises to further optimize your deployment pipeline.

8.4 Dockerizing and Containerizing PyTorch Models

Deploying PyTorch models in production often requires creating an isolated, reproducible environment that encapsulates all dependencies, configurations, and code. Docker provides a way to package applications and their environments into containers, ensuring that the model runs consistently across different systems—whether on local machines, cloud servers, or edge devices. In this section, we will:

- Introduce Docker concepts relevant to model deployment.
- Demonstrate how to write a Dockerfile for a PyTorch-based API or inference script.
- Discuss best practices for containerizing PyTorch models.
- Provide examples and exercises to help you get started.

Key Concepts

1. **Docker Basics:**
   - **Image:** A lightweight, standalone, and executable package that includes everything needed to run a piece of software (code, runtime, libraries, environment variables, and configuration files).
   - **Container:** A runtime instance of an image. Containers run isolated from one another and the host system.
   - **Dockerfile:** A script containing instructions to build a Docker image.
2. **Benefits of Containerization:**
   - **Reproducibility:** Ensures that the model and its dependencies are packaged together.
   - **Portability:** Easily move and deploy containers across various environments.
   - **Scalability:** Integrate with orchestration tools (e.g., Kubernetes) to manage multiple container instances.
   - **Isolation:** Separate the application from the host system to avoid conflicts between dependencies.
3. **Integrating PyTorch Models:**

- o Ensure the PyTorch model is saved (e.g., using `torch.save` or TorchScript).
- o Package the inference code (e.g., a FastAPI or Flask application) along with the model.

Step-by-Step Guide to Dockerizing a PyTorch Model

1. Prepare Your PyTorch Application

Ensure your PyTorch model and inference script are working as expected. For example, you might have an inference script (`app.py`) that loads the model and serves predictions via FastAPI.

Example `app.py`:

```python
from fastapi import FastAPI, HTTPException
from pydantic import BaseModel
import torch
from transformers import GPT2LMHeadModel, GPT2Tokenizer

app = FastAPI(title="PyTorch Model Inference API")

# Load model and tokenizer (example using GPT-2)
model = GPT2LMHeadModel.from_pretrained("gpt2")
tokenizer = GPT2LMHeadModel.from_pretrained("gpt2")
# This line would typically load the tokenizer
model.eval()
device = torch.device("cuda" if torch.cuda.is_available() else "cpu")
model.to(device)

class InferenceRequest(BaseModel):
    prompt: str
    max_length: int = 50
    temperature: float = 0.7

@app.post("/predict")
```

```python
async def predict(request: InferenceRequest):
    if not request.prompt:
        raise HTTPException(status_code=400,
detail="Prompt cannot be empty.")
    input_ids = tokenizer.encode(request.prompt,
return_tensors="pt").to(device)
    with torch.no_grad():
        outputs = model.generate(input_ids,
max_length=request.max_length, do_sample=True,
temperature=request.temperature)
    generated_text = tokenizer.decode(outputs[0],
skip_special_tokens=True)
    return {"generated_text": generated_text}

if __name__ == "__main__":
    import uvicorn
    uvicorn.run(app, host="0.0.0.0", port=8000)
```

Note: Replace the model and tokenizer with your specific PyTorch model if needed.

---

2. Write a Dockerfile

Create a file named `Dockerfile` in your project directory. The Dockerfile defines how to build the Docker image.

Example Dockerfile:

```dockerfile
dockerfile

# Use an official Python runtime as a base image
FROM python:3.9-slim

# Set the working directory in the container
WORKDIR /app

# Copy requirements file and install dependencies
COPY requirements.txt .
RUN pip install --no-cache-dir -r requirements.txt
```

```
# Copy the rest of the application code
COPY . .

# Expose port 8000 for the FastAPI application
EXPOSE 8000

# Command to run the application with Uvicorn
CMD ["uvicorn", "app:app", "--host", "0.0.0.0", "--port", "8000"]
```

Example requirements.txt:

```plaintext

fastapi
uvicorn
torch
transformers
pydantic
```

3. Build and Run the Docker Container

Open your terminal and navigate to your project directory, then run:

```bash

# Build the Docker image
docker build -t pytorch-inference-api .

# Run the Docker container
docker run -p 8000:8000 pytorch-inference-api
```

This command builds an image named `pytorch-inference-api` and maps port 8000 of the container to port 8000 on your host machine.

Best Practices and Troubleshooting

- **Optimize Dependencies:**
  Use a slim base image and only install necessary dependencies to reduce image size and improve build times.
- **Cache Management:**
  Leverage Docker caching by ordering instructions in the Dockerfile so that frequently changing files (e.g., application code) are copied later, minimizing rebuild time.
- **GPU Support:**
  If deploying on GPU-enabled servers, use the appropriate base images (e.g., `nvidia/cuda`) and configure Docker to use GPU resources with NVIDIA Container Toolkit.
- **Logging and Monitoring:**
  Integrate logging (e.g., Python logging module) and health checks in your containerized application for better monitoring in production.
- **Security:**
  Ensure that your container does not run as the root user and follow security best practices when deploying in production.
- **Testing:**
  Thoroughly test the Docker container locally before deploying it to production environments. Use tools like Docker Compose for multi-container applications if needed.

Exercises

1. **Custom Requirements File:**
   Create a `requirements.txt` that only includes necessary dependencies and experiment with using a smaller base image to reduce the final Docker image size.
2. **Multi-Stage Builds:**
   Modify the Dockerfile to use multi-stage builds for even leaner production images.
3. **GPU-Enabled Container:**
   Adapt the Dockerfile to support GPU usage by using an NVIDIA base image and running a simple inference test on a GPU instance.
4. **Performance Benchmarking:**
   Deploy the container locally and benchmark the inference latency using tools like Apache JMeter or Locust. Compare the performance of the containerized model with the native environment.
5. **Container Orchestration:**
   Write a simple Docker Compose file to run your FastAPI application

along with a monitoring service (e.g., Prometheus) and experiment with scaling the application.

Dockerizing and containerizing PyTorch models is a critical step for scalable and reproducible deployment. By encapsulating your model, dependencies, and inference code into a Docker container, you ensure that your application runs consistently across different environments. This section provided a detailed guide to writing a Dockerfile, building and running a container, and best practices for optimizing the deployment process. With these skills, you can confidently package and deploy your PyTorch models in production.

8.5 Deploying PyTorch Models in Cloud

Deploying machine learning models in the cloud enables you to leverage scalable infrastructure, manage resources efficiently, and provide robust APIs for real-time inference. In this section, we explore three leading cloud platforms for deploying PyTorch models:

- **AWS SageMaker:**
  A fully managed service that simplifies building, training, and deploying machine learning models at scale. SageMaker offers model hosting, automatic scaling, and built-in monitoring.
- **GCP Vertex AI:**
  Google Cloud's unified machine learning platform that supports training and deploying models with ease. Vertex AI integrates well with other Google Cloud services and offers advanced model monitoring and management features.
- **Azure ML:**
  Microsoft's cloud platform for managing the end-to-end machine learning lifecycle. Azure ML provides tools for model training, deployment, and scalable inference, along with integration into the broader Azure ecosystem.

1. AWS SageMaker

Overview

AWS SageMaker provides a comprehensive environment to train and deploy models without managing infrastructure. Key features include:

- **Managed Endpoints:**
  Easily deploy models as REST APIs with auto-scaling.
- **Model Hosting:**
  Supports batch and real-time inference.
- **Built-in Algorithms and Framework Support:**
  Direct support for PyTorch with pre-configured containers.

Deployment Workflow

1. **Prepare Your Model:**
   Save your PyTorch model (or convert it to TorchScript) and package any necessary dependencies.
2. **Create a Model Artifact:**
   Upload your model artifact to Amazon S3.
3. **Deploy via SageMaker:**
   Use the SageMaker Python SDK or AWS Console to create a model, then deploy it as a real-time endpoint.

Code Example (using SageMaker Python SDK):

```python
import sagemaker
from sagemaker.pytorch import PyTorchModel

# Initialize SageMaker session and role (ensure
your role has appropriate permissions)
sagemaker_session = sagemaker.Session()
role =
"arn:aws:iam::YOUR_ACCOUNT_ID:role/YOUR_SAGEMAKER_ROLE"

# Create a PyTorchModel object; assume model.tar.gz
contains your serialized model and inference code
pytorch_model = PyTorchModel(model_data="s3://your-bucket/model.tar.gz",
                             role=role,

entry_point="inference.py",
```

```
framework_version="1.9.0",
                            py_version="py38")

# Deploy the model to a real-time endpoint
predictor =
pytorch_model.deploy(initial_instance_count=1,
instance_type="ml.m5.large")

# Make a prediction
result = predictor.predict({"data": [1.0, 2.0,
3.0]})
print("Prediction:", result)

# To clean up resources:
predictor.delete_endpoint()
```

2. GCP Vertex AI

Overview

Vertex AI streamlines the ML workflow on Google Cloud. It supports custom training and model deployment and integrates with services like BigQuery and Dataflow.

Deployment Workflow

1. **Prepare and Containerize Your Model:**
   Create a Docker container with your PyTorch model and inference code, or use a pre-built container.
2. **Upload to Google Cloud Storage (GCS):**
   Store your model artifact in GCS.
3. **Deploy via Vertex AI:**
   Use the Vertex AI console or Python SDK to create a model resource and deploy it to an endpoint.

Code Example (using Vertex AI Python SDK):

```python
from google.cloud import aiplatform
```

```
# Initialize Vertex AI
aiplatform.init(project="YOUR_PROJECT_ID",
location="us-central1")

# Upload your model to Vertex AI
model = aiplatform.Model.upload(
    display_name="pytorch_model",
    artifact_uri="gs://your-
bucket/model_directory",
    serving_container_image_uri="gcr.io/cloud-
aiplatform/pytorch:1.9",
)

# Deploy the model to an endpoint
endpoint = model.deploy(
    machine_type="n1-standard-4",
    min_replica_count=1,
    max_replica_count=3,
)

# To make a prediction, use the endpoint's predict
method
response = endpoint.predict(instances=[[1.0, 2.0,
3.0]])
print("Prediction:", response)

# Clean up by undeploying the model
endpoint.undeploy_all()
```

3. Azure ML

Overview

Azure ML provides an end-to-end platform for building, training, and deploying machine learning models. It supports model versioning, real-time inferencing, and integration with Azure Kubernetes Service (AKS) for scalable deployments.

Deployment Workflow

1. **Prepare Your Model:**
   Save your PyTorch model and any associated inference scripts.
2. **Register the Model:**
   Use the Azure ML SDK to register your model in your workspace.
3. **Create an Inference Configuration:**
   Specify the environment (dependencies, Dockerfile) and the scoring script.
4. **Deploy as a Web Service:**
   Deploy the model to an AKS cluster or Azure Container Instances (ACI) for real-time inference.

Code Example (using Azure ML SDK):

```python
from azureml.core import Workspace, Model,
Environment, InferenceConfig
from azureml.core.webservice import AciWebservice,
Webservice

# Connect to your Azure ML workspace
ws = Workspace.from_config()

# Register your PyTorch model (if not already
registered)
model = Model.register(workspace=ws,
model_path="model.pth", model_name="pytorch_model")

# Create an environment with required dependencies
env =
Environment.from_conda_specification(name="pytorch-
env", file_path="conda_dependencies.yml")

# Define inference configuration
inference_config =
InferenceConfig(entry_script="score.py",
environment=env)

# Define deployment configuration (using ACI for
simplicity)
```

```
deployment_config =
AciWebservice.deploy_configuration(cpu_cores=1,
memory_gb=1)

# Deploy the model as a web service
service = Model.deploy(workspace=ws,
                       name="pytorch-model-
service",
                       models=[model],

inference_config=inference_config,

deployment_config=deployment_config)
service.wait_for_deployment(show_output=True)
print("Service state:", service.state)

# Make a prediction
input_data = {"data": [1.0, 2.0, 3.0]}
prediction = service.run(input_data=input_data)
print("Prediction:", prediction)

# Clean up
service.delete()
```

Note:

- The `conda_dependencies.yml` file should list all required packages.
- The `score.py` script contains the model loading and inference logic.

Best Practices and Considerations

- **Resource Management:**
  Choose appropriate instance types and scaling configurations based on your model's requirements and expected traffic.
- **Model Monitoring:**
  Implement logging and monitoring (e.g., AWS CloudWatch, GCP Stackdriver, Azure Monitor) to track model performance and resource usage.

- **Security:**
  Secure your endpoints with authentication, encryption, and proper network configurations.
- **Cost Optimization:**
  Balance performance and cost by choosing appropriate scaling policies and leveraging spot instances or reserved capacity where possible.
- **Testing and Validation:**
  Test your deployed endpoints thoroughly with realistic workloads before production deployment.

Exercises

1. **Compare Cloud Platforms:**
   Deploy the same PyTorch model on AWS SageMaker, GCP Vertex AI, and Azure ML. Compare deployment times, inference latencies, and ease of integration.
2. **Load Testing:**
   Use cloud-native load testing tools to simulate high traffic on your deployed endpoints. Analyze performance and identify potential bottlenecks.
3. **Security Hardening:**
   Implement security best practices for your deployed model, including API authentication and network security, and test these measures.
4. **Cost Analysis:**
   Monitor the cost of running your deployments on different platforms over a period. Evaluate which platform offers the best balance between performance and cost.
5. **End-to-End Pipeline:**
   Develop a complete end-to-end pipeline that includes model training, packaging, deployment, and monitoring. Automate the pipeline using cloud-native orchestration tools.

Deploying PyTorch models in the cloud using services like AWS SageMaker, GCP Vertex AI, and Azure ML enables scalable, efficient, and secure inference solutions. Each cloud platform offers unique tools and features that cater to different deployment needs. By understanding the workflows and best practices for each service, you can select the best option for your application and ensure that your models are deployed robustly and cost-effectively. Experiment with the provided exercises to further refine your deployment strategy and optimize your model serving in production.

8.6 Project: Deploying a Real-time Object Detection Model on AWS

Real-time object detection is a critical capability for numerous applications including surveillance, autonomous driving, and industrial automation. Deploying such models in production requires a scalable and reliable infrastructure that can handle high-throughput inference with low latency. AWS SageMaker offers a fully managed service for deploying PyTorch models with automatic scaling and robust monitoring. In this project, you will:

- Prepare an object detection model (e.g., Faster R-CNN or YOLO) trained with PyTorch.
- Package and upload the model to AWS S3.
- Use AWS SageMaker to create and deploy a real-time inference endpoint.
- Test and monitor the endpoint using AWS tools and REST API calls.

2. Project Objectives

- **Model Packaging:** Serialize your PyTorch object detection model and package any custom inference code.
- **Artifact Management:** Upload the packaged model (model archive) to AWS S3.
- **Endpoint Deployment:** Deploy the model on AWS SageMaker, ensuring low-latency, high-availability real-time inference.
- **API Integration:** Test the deployed endpoint with sample images and integrate the endpoint into an application.
- **Monitoring:** Utilize AWS CloudWatch and SageMaker's built-in monitoring for performance and error tracking.

3. Model Preparation and Packaging

a. Serialize Your PyTorch Model

Ensure your model is in evaluation mode and saved appropriately. If you have a custom object detection model (e.g., based on Faster R-CNN), save the state dictionary or convert it to TorchScript.

```python
import torch
import torch.nn as nn

# Assume we have a pre-trained object detection
model (for example, Faster R-CNN)
# Here we use a placeholder for illustration;
replace with your actual model
class ObjectDetectionModel(nn.Module):
    def __init__(self):
        super(ObjectDetectionModel,
self).__init__()
        # Define layers of your model here
        self.fc = nn.Linear(1024, 91)  # Example:
91 classes (COCO dataset)

    def forward(self, x):
        # Forward pass of your model
        return self.fc(x)

# Instantiate and set the model to evaluation mode
model = ObjectDetectionModel()
model.eval()

# Save the model state dictionary
torch.save(model.state_dict(),
"object_detection_model.pth")
```

b. Create a Model Archive

Use the `torch-model-archiver` to package your model along with a custom handler if needed. The handler should contain the logic for loading the model and processing inference requests.

Example command (run in terminal):

```bash
torch-model-archiver --model-name
object_detection_model \
    --version 1.0 \
    --serialized-file object_detection_model.pth \
    --handler object_detection_handler.py \
    --extra-files "object_detection_model.py,
class_map.json" \
    --export-path model_store
```

Notes:

- **object_detection_handler.py**: A custom handler that implements methods like `preprocess`, `inference`, and `postprocess` for object detection.
- **class_map.json**: Maps class indices to human-readable names (if applicable).

---

4. Uploading the Model Artifact to AWS S3

Upload your model archive (`object_detection_model.mar`) to an S3 bucket using the AWS CLI or SDK.

```bash
aws s3 cp model_store/object_detection_model.mar
s3://your-s3-bucket/model_store/
```

---

5. Deploying the Model on AWS SageMaker

Use the SageMaker Python SDK to deploy your model. Below is an example using SageMaker's PyTorchModel class.

```python
import sagemaker
from sagemaker.pytorch import PyTorchModel

# Initialize SageMaker session and IAM role
(replace with your details)
sagemaker_session = sagemaker.Session()
role =
"arn:aws:iam::YOUR_ACCOUNT_ID:role/YOUR_SAGEMAKER_R
OLE"

# Create a PyTorchModel object
pytorch_model = PyTorchModel(model_data="s3://your-
s3-bucket/model_store/object_detection_model.mar",
                            role=role,

entry_point="object_detection_handler.py",

framework_version="1.9.0",
                                py_version="py38")

# Deploy the model as a real-time endpoint
predictor =
pytorch_model.deploy(initial_instance_count=1,
instance_type="ml.m5.xlarge")
```

Notes:

- **initial_instance_count**: Adjust based on expected traffic.
- **instance_type**: Choose based on model complexity and latency requirements.

6. Testing the Deployed Endpoint

Once the endpoint is live, test it by sending a POST request with an image. You can use AWS SageMaker's Predictor or tools like `curl`.

```python
python

# Example using the SageMaker Predictor API
import numpy as np
from PIL import Image
import io

# Load an image and preprocess it (ensure it meets
your handler's expectations)
with open("sample_image.jpg", "rb") as f:
    image_bytes = f.read()

# Send the image to the endpoint
result = predictor.predict(image_bytes)
print("Detection Result:", result)
```

Alternatively, using `curl`:

```bash
bash

curl -X POST \
  -H "Content-Type: application/octet-stream" \
  --data-binary "@sample_image.jpg" \
  https://<endpoint-
url>/predictions/object_detection_model
```

7. Monitoring and Scaling

- **CloudWatch:**
  Use AWS CloudWatch to monitor endpoint metrics like latency, throughput, and error rates.
- **Auto Scaling:**
  Configure auto-scaling policies within SageMaker to automatically adjust the number of instances based on demand.

Best Practices and Troubleshooting

- **Preprocessing Consistency:**
  Ensure that the preprocessing in your handler matches what was used during training.
- **Latency Optimization:**
  Use appropriate instance types and enable model batch processing if applicable.
- **Error Handling:**
  Implement robust error handling in your custom handler to return meaningful error messages.
- **Cost Management:**
  Monitor usage and set up auto-scaling to balance performance with cost efficiency.
- **Testing:**
  Thoroughly test the endpoint with diverse images to ensure robustness across various scenarios.

Exercises

1. **Custom Handler Development:**
   Develop a custom inference handler for your object detection model that includes image resizing, normalization, and postprocessing to format detection results (bounding boxes, class labels, confidence scores).
2. **Benchmarking:**
   Conduct load testing on your deployed endpoint using tools like Apache JMeter or Locust. Measure latency and throughput, and adjust the instance type or count as needed.
3. **Auto Scaling Setup:**
   Configure auto-scaling for your SageMaker endpoint and simulate varying loads to observe how the endpoint scales.
4. **Error Analysis:**
   Test the endpoint with invalid inputs (e.g., non-image data) to ensure that your error handling in the handler works as expected.
5. **Cost Analysis:**
   Monitor the cost implications of your deployment over a period and evaluate the impact of different instance types and scaling policies.

Deploying a real-time object detection model on AWS using SageMaker offers a robust and scalable solution for production-level inference. By following this project guide, you have learned how to package a PyTorch model, create a model archive, upload it to S3, deploy it as a SageMaker endpoint, and test it with real-world data. Implementing best practices for monitoring, scaling, and error handling ensures that your deployment remains efficient and reliable. Experiment with the exercises to further optimize your deployment and adapt it to your specific application needs.

8.7 Exercise: CI/CD for PyTorch Applications with GitHub Actions

In modern machine learning workflows, ensuring that your PyTorch code is robust, reproducible, and deployable is critical. CI/CD pipelines help automate these processes by continuously integrating code changes, running tests, building artifacts, and deploying them to production environments. In this exercise, you'll create a GitHub Actions workflow that performs the following tasks:

- **Run Unit Tests and Linting:** Automatically test your PyTorch code to catch bugs and enforce code quality standards.
- **Build and Push Docker Images:** Containerize your PyTorch application to ensure consistent deployment across environments.
- **Deploy the Application:** (Optional) Automate deployment steps to a staging or production environment.

Project Objectives

- **Automated Testing:**
  Run unit tests using a testing framework like `pytest` to ensure your code behaves as expected.
- **Linting and Code Quality:**
  Use linters (e.g., `flake8`) to maintain code quality and consistency.
- **Docker Image Building:**
  Build a Docker image of your PyTorch application and optionally push it to a container registry (e.g., Docker Hub).

- **Deployment Integration:**
  Set up deployment steps that could push the updated model or application to a cloud service or server.

Step-by-Step Guide

1. Prepare Your PyTorch Application Repository

Ensure your repository includes:

- Your PyTorch model code (e.g., `model.py`).
- An inference script or API (e.g., `app.py`).
- Unit tests (e.g., in a `tests/` directory using `pytest`).
- A `Dockerfile` for containerizing your application.
- A `requirements.txt` or `environment.yml` file listing dependencies.

2. Create a GitHub Actions Workflow File

Create a file in your repository under `.github/workflows/ci-cd.yml` with the following content:

```yaml
name: CI/CD Pipeline for PyTorch Application

on:
  push:
    branches:
      - main
  pull_request:
    branches:
      - main

jobs:
  build-and-test:
    runs-on: ubuntu-latest

    steps:
```

```yaml
    - name: Checkout Code
      uses: actions/checkout@v3

    - name: Set up Python 3.9
      uses: actions/setup-python@v4
      with:
        python-version: '3.9'

    - name: Install Dependencies
      run: |
        python -m pip install --upgrade pip
        pip install -r requirements.txt
        pip install flake8 pytest

    - name: Lint with flake8
      run: |
        flake8 .

    - name: Run Unit Tests with pytest
      run: |
        pytest

docker-build:
  runs-on: ubuntu-latest
  needs: build-and-test

  steps:
    - name: Checkout Code
      uses: actions/checkout@v3

    - name: Set up Docker Buildx
      uses: docker/setup-buildx-action@v2

    - name: Login to Docker Hub
      uses: docker/login-action@v2
      with:
        username: ${{ secrets.DOCKER_USERNAME }}
        password: ${{ secrets.DOCKER_PASSWORD }}

    - name: Build and Push Docker Image
      uses: docker/build-push-action@v4
      with:
```

```
          context: .
          file: Dockerfile
          push: true
          tags: your-dockerhub-username/your-
app:latest

  deploy:
    runs-on: ubuntu-latest
    needs: docker-build

    steps:
      - name: Checkout Code
        uses: actions/checkout@v3

      # Example deployment step (customize as
needed)
      - name: Deploy to Your Server or Cloud
Service
        run: |
          echo "Deploying the application..."
          # Insert your deployment commands here,
e.g., SSH commands, cloud CLI commands, etc.
```

3. Configure Secrets in GitHub

- **DOCKER_USERNAME and DOCKER_PASSWORD:**
  In your GitHub repository, go to **Settings > Secrets and variables >
  Actions** and add secrets for your Docker Hub credentials.
- **Additional Secrets:**
  If your deployment step requires credentials (e.g., SSH keys, cloud
  API keys), add them as repository secrets.

4. Customize the Deployment Step

The provided workflow includes a placeholder for the deployment job. You
can customize this step to deploy your Docker container to a cloud provider
(AWS, GCP, Azure) or your own server. For example, you might use AWS
CLI commands to update an ECS service or use Kubernetes commands to
update a deployment.

Best Practices and Troubleshooting

- **Test Locally:**
  Before pushing changes, run tests and linting locally to catch issues early.
- **Modular Workflow:**
  Separate jobs for testing, building, and deployment help isolate failures and speed up the CI/CD pipeline.
- **Caching Dependencies:**
  Consider caching pip dependencies to reduce build times. Use the `actions/cache` action for pip cache.
- **Monitoring and Notifications:**
  Set up notifications (e.g., via Slack or email) to alert you of failed builds or deployments.
- **Security:**
  Store sensitive information (e.g., API keys, passwords) as GitHub Secrets to protect them.
- **Error Handling:**
  Use GitHub Actions' logging and output to troubleshoot failures in any step of the pipeline.

Exercises

1. **Extend Testing Coverage:**
   Add more unit tests to cover different components of your PyTorch application, and update the workflow to run these tests.
2. **Implement Dependency Caching:**
   Modify the workflow to cache pip packages between builds. Compare build times before and after caching.
3. **Custom Deployment Script:**
   Write a custom deployment script (e.g., a Bash script) that updates a Kubernetes deployment or an AWS ECS service, and integrate it into the GitHub Actions workflow.
4. **Multi-Stage Docker Build:**
   Update your Dockerfile to use multi-stage builds for a smaller production image. Test that the new image works with your CI/CD pipeline.
5. **Integration with Monitoring:**
   Integrate a monitoring solution (e.g., Prometheus with Grafana) into

your deployment and configure your workflow to send notifications if the deployment fails or if key metrics exceed thresholds.

Setting up a CI/CD pipeline using GitHub Actions for your PyTorch applications streamlines the development-to-deployment process. By automating testing, building Docker images, and deploying your models, you ensure that your code is consistently reliable and production-ready. Experiment with the provided exercises to further enhance your pipeline, optimize performance, and maintain high-quality deployments. With a robust CI/CD process in place, you can confidently iterate on your models and rapidly deploy improvements to your applications.

Chapter 9: Performance Optimization and Scaling

9.1 Advanced GPU Utilization and Optimization

Modern deep learning models require significant computational power, and GPUs are indispensable for accelerating training and inference. However, to harness their full potential, it's essential to optimize how you use these resources. In this section, we cover advanced techniques for GPU utilization and optimization, including:

- Efficient data loading and memory management.
- Leveraging asynchronous GPU execution.
- Mixed precision training with automatic mixed precision (AMP).
- Multi-GPU and distributed training strategies.
- Profiling and debugging tools to identify and resolve performance bottlenecks.

Key Concepts and Techniques

1. Asynchronous GPU Execution and Memory Management

- **Asynchronous Execution:**
  GPU operations in PyTorch are asynchronous, meaning that when you enqueue an operation, control returns to the CPU immediately without waiting for GPU computations to complete. This requires explicit synchronization (using `torch.cuda.synchronize()`) when measuring performance.
- **Memory Management:**
  - **Pin Memory:** Use the DataLoader's `pin_memory=True` to speed up CPU-to-GPU data transfers.
  - **Efficient Data Loading:** Utilize multiple workers (`num_workers`) to overlap data loading with GPU computation.
  - **Memory Profiling:** Monitor memory usage with `torch.cuda.memory_allocated()` and `torch.cuda.max_memory_allocated()` to identify memory leaks or inefficiencies.

2. Mixed Precision Training

- **Concept:**
  Mixed precision training uses lower precision (FP16) for most computations while keeping critical operations in FP32. This reduces memory usage and can significantly speed up training on GPUs with Tensor Cores.
- **Implementation with AMP:**
  PyTorch's `torch.cuda.amp` module automates mixed precision training with the `autocast` context manager and `GradScaler` for maintaining numerical stability.

3. Multi-GPU and Distributed Training

- **Data Parallelism vs. Distributed Data Parallel (DDP):**
    - **Data Parallelism:** Uses `torch.nn.DataParallel` to split batches across multiple GPUs. It is simple but less efficient due to replication overhead.
    - **Distributed Data Parallel (DDP):** Preferred for scalability, DDP synchronizes gradients across GPUs more efficiently, both on a single node and across multiple nodes.
- **Distributed Training Frameworks:**
  Tools like Horovod or PyTorch's native DDP facilitate scaling training to multiple GPUs, minimizing communication overhead.

4. Profiling and Optimization Tools

- **PyTorch Profiler:**
  Use `torch.profiler` to trace operations and identify bottlenecks in your training or inference pipeline.
- **NVIDIA Nsight Systems:**
  A powerful tool to visualize GPU utilization and track kernel performance.
- **Monitoring GPU Utilization:**
  Tools such as `nvidia-smi` help monitor memory usage and GPU utilization in real time.

Code Examples

Example 1: Mixed Precision Training with AMP

```python
import torch
from torch import nn, optim
from torch.cuda.amp import autocast, GradScaler

# Define a simple model and move it to GPU
model = nn.Linear(1024, 10).cuda()
optimizer = optim.Adam(model.parameters(),
lr=0.001)
scaler = GradScaler()

# Dummy input data
inputs = torch.randn(64, 1024).cuda()
labels = torch.randint(0, 10, (64,)).cuda()
criterion = nn.CrossEntropyLoss()

# Training loop with AMP
for epoch in range(10):
    optimizer.zero_grad()
    with autocast():
        outputs = model(inputs)
        loss = criterion(outputs, labels)
    scaler.scale(loss).backward()
    scaler.step(optimizer)
    scaler.update()
    print(f"Epoch {epoch+1}, Loss:
{loss.item():.4f}")
```

Example 2: Distributed Data Parallel (DDP) Setup

```python
import os
import torch
import torch.distributed as dist
from torch.nn.parallel import
DistributedDataParallel as DDP
```

```python
from torch import nn, optim

def setup(rank, world_size):
    os.environ['MASTER_ADDR'] = 'localhost'
    os.environ['MASTER_PORT'] = '12355'
    dist.init_process_group("nccl", rank=rank,
world_size=world_size)

def cleanup():
    dist.destroy_process_group()

def train_ddp(rank, world_size):
    setup(rank, world_size)
    model = nn.Linear(1024, 10).cuda(rank)
    ddp_model = DDP(model, device_ids=[rank])
    optimizer = optim.Adam(ddp_model.parameters(),
lr=0.001)
    inputs = torch.randn(64, 1024).cuda(rank)
    labels = torch.randint(0, 10, (64,)).cuda(rank)
    criterion = nn.CrossEntropyLoss()
    for _ in range(10):
        optimizer.zero_grad()
        outputs = ddp_model(inputs)
        loss = criterion(outputs, labels)
        loss.backward()
        optimizer.step()
        print(f"Rank {rank}, Loss:
{loss.item():.4f}")
    cleanup()

# To run DDP, launch multiple processes with
appropriate rank and world_size.
# For example, using torch.multiprocessing.spawn:
if __name__ == "__main__":
    import torch.multiprocessing as mp
    world_size = 2  # Number of GPUs
    mp.spawn(train_ddp, args=(world_size,),
nprocs=world_size, join=True)
```

Best Practices and Tips

- **Asynchronous Execution:**
  Synchronize GPU operations when benchmarking by calling
  `torch.cuda.synchronize()` before and after timed sections.
- **Efficient Data Loading:**
  Increase `num_workers` in your DataLoader and use
  `pin_memory=True` to optimize data transfer from CPU to GPU.
- **Monitoring Tools:**
  Regularly use `nvidia-smi` and PyTorch profiling to track GPU
  usage and memory consumption.
- **Gradient Accumulation:**
  If you face GPU memory constraints, accumulate gradients over
  multiple mini-batches before updating model weights.
- **Distributed Training:**
  Prefer DDP over DataParallel for multi-GPU setups due to its
  scalability and efficiency in gradient synchronization.
- **Mixed Precision Tuning:**
  Monitor the effect of mixed precision on model accuracy; sometimes
  slight adjustments in the loss scaling factor are necessary.

Exercises

1. **Experiment with AMP:**
   Train a deep neural network using both full precision and mixed
   precision (AMP). Compare training times, GPU memory usage, and
   model performance.
2. **Profiling Analysis:**
   Use `torch.profiler` to profile a training loop and identify
   bottlenecks. Experiment with optimizations (e.g., increasing
   DataLoader workers) to improve performance.
3. **Distributed Training Comparison:**
   Implement a simple model training using both DataParallel and DDP.
   Measure the training speedup and discuss the benefits of DDP.
4. **Memory Optimization:**
   Monitor and log GPU memory usage during training with various
   batch sizes and gradient accumulation steps. Determine the optimal
   configuration for maximum GPU utilization without running out of
   memory.

5. **Asynchronous Performance:**
   Write a script that measures inference latency with and without
   explicit synchronization using `torch.cuda.synchronize()`.
   Analyze how asynchronous operations affect timing measurements.

Advanced GPU utilization and optimization are critical for training large-scale deep learning models efficiently. By employing mixed precision training, distributed data parallelism, and efficient data loading strategies, you can significantly reduce training time and memory consumption. Profiling tools and best practices help in identifying and eliminating bottlenecks, ensuring that your GPU resources are fully leveraged. Experimenting with these techniques will empower you to scale your PyTorch applications to handle increasingly complex tasks and larger datasets.

9.2 Distributed Training Techniques

As deep learning models grow in size and complexity, training them on a single GPU often becomes impractical due to memory limitations and long training times. Distributed training techniques enable you to scale training across multiple GPUs or even multiple nodes, thus reducing training time and allowing you to work with larger models and datasets. In this section, we cover three key distributed training strategies:

- **Data Parallelism:** Splitting the input data across multiple GPUs, each running a full replica of the model.
- **Model Parallelism:** Dividing the model itself across multiple GPUs, which is useful when a single model cannot fit into one GPU's memory.
- **Pipeline Parallelism:** Splitting the model into sequential stages and assigning each stage to different GPUs, which allows for concurrent processing of different mini-batches in a pipeline fashion.

1. Data Parallelism

Overview

Data parallelism is one of the most common distributed training methods. In this approach, the entire model is replicated on each GPU, and each replica processes a different subset (batch) of the data. After computing the gradients, the model parameters are synchronized (usually via an all-reduce operation).

Advantages

- **Simplicity:** Easy to implement using PyTorch's built-in `DataParallel` or, preferably, `DistributedDataParallel` (DDP).
- **Scalability:** Well-suited for scenarios where the model fits in the memory of one GPU but the dataset is large.

Code Example using DDP

```python
import os
import torch
import torch.distributed as dist
from torch.nn.parallel import
DistributedDataParallel as DDP
from torch import nn, optim
from torch.utils.data import DataLoader,
DistributedSampler, TensorDataset

def setup(rank, world_size):
    os.environ['MASTER_ADDR'] = 'localhost'
    os.environ['MASTER_PORT'] = '12355'
    dist.init_process_group("nccl", rank=rank,
world_size=world_size)

def cleanup():
    dist.destroy_process_group()

# Define a simple model
class SimpleModel(nn.Module):
```

```python
    def __init__(self, input_dim, output_dim):
        super(SimpleModel, self).__init__()
        self.fc = nn.Linear(input_dim, output_dim)

    def forward(self, x):
        return self.fc(x)

def train_ddp(rank, world_size):
    setup(rank, world_size)

    # Create model and move it to the appropriate device
    model = SimpleModel(input_dim=100, output_dim=10).to(rank)
    ddp_model = DDP(model, device_ids=[rank])

    # Dummy dataset
    data = torch.randn(1000, 100)
    targets = torch.randint(0, 10, (1000,))
    dataset = TensorDataset(data, targets)
    sampler = DistributedSampler(dataset, num_replicas=world_size, rank=rank)
    dataloader = DataLoader(dataset, batch_size=32, sampler=sampler)

    optimizer = optim.Adam(ddp_model.parameters(), lr=0.001)
    criterion = nn.CrossEntropyLoss()

    for epoch in range(5):
        sampler.set_epoch(epoch)
        epoch_loss = 0.0
        for batch_data, batch_targets in dataloader:
            batch_data = batch_data.to(rank)
            batch_targets = batch_targets.to(rank)
            optimizer.zero_grad()
            outputs = ddp_model(batch_data)
            loss = criterion(outputs, batch_targets)
            loss.backward()
            optimizer.step()
```

```
            epoch_loss += loss.item()
        print(f"Rank {rank}, Epoch {epoch+1}, Loss:
{epoch_loss/len(dataloader):.4f}")

    cleanup()

if __name__ == "__main__":
    import torch.multiprocessing as mp
    world_size = 2   # Number of GPUs
    mp.spawn(train_ddp, args=(world_size,),
nprocs=world_size, join=True)
```

---

2. Model Parallelism

Overview

Model parallelism is used when a single model is too large to fit into the memory of one GPU. In this approach, different parts of the model are assigned to different GPUs. During the forward and backward passes, intermediate activations are transferred between devices as needed.

Advantages

- **Memory Efficiency:**
  Enables training of very large models by splitting them across multiple GPUs.
- **Flexibility:**
  Allows for fine-grained distribution of model components based on computational and memory requirements.

Implementation Considerations

Model parallelism often requires manual partitioning of the model. For example, you might place the initial layers on one GPU and the deeper layers on another. This method requires careful management of data transfers between GPUs.

Example Outline

```
python
```

```python
import torch
import torch.nn as nn

class ModelParallelNet(nn.Module):
    def __init__(self):
        super(ModelParallelNet, self).__init__()
        # Define parts of the model on different
devices
        self.part1 = nn.Linear(100,
50).to("cuda:0")
        self.part2 = nn.Linear(50, 10).to("cuda:1")

    def forward(self, x):
        x = x.to("cuda:0")
        x = torch.relu(self.part1(x))
        x = x.to("cuda:1")
        x = self.part2(x)
        return x

model = ModelParallelNet()
input_data = torch.randn(32, 100)
output = model(input_data)
print("Model Parallel Output Shape:", output.shape)
```

3. Pipeline Parallelism

Overview

Pipeline parallelism divides the model into sequential stages and assigns each stage to a different GPU. Instead of processing one batch at a time, pipeline parallelism allows different GPUs to work concurrently on different mini-batches, akin to an assembly line.

Advantages

- **Increased Throughput:**
  Enables concurrent processing, reducing idle times across GPUs.
- **Efficient Utilization:**
  Can help balance computational load when layers have varying complexities.

Implementation Considerations

Implementing pipeline parallelism requires partitioning the model into discrete stages and managing the flow of data between these stages. PyTorch offers experimental support for pipeline parallelism, and libraries like DeepSpeed provide additional tools.

Example Outline

```python
import torch
import torch.nn as nn
import torch.distributed.pipeline.sync as pipeline

# Define a simple model and split it into stages
class Stage1(nn.Module):
    def __init__(self):
        super(Stage1, self).__init__()
        self.fc1 = nn.Linear(100, 50)

    def forward(self, x):
        return torch.relu(self.fc1(x))

class Stage2(nn.Module):
    def __init__(self):
        super(Stage2, self).__init__()
        self.fc2 = nn.Linear(50, 10)

    def forward(self, x):
        return self.fc2(x)

# Create the sequential model split into stages
model = nn.Sequential(Stage1(), Stage2())
# Wrap the model with pipeline parallelism
(assuming 2 GPUs)
model = pipeline.Pipe(model, chunks=4,
devices=["cuda:0", "cuda:1"])
input_data = torch.randn(32, 100).to("cuda:0")
output = model(input_data)
print("Pipeline Parallel Output Shape:",
output.shape)
```

Best Practices and Troubleshooting

- **Balancing Workload:**
  In model and pipeline parallelism, ensure that the computational load is balanced across GPUs to minimize bottlenecks.
- **Minimizing Data Transfer:**
  Efficiently manage data transfers between devices, as frequent transfers can degrade performance.
- **Synchronization:**
  Use appropriate synchronization methods to ensure correct gradient updates when using distributed techniques.
- **Monitoring:**
  Profile GPU utilization with tools like `nvidia-smi` and PyTorch Profiler to identify and address performance bottlenecks.
- **Error Handling:**
  Distributed training can introduce complex debugging challenges; ensure robust logging and exception handling to track issues.

Exercises

1. **Data Parallel vs. DDP:**
   Implement the same training loop using both `DataParallel` and `DistributedDataParallel` (DDP). Compare training times and scalability.
2. **Model Parallel Partitioning:**
   Manually partition a large model (e.g., a Transformer) across two GPUs. Experiment with different partition points and analyze the impact on memory usage and training speed.
3. **Pipeline Parallelism Optimization:**
   Implement pipeline parallelism on a multi-stage model and measure the throughput improvement by varying the number of micro-batches (chunks). Evaluate the trade-off between throughput and latency.
4. **Hybrid Distributed Training:**
   Combine data parallelism with model parallelism (hybrid parallelism) for a very large model. Evaluate how this approach scales on multiple nodes with multiple GPUs.
5. **Profiling and Debugging:**
   Use PyTorch's profiling tools to analyze a distributed training run.

Identify and optimize parts of the pipeline that cause communication overhead or imbalance.

Distributed training techniques are essential for scaling deep learning workloads across multiple GPUs and nodes. Data parallelism offers a straightforward method for scaling with minimal changes to the model, while model parallelism and pipeline parallelism provide solutions for training extremely large models and optimizing throughput. By understanding these techniques and experimenting with the provided exercises, you can optimize the training of your PyTorch models, significantly reducing training time and enabling the handling of more complex and larger-scale tasks.

9.3 Accelerating PyTorch with JIT Compilation and ONNX Runtime

As deep learning models become more complex, optimizing inference performance is critical for deployment. Two powerful tools for accelerating PyTorch models are:

- **TorchScript (JIT Compilation):**
  Converts dynamic PyTorch models into a statically-typed, optimized intermediate representation. This enables ahead-of-time (AOT) compilation, better runtime performance, and deployment in environments where Python may not be available.
- **ONNX Runtime:**
  Provides a high-performance inference engine that runs ONNX (Open Neural Network Exchange) models across different platforms. Converting PyTorch models to ONNX allows you to leverage hardware optimizations and deploy models in diverse production environments.

This section covers the conversion process using TorchScript, exporting to ONNX, and running the optimized models with ONNX Runtime.

1. TorchScript and JIT Compilation

What is TorchScript?

TorchScript is an intermediate representation of a PyTorch model that can be run independently from Python. It allows you to:

- Optimize model execution by performing compile-time optimizations.
- Serialize models to files (.pt) for deployment.
- Run models in C++ environments using LibTorch.

Converting a Model using TorchScript

There are two main methods:

- **Tracing:** Captures the operations performed on a sample input. Best for models with static control flow.
- **Scripting:** Converts the model by analyzing its source code, supporting dynamic control flows (e.g., loops, conditionals).

Example – Tracing a Model:

python

```python
import torch
import torch.nn as nn

# Define a simple model for demonstration
class SimpleModel(nn.Module):
    def __init__(self, input_dim, output_dim):
        super(SimpleModel, self).__init__()
        self.fc = nn.Linear(input_dim, output_dim)

    def forward(self, x):
        return torch.relu(self.fc(x))

model = SimpleModel(input_dim=10, output_dim=5)
model.eval()   # Set to evaluation mode

# Create a sample input tensor
sample_input = torch.randn(1, 10)

# Trace the model
traced_model = torch.jit.trace(model, sample_input)
traced_model.save("simple_model_traced.pt")
```

```
print("Traced model saved as
'simple_model_traced.pt'.")
```

Example – Scripting a Model:

```python
python

import torch
import torch.nn as nn

class DynamicModel(nn.Module):
    def __init__(self):
        super(DynamicModel, self).__init__()
        self.fc = nn.Linear(10, 10)

    def forward(self, x):
        # Demonstrate dynamic behavior with a loop
based on input sum
        for _ in range(int(x.sum().item()) % 3 +
1):
            x = torch.relu(self.fc(x))
        return x

model = DynamicModel()
model.eval()

# Script the model to support dynamic control flow
scripted_model = torch.jit.script(model)
scripted_model.save("dynamic_model_scripted.pt")
print("Scripted model saved as
'dynamic_model_scripted.pt'.")
```

2. Exporting PyTorch Models to ONNX

ONNX (Open Neural Network Exchange) is a format that allows models to be transferred between different deep learning frameworks. Exporting a PyTorch model to ONNX lets you use ONNX Runtime for inference, which can provide additional performance benefits and cross-platform compatibility.

Exporting a Model to ONNX

Example:

```python
import torch
import torch.nn as nn

# Define a simple model
class SimpleModel(nn.Module):
    def __init__(self, input_dim, output_dim):
        super(SimpleModel, self).__init__()
        self.fc = nn.Linear(input_dim, output_dim)

    def forward(self, x):
        return torch.relu(self.fc(x))

model = SimpleModel(input_dim=10, output_dim=5)
model.eval()

# Sample input for export
sample_input = torch.randn(1, 10)

# Export the model to ONNX
torch.onnx.export(model, sample_input,
"simple_model.onnx",
                  export_params=True,
                  opset_version=12,
                  do_constant_folding=True,
                  input_names=["input"],
                  output_names=["output"])
print("Model exported to 'simple_model.onnx'.")
```

3. Accelerating Inference with ONNX Runtime

ONNX Runtime is a high-performance engine designed for executing ONNX models. It supports hardware acceleration and optimizations that can significantly speed up inference.

Using ONNX Runtime for Inference

Example:

python

```python
import onnxruntime as ort
import numpy as np

# Load the ONNX model
ort_session =
ort.InferenceSession("simple_model.onnx")

# Prepare input (convert PyTorch tensor to numpy
array)
input_data = np.random.randn(1,
10).astype(np.float32)
ort_inputs = {ort_session.get_inputs()[0].name:
input_data}

# Run inference
ort_outs = ort_session.run(None, ort_inputs)
print("ONNX Runtime output:", ort_outs[0])
```

Best Practices and Troubleshooting

- **Choose the Right Conversion Method:**
  Use tracing for models with static control flow and scripting for
  models with dynamic behavior. Test both if unsure.
- **Validate Model Equivalence:**
  After converting to TorchScript or ONNX, verify that the outputs
  match those of the original PyTorch model using the same sample
  input.
- **Optimize ONNX Model:**
  Use ONNX Runtime's optimization tools (e.g., ONNX Graph
  Optimizer) to further improve performance.
- **Hardware Considerations:**
  ONNX Runtime supports different execution providers (e.g., CPU,
  CUDA, TensorRT). Experiment with these providers to maximize
  inference speed.

- **Version Compatibility:**
  Ensure compatibility between PyTorch, ONNX, and ONNX Runtime versions to avoid conversion errors or runtime issues.

Exercises

1. **Model Equivalence Testing:**
   Convert a complex model using both TorchScript tracing and scripting. Compare their outputs with the original model for a variety of inputs.
2. **ONNX Conversion Challenge:**
   Export a model with dynamic control flow to ONNX and troubleshoot any issues that arise during the export process.
3. **Inference Benchmarking:**
   Benchmark inference times for a model using pure PyTorch, TorchScript, and ONNX Runtime. Compare the results across different hardware configurations.
4. **Optimize with Execution Providers:**
   Use ONNX Runtime to run inference on a GPU with the CUDA execution provider. Compare performance with CPU inference.
5. **Advanced ONNX Optimization:**
   Experiment with ONNX Runtime's optimization flags and tools (e.g., enabling FP16 precision) and measure the impact on inference latency and accuracy.

Accelerating PyTorch models with TorchScript and ONNX Runtime can lead to significant improvements in inference speed and deployment flexibility. TorchScript allows you to convert your dynamic models into optimized static graphs, while ONNX Runtime enables cross-platform, high-performance inference. By following best practices and experimenting with the provided exercises, you can optimize your model's performance, reduce latency, and prepare it for efficient production deployment.

9.4 Profiling, Benchmarking, and Performance Debugging

Optimizing the performance of deep learning models requires a thorough understanding of where bottlenecks occur during training and inference.

Profiling and benchmarking provide insights into resource utilization, execution time, and memory usage. With these insights, you can target improvements in your code and hardware utilization. In this section, we will discuss:

- **Profiling Tools:** Tools like PyTorch Profiler and NVIDIA Nsight Systems help capture detailed performance metrics.
- **Benchmarking Strategies:** Techniques for measuring inference and training speed under various conditions.
- **Performance Debugging:** Best practices for identifying and fixing inefficiencies in your code.

---

1. Profiling Tools and Techniques

PyTorch Profiler

PyTorch provides a built-in profiler (`torch.profiler`) that allows you to record the operations executed during a training or inference run. The profiler helps identify which operations are taking the most time, how GPU and CPU resources are being utilized, and where memory bottlenecks may exist.

Example: Using PyTorch Profiler

```python
import torch
import torch.nn as nn
import torch.optim as optim
from torch.profiler import profile,
record_function, ProfilerActivity

# Define a simple model
class SimpleModel(nn.Module):
    def __init__(self):
        super(SimpleModel, self).__init__()
        self.fc1 = nn.Linear(1024, 512)
        self.fc2 = nn.Linear(512, 10)

    def forward(self, x):
```

```
        x = torch.relu(self.fc1(x))
        x = self.fc2(x)
        return x

model = SimpleModel().cuda()
optimizer = optim.Adam(model.parameters(), lr=1e-3)
criterion = nn.CrossEntropyLoss()

# Dummy input and target
inputs = torch.randn(64, 1024).cuda()
targets = torch.randint(0, 10, (64,)).cuda()

# Profiling the training step
with profile(activities=[ProfilerActivity.CPU,
ProfilerActivity.CUDA], record_shapes=True) as
prof:
    with record_function("model_inference"):
        optimizer.zero_grad()
        outputs = model(inputs)
        loss = criterion(outputs, targets)
        loss.backward()
        optimizer.step()

print(prof.key_averages().table(sort_by="cuda_time_
total", row_limit=10))
```

Key Points:

- **ProfilerActivity:** Specify whether to profile CPU, CUDA, or both.
- **Record Function:** Mark sections of your code to group operations logically.
- **Key Averages Table:** Provides a summary of operations sorted by CUDA time, CPU time, or memory usage.

NVIDIA Tools

For GPU-specific profiling, NVIDIA offers tools such as:

- **nvidia-smi:** Command-line tool to monitor GPU utilization, memory usage, and temperature in real time.

- **Nsight Systems and Nsight Compute:** Advanced profiling tools that provide detailed analysis of GPU kernel performance and memory throughput.

Example: Using nvidia-smi

Run the following command in your terminal during model training to monitor GPU utilization:

```bash
nvidia-smi --query-gpu=timestamp,name,utilization.gpu,utilization.memory,memory.total,memory.free --format=csv -l 2
```

2. Benchmarking Strategies

Benchmarking involves measuring the performance of your model under specific conditions. Key metrics include:

- **Latency:** Time taken for a single inference pass.
- **Throughput:** Number of inferences per unit time (e.g., images per second).
- **Memory Usage:** Peak memory consumption during training or inference.

Benchmarking Inference

Example: Measuring Inference Latency

```python
import time

model.eval()
input_tensor = torch.randn(1, 1024).cuda()

# Warm-up run
for _ in range(10):
    _ = model(input_tensor)
```

```
# Measure latency
start_time = time.time()
with torch.no_grad():
    _ = model(input_tensor)
torch.cuda.synchronize()  # Ensure all operations
are finished
end_time = time.time()
latency = end_time - start_time
print(f"Inference Latency: {latency * 1000:.2f}
ms")
```

Benchmarking Training

Measure the time per epoch or per batch to understand training speed. Use `torch.cuda.synchronize()` to ensure accurate measurements.

Example: Benchmarking a Training Epoch

python

```
num_batches = len(dataloader)
start_epoch = time.time()
for inputs, targets in dataloader:
    inputs, targets = inputs.cuda(), targets.cuda()
    optimizer.zero_grad()
    outputs = model(inputs)
    loss = criterion(outputs, targets)
    loss.backward()
    optimizer.step()
    torch.cuda.synchronize()
end_epoch = time.time()
print(f"Epoch Time: {end_epoch - start_epoch:.2f}
seconds")
print(f"Average Time per Batch: {(end_epoch -
start_epoch) / num_batches * 1000:.2f} ms")
```

3. Performance Debugging

When performance is not as expected, consider the following steps:

- **Identify Bottlenecks:**
  Use profiling outputs to pinpoint operations that consume the most time or memory.
- **Optimize Data Loading:**
  Increase `num_workers` in your DataLoader and use `pin_memory=True` to improve data transfer speeds.
- **Reduce Synchronization Overhead:**
  Avoid unnecessary synchronization calls; use them only when measuring performance.
- **Model Optimization Techniques:**
  Explore mixed precision training, model pruning, or quantization to reduce memory usage and accelerate computation.
- **Check Hardware Utilization:**
  Use tools like `nvidia-smi` to ensure GPUs are fully utilized. Underutilization may indicate bottlenecks in data loading or CPU-bound preprocessing.

Best Practices

- **Regular Profiling:**
  Integrate profiling into your development workflow to catch performance regressions early.
- **Incremental Changes:**
  Optimize one component at a time (data loading, model architecture, training loop) and measure improvements incrementally.
- **Use Caching:**
  Cache preprocessed data where possible to reduce redundant computations.
- **Documentation:**
  Keep detailed logs of benchmarking results and configuration changes to understand their impact over time.

Exercises

1. **Comprehensive Profiling:**
   Profile a full training epoch of your model using

`torch.profiler`. Identify the top 5 operations by GPU and CPU time and suggest optimizations.

2. **Inference Benchmarking:**
   Benchmark your model's inference latency under different batch sizes. Analyze how batch size affects throughput and latency.

3. **DataLoader Optimization:**
   Experiment with different numbers of DataLoader workers and measure their effect on training speed. Determine the optimal configuration for your hardware.

4. **Mixed Precision Impact:**
   Train your model with and without mixed precision (using AMP) and compare GPU memory usage, training speed, and final model accuracy.

5. **End-to-End Pipeline Evaluation:**
   Use both PyTorch profiling and external tools like NVIDIA Nsight Systems to evaluate an end-to-end training pipeline. Document any identified bottlenecks and propose solutions.

Profiling, benchmarking, and performance debugging are critical steps in optimizing deep learning models for efficient training and inference. By leveraging tools like PyTorch Profiler, NVIDIA monitoring utilities, and systematic benchmarking strategies, you can identify and address performance bottlenecks in your models. Implementing best practices and performing regular performance evaluations ensures that your deep learning applications are both scalable and efficient. Experiment with the provided exercises to gain deeper insights and fine-tune your optimization techniques.

Would you like to review any part of this section further, or shall we proceed to the next section or chapter?

9.5 Project: Distributed Training of Large Models on GPU Clusters

As deep learning models increase in complexity and size, training them on a single GPU becomes impractical due to memory constraints and prolonged training times. Distributed training allows you to leverage multiple GPUs—potentially across several nodes—to accelerate training and handle larger models. This project focuses on implementing distributed training using PyTorch's DistributedDataParallel (DDP). You will learn to:

- Configure a multi-GPU training environment.
- Partition and load data efficiently using DistributedSampler.
- Synchronize gradient updates across GPUs.
- Monitor training performance and optimize resource utilization.

Project Objectives

- **Scalability:**
  Train large models efficiently by distributing the workload across multiple GPUs.
- **Efficiency:**
  Reduce training time through parallel processing and effective data partitioning.
- **Robustness:**
  Ensure model convergence and stability by properly synchronizing gradients and managing data.
- **Experimentation:**
  Evaluate the benefits of distributed training on model performance and training speed.

Key Components

1. Environment Setup

- **Hardware:**
  A GPU cluster with multiple GPUs per node. Use the NCCL backend for efficient GPU-to-GPU communication.
- **Software:**
  PyTorch (with distributed training support), and a cluster management system (e.g., SLURM, Kubernetes, or manual multi-GPU setup).

2. Distributed Data Loading

- **DistributedSampler:**
  Utilize `torch.utils.data.DistributedSampler` to partition your dataset across multiple processes, ensuring each process sees a unique subset of the data.
- **Batch Management:**
  Maintain consistent batch sizes per GPU to balance workload and synchronize gradients properly.

3. Model Parallelism via DistributedDataParallel (DDP)

- **DDP Overview:**
  Wrap your model in `DistributedDataParallel` (DDP) to automatically handle gradient synchronization across GPUs.
- **Initialization:**
  Use environment variables or launch scripts to set up the distributed training environment (master address, port, rank, world size).

4. Synchronization and Profiling

- **Synchronization:**
  Ensure correct timing measurements by using `torch.cuda.synchronize()` when benchmarking.
- **Profiling:**
  Monitor GPU utilization and communication overhead with tools like `nvidia-smi` and PyTorch Profiler.

Hands-On Code Example

Below is a simplified example that demonstrates distributed training using DDP on a multi-GPU setup. This example uses a simple model and synthetic data for illustration.

```python
import os
import torch
import torch.nn as nn
import torch.optim as optim
import torch.distributed as dist
```

```python
from torch.nn.parallel import
DistributedDataParallel as DDP
from torch.utils.data import DataLoader,
DistributedSampler, TensorDataset

def setup_distributed(rank, world_size):
    os.environ['MASTER_ADDR'] = 'localhost'
    os.environ['MASTER_PORT'] = '12355'
    dist.init_process_group(backend="nccl",
rank=rank, world_size=world_size)

def cleanup_distributed():
    dist.destroy_process_group()

# Define a simple model for demonstration
class SimpleModel(nn.Module):
    def __init__(self, input_dim=100,
output_dim=10):
        super(SimpleModel, self).__init__()
        self.fc1 = nn.Linear(input_dim, 256)
        self.fc2 = nn.Linear(256, output_dim)

    def forward(self, x):
        x = torch.relu(self.fc1(x))
        return self.fc2(x)

def train_ddp(rank, world_size):
    setup_distributed(rank, world_size)

    # Create synthetic dataset
    data = torch.randn(1000, 100)
    targets = torch.randint(0, 10, (1000,))
    dataset = TensorDataset(data, targets)
    sampler = DistributedSampler(dataset,
num_replicas=world_size, rank=rank)
    dataloader = DataLoader(dataset, batch_size=32,
sampler=sampler)

    # Initialize model and move to correct GPU
    model = SimpleModel().to(rank)
    ddp_model = DDP(model, device_ids=[rank])
```

```
    optimizer = optim.Adam(ddp_model.parameters(),
lr=0.001)
    criterion = nn.CrossEntropyLoss()

    # Training loop
    num_epochs = 5
    for epoch in range(num_epochs):
        sampler.set_epoch(epoch)
        total_loss = 0.0
        for batch_data, batch_targets in
dataloader:
            batch_data = batch_data.to(rank)
            batch_targets = batch_targets.to(rank)
            optimizer.zero_grad()
            outputs = ddp_model(batch_data)
            loss = criterion(outputs,
batch_targets)
            loss.backward()
            optimizer.step()
            total_loss += loss.item()
        avg_loss = total_loss / len(dataloader)
        print(f"Rank {rank}, Epoch {epoch+1}, Loss:
{avg_loss:.4f}")

    cleanup_distributed()

if __name__ == "__main__":
    import torch.multiprocessing as mp
    world_size = torch.cuda.device_count()  #
Number of GPUs available
    mp.spawn(train_ddp, args=(world_size,),
nprocs=world_size, join=True)
```

Best Practices and Tips

- **Proper Initialization:**
  Always initialize the distributed process group before creating data loaders and models. Use torch.multiprocessing.spawn or a similar mechanism to launch multiple processes.

- **DistributedSampler:**
  Use `DistributedSampler` to partition data across processes. Set the epoch for the sampler each epoch to ensure shuffling.
- **Gradient Synchronization:**
  Wrap your model with DDP to ensure efficient gradient averaging. Avoid using `DataParallel` in multi-node environments.
- **Monitoring Performance:**
  Use profiling tools (e.g., `nvidia-smi`, PyTorch Profiler) to monitor GPU utilization and detect communication bottlenecks.
- **Error Handling:**
  Distributed training can introduce complex debugging scenarios. Ensure robust logging and exception handling in each process.
- **Scalability Considerations:**
  Experiment with different batch sizes, learning rates, and communication backends (e.g., NCCL for GPUs) to optimize distributed training performance.

Exercises

1. **Data Parallel vs. DDP:**
   Implement a simple training loop using both `torch.nn.DataParallel` and DDP. Measure and compare the training time and scalability as you increase the number of GPUs.
2. **Scaling to Multiple Nodes:**
   If available, extend your DDP implementation to multiple nodes. Analyze the communication overhead and its impact on training speed.
3. **Profiling Distributed Training:**
   Use PyTorch's profiler to record a distributed training run. Identify the most time-consuming operations and propose optimizations.
4. **Memory Optimization:**
   Experiment with gradient accumulation to handle larger batch sizes without exceeding GPU memory limits. Evaluate the trade-off between gradient accumulation and training time.
5. **Hybrid Parallelism:**
   Explore combining data parallelism with model parallelism for a very large model. Design a small-scale experiment and document the performance improvements and challenges.

Distributed training is essential for scaling deep learning models, especially as they grow in complexity and size. By leveraging techniques like Data Parallelism with DistributedDataParallel (DDP), you can significantly reduce training times and enable the handling of large models on GPU clusters. This project provided an end-to-end guide—from environment setup and data loading to model training and performance profiling—equipping you with the tools and best practices needed to optimize distributed training workflows. Experimenting with the provided exercises will further enhance your ability to scale PyTorch models efficiently across multiple GPUs and nodes.

9.6 Optimizing Model Serving Performance and Latency

Efficient model serving is crucial for real-time applications where latency and throughput directly affect user experience. Whether you're deploying a model for object detection, sentiment analysis, or any other inference task, reducing response time and maximizing resource utilization are key goals. This section outlines techniques to optimize model serving performance, including:

- **Batch Processing and Asynchronous Execution:**
  Combine multiple requests into a batch and use asynchronous frameworks to minimize wait times.
- **Model Conversion and Optimization:**
  Convert models to optimized formats (e.g., TorchScript, ONNX) and use quantization to accelerate inference.
- **Hardware Utilization:**
  Optimize the use of GPUs or other accelerators and manage memory effectively.
- **Monitoring and Benchmarking:**
  Continuously monitor latency and throughput using profiling tools to identify bottlenecks and optimize the deployment pipeline.

Key Concepts and Techniques

1. Batch Processing

- **Rationale:**
  Aggregating several inference requests into a single batch can

dramatically reduce per-sample latency by leveraging parallelism on the GPU.

- **Implementation:**
  In serving environments, accumulate requests for a short time window before processing them together.

2. Asynchronous Processing

- **Rationale:**
  Asynchronous frameworks (like FastAPI) can handle multiple requests concurrently, reducing idle time and improving overall throughput.
- **Implementation:**
  Use asynchronous endpoints to process I/O-bound tasks and offload blocking model inference operations to a separate thread pool if necessary.

3. Model Optimization

- **Model Conversion:**
  Convert your model to TorchScript or ONNX to benefit from optimizations such as kernel fusion and reduced Python overhead.
- **Quantization:**
  Lower the precision of the model (e.g., using dynamic quantization) to reduce computation and memory usage, leading to faster inference.
- **Caching and Warm-Up:**
  Cache model outputs for frequent requests and perform warm-up runs to ensure that the model is fully loaded and optimized before handling live traffic.

4. Hardware Utilization

- **GPU Acceleration:**
  Ensure that your model serving environment is configured to use available GPUs effectively, and monitor utilization with tools like `nvidia-smi`.
- **Memory Management:**
  Optimize data transfer between CPU and GPU by using pinned memory and asynchronous data loading.

Hands-On Code Example

Below is an example of a FastAPI application that demonstrates batch processing and asynchronous inference using a TorchScript model. This example simulates serving a model that performs inference on batched input data, and it measures latency to help identify performance improvements.

python

```python
from fastapi import FastAPI, HTTPException
from pydantic import BaseModel
import torch
import uvicorn
import time
from typing import List

# Define the input schema
class InferenceRequest(BaseModel):
    inputs: List[List[float]]  # List of input
feature vectors (each of size 10)

# Load the TorchScript model (assume model has been
converted and saved)
model = torch.jit.load("simple_model_traced.pt",
map_location=torch.device("cuda" if
torch.cuda.is_available() else "cpu"))
model.eval()
device = torch.device("cuda" if
torch.cuda.is_available() else "cpu")
model.to(device)

app = FastAPI(title="Optimized Model Serving API")

@app.post("/predict")
async def predict(request: InferenceRequest):
    if not request.inputs:
        raise HTTPException(status_code=400,
detail="No input data provided.")

    # Convert input data to a tensor and move to
the appropriate device
    try:
```

```
        input_tensor = torch.tensor(request.inputs,
dtype=torch.float32).to(device)
    except Exception as e:
        raise HTTPException(status_code=400,
detail=f"Invalid input data: {e}")

    # Start timing the inference
    start_time = time.time()
    with torch.no_grad():
        output = model(input_tensor)
    # Ensure all GPU operations are complete
    if device.type == "cuda":
        torch.cuda.synchronize()
    latency = time.time() - start_time

    return {"predictions": output.cpu().tolist(),
"inference_latency_ms": latency * 1000}

if __name__ == "__main__":
    uvicorn.run(app, host="0.0.0.0", port=8000)
```

Explanation:

- **Batch Processing:**
  The endpoint accepts a list of input feature vectors and processes
  them in a batch, taking advantage of parallel computation on GPUs.
- **Asynchronous Endpoint:**
  FastAPI's async capabilities allow the server to handle multiple
  requests concurrently.
- **Latency Measurement:**
  The code measures inference time and returns it with the predictions,
  providing useful metrics for monitoring performance.

Best Practices and Troubleshooting

- **Warm-Up the Model:**
  Run several warm-up inferences during startup to load and optimize
  the model before serving real requests.

- **Monitor GPU Utilization:**
  Use `nvidia-smi` or similar tools to ensure that GPUs are fully utilized during inference.
- **Efficient Data Conversion:**
  Convert incoming JSON data to tensors efficiently, and consider using pre-allocated buffers or caching strategies for recurring requests.
- **Asynchronous Offloading:**
  If model inference is blocking, offload it to a separate thread or process to keep the API responsive.
- **Load Testing:**
  Simulate high concurrency using tools like Locust or Apache JMeter to identify bottlenecks and adjust batch sizes or server configurations accordingly.

Exercises

1. **Batch Size Experiment:**
   Modify the API to process different batch sizes and measure the effect on average inference latency and throughput.
2. **Asynchronous Model Inference:**
   Implement an asynchronous inference mechanism using a thread pool (e.g., `concurrent.futures.ThreadPoolExecutor`) and compare its performance with the synchronous approach.
3. **Quantization Comparison:**
   Convert the model to a quantized version (e.g., using dynamic quantization) and compare the inference speed and accuracy between full-precision and quantized models.
4. **Load Testing:**
   Simulate a high load scenario using Locust. Measure the API's response times and identify any performance bottlenecks.
5. **Profiling Integration:**
   Integrate a simple logging mechanism that records the inference latency of each request. Analyze the logs to detect any anomalies or slowdowns over time.

Optimizing model serving performance and latency is vital for delivering real-time, scalable deep learning applications. By implementing batch processing, leveraging asynchronous APIs, and applying model optimization techniques such as quantization, you can significantly reduce inference latency and improve throughput. Regular profiling, monitoring, and load testing are essential to maintain optimal performance as demand scales. Experiment with the provided exercises to further refine your serving pipeline and ensure that your deployed models meet production performance requirements.

Chapter 10: Ethical AI, Model Interpretability, and Fairness

10.1 Ethical Considerations in Deep Learning Deployment

As deep learning systems become more integrated into society, the ethical implications of their deployment have become a central concern. Beyond technical performance, models must be designed and deployed in a way that is fair, transparent, and accountable. This section discusses key ethical considerations, including bias and fairness, privacy, transparency, and accountability, and provides guidelines for responsible AI deployment.

Key Ethical Considerations

1. Fairness and Bias

- **Definition:**
  Fairness in AI means ensuring that models perform equitably across different demographic groups without perpetuating existing biases.
- **Sources of Bias:**
  - **Data Bias:** Historical or sampling biases in training data.
  - **Algorithmic Bias:** Biases arising from model design or training objectives.
  - **Feedback Loops:** Models that reinforce biased decisions over time.
- **Mitigation Strategies:**
  - **Diverse and Representative Data:** Ensure your training data reflects the diversity of the population.
  - **Bias Audits:** Regularly evaluate models for disparate performance across groups.
  - **Fairness Metrics:** Use metrics like demographic parity, equal opportunity, or disparate impact to quantify fairness.

2. Transparency and Explainability

- **Importance:**
  Transparent models enable stakeholders to understand how decisions

are made, which is critical for building trust, especially in sensitive applications such as healthcare or finance.

- **Techniques:**
    - **Model Interpretability Tools:** Use tools like Grad-CAM, LIME, or SHAP to provide insights into model behavior.
    - **Documentation:** Maintain thorough documentation of model development, training data, and decision-making processes.
    - **Open Communication:** Clearly communicate the limitations and uncertainties of your model to end users.

3. Privacy and Data Security

- **Data Protection:**
  Safeguard sensitive data through anonymization, encryption, and secure data storage practices.
- **User Consent:**
  Ensure that data collection complies with relevant privacy regulations (e.g., GDPR, CCPA) and that users provide informed consent.
- **Techniques:**
    - **Differential Privacy:** Incorporate methods that ensure individual data points cannot be re-identified.
    - **Federated Learning:** Train models across decentralized data sources without aggregating sensitive data centrally.

4. Accountability and Governance

- **Responsibility:**
  Establish clear lines of accountability for model decisions and their societal impact. This includes monitoring model performance and addressing any unintended consequences.
- **Regulatory Compliance:**
  Adhere to legal and ethical guidelines relevant to your industry. Engage with regulatory bodies and independent auditors to ensure compliance.
- **Governance Practices:**
    - **Ethical Review Boards:** Establish committees to review and guide AI deployment.
    - **Continuous Monitoring:** Implement systems to monitor model behavior in production and to update models as needed.
    - **User Feedback Mechanisms:** Enable channels for users to report issues or biases in model outputs.

Best Practices for Ethical AI Deployment

- **Proactive Bias Assessment:**
  Integrate fairness audits into the development pipeline, regularly testing for bias and implementing corrective measures.
- **Transparency Documentation:**
  Publish model cards or similar documentation detailing the model's purpose, data sources, intended use cases, limitations, and performance across different demographic groups.
- **Privacy by Design:**
  Embed privacy protection mechanisms into your model development process from the start, rather than as an afterthought.
- **Robust Governance:**
  Create multidisciplinary teams including ethicists, domain experts, and technical staff to oversee AI deployment and ensure accountability.
- **Continuous Improvement:**
  View ethical AI deployment as an ongoing process that requires continuous monitoring, evaluation, and improvement based on user feedback and new insights.

Exercises

1. **Bias Audit:**
   Choose a dataset and model, then conduct a bias audit using fairness metrics. Report any disparities and propose methods to mitigate them.
2. **Transparency Documentation:**
   Create a model card for a deep learning model. Include details on its training data, performance metrics, limitations, and ethical considerations.
3. **Privacy Impact Assessment:**
   Analyze the data collection and processing methods in your project. Identify potential privacy risks and suggest mitigation strategies (e.g., differential privacy techniques).
4. **User Feedback Simulation:**
   Design a process for collecting and integrating user feedback on

model outputs, focusing on detecting and mitigating bias and fairness issues.
5. **Ethical Governance Plan:**
   Draft an outline for an ethical review board or governance framework for your organization's AI projects, detailing roles, responsibilities, and evaluation procedures.

Ethical considerations are paramount in the deployment of deep learning models. By addressing fairness, transparency, privacy, and accountability, you can build AI systems that not only perform well but also contribute positively to society. Adopting ethical best practices, conducting regular audits, and maintaining open channels for user feedback are essential steps towards responsible AI deployment. As you continue to develop and deploy models, these ethical guidelines will help ensure that your work benefits all stakeholders fairly and transparently.

10.2 Fairness and Bias Mitigation Strategies

As AI models become increasingly integrated into decision-making systems, ensuring fairness and mitigating bias is crucial to prevent adverse societal impacts. Bias can manifest in various ways, stemming from data, model architecture, or deployment practices, and can lead to unequal treatment of different demographic groups. This section outlines strategies to detect bias, measure fairness, and apply techniques to reduce bias in deep learning models.

Key Concepts

1. Sources of Bias

- **Data Bias:**
  Arises from non-representative or imbalanced training data. For instance, if certain demographic groups are underrepresented, the model may perform poorly for these groups.
- **Algorithmic Bias:**
  Occurs when model design, loss functions, or training procedures inadvertently favor one group over another.

- **Societal Bias:**
  Biases embedded in historical data and societal norms can be perpetuated by AI systems.

2. Fairness Metrics

- **Demographic Parity:**
  The model's predictions should be independent of sensitive attributes (e.g., gender, race).
- **Equal Opportunity:**
  The true positive rate should be equal across different groups.
- **Equalized Odds:**
  Both the true positive rate and false positive rate should be similar across groups.
- **Disparate Impact:**
  The ratio of favorable outcomes should be approximately equal across groups.

Quantitative evaluation using these metrics is critical for understanding and mitigating bias.

Bias Mitigation Techniques

1. Data-Level Interventions

- **Data Collection:**
  Ensure that your training dataset is diverse and representative of the population the model will serve.
- **Data Augmentation:**
  Use augmentation techniques to balance datasets, especially for underrepresented classes.
- **Re-sampling and Re-weighting:**
  Adjust the training data by over-sampling minority classes or re-weighting instances during training.

2. Algorithm-Level Interventions

- **Adversarial Debiasing:**
  Train an adversarial network to predict sensitive attributes from the model's representations and use its loss to discourage biased features.

- **Regularization Techniques:**
  Add fairness regularizers to the loss function to penalize disparate performance across groups.
- **Fair Representation Learning:**
  Learn latent representations that are invariant to sensitive attributes by employing techniques like disentanglement or contrastive learning.

3. Post-Processing Techniques

- **Calibrated Thresholding:**
  Adjust decision thresholds for different groups to achieve balanced performance metrics.
- **Re-ranking:**
  Apply post-processing to model outputs (e.g., in recommendation systems) to ensure fairness in the final decision.

Practical Code Example: Re-weighting for Imbalanced Data

Below is an example of how to apply instance re-weighting during training to mitigate bias due to imbalanced data. In this case, we assume a simple classification task where the dataset has imbalanced classes.

```python
import torch
import torch.nn as nn
import torch.optim as optim
from torch.utils.data import DataLoader,
TensorDataset
import numpy as np

# Create synthetic imbalanced data
# 1000 samples with 90% of class 0 and 10% of class
1
num_samples = 1000
data = torch.randn(num_samples, 10)
labels = torch.cat((torch.zeros(int(num_samples *
0.9), dtype=torch.long),
```

```python
                    torch.ones(int(num_samples *
0.1), dtype=torch.long)))
dataset = TensorDataset(data, labels)
dataloader = DataLoader(dataset, batch_size=32,
shuffle=True)

# Simple classification model
class SimpleClassifier(nn.Module):
    def __init__(self, input_dim, output_dim):
        super(SimpleClassifier, self).__init__()
        self.fc = nn.Linear(input_dim, output_dim)

    def forward(self, x):
        return self.fc(x)

model = SimpleClassifier(10, 2)
criterion = nn.CrossEntropyLoss(reduction='none')
# We'll compute per-sample loss
optimizer = optim.Adam(model.parameters(),
lr=0.001)

# Compute class weights inversely proportional to
class frequency
class_counts = np.bincount(labels.numpy())
class_weights = 1.0 / class_counts
weights = torch.tensor([class_weights[label] for
label in labels], dtype=torch.float32)

# Training loop with re-weighting
num_epochs = 10
for epoch in range(num_epochs):
    total_loss = 0.0
    for batch_data, batch_labels in dataloader:
        optimizer.zero_grad()
        outputs = model(batch_data)
        loss = criterion(outputs, batch_labels)
        # Get weights for current batch
        batch_weights =
torch.tensor([class_weights[label.item()] for label
in batch_labels], dtype=torch.float32)
        weighted_loss = (loss *
batch_weights.to(loss.device)).mean()
```

```
        weighted_loss.backward()
        optimizer.step()
        total_loss += weighted_loss.item()
    print(f"Epoch {epoch+1}, Average Loss:
{total_loss/len(dataloader):.4f}")
```

Explanation:

- We compute class weights inversely proportional to class frequencies.
- The per-sample loss is weighted by the corresponding class weight, mitigating bias from imbalanced data.

Best Practices and Troubleshooting

- **Regular Auditing:**
  Perform periodic audits using fairness metrics to ensure that bias does not creep into your model as data or usage patterns change.
- **Holistic Approach:**
  Address bias at multiple stages: data collection, model training, and post-processing. Use a combination of techniques for robust mitigation.
- **Transparent Reporting:**
  Document and report fairness metrics and mitigation strategies in model cards or technical reports.
- **User Feedback:**
  Incorporate mechanisms to collect and address user feedback regarding model fairness and performance.
- **Continuous Monitoring:**
  Monitor model outputs continuously after deployment to catch any drifting biases and update models accordingly.

Exercises

1. **Bias Measurement:**
   Select a dataset and a classification model. Compute fairness metrics such as demographic parity and equalized odds. Analyze the model's performance across different groups.

2. **Adversarial Debiasing Implementation:**
   Implement a simple adversarial debiasing setup where an auxiliary network attempts to predict sensitive attributes from model representations. Adjust the training loss to reduce the accuracy of the adversary.
3. **Re-sampling Experiment:**
   Experiment with over-sampling and under-sampling strategies on an imbalanced dataset. Compare model performance and fairness metrics across different sampling techniques.
4. **Post-Processing Thresholds:**
   Develop a post-processing method to adjust classification thresholds for different groups. Evaluate how this impacts fairness metrics.
5. **Case Study Analysis:**
   Choose a real-world application (e.g., loan approval or hiring) and design a bias mitigation strategy. Document your approach, chosen metrics, and expected impact.

Ensuring fairness and mitigating bias in deep learning models is a multifaceted challenge that requires interventions at various stages of the machine learning lifecycle. By adopting a combination of data-level, algorithm-level, and post-processing techniques, you can build models that are more equitable and aligned with ethical standards. Regular audits, transparent reporting, and continuous monitoring are essential practices for maintaining fairness in AI systems. The strategies and exercises provided in this section aim to equip you with the tools and insights necessary to address bias in your models effectively.

10.3 Explainability Tools and Methods for PyTorch Models

As deep learning models become increasingly complex, understanding their decision-making process is crucial for building trust, diagnosing errors, and ensuring accountability. Explainability tools help demystify black-box models by revealing which features or input regions contribute most to a prediction. In PyTorch, several methods have been developed to interpret model behavior, ranging from gradient-based techniques to model-agnostic methods. This section covers the key tools and methods for explainability, including:

- **Gradient-Based Methods:** Such as Grad-CAM, Integrated Gradients, and Saliency Maps.
- **Model-Agnostic Approaches:** Such as LIME (Local Interpretable Model-agnostic Explanations) and SHAP (SHapley Additive exPlanations).

We also discuss best practices for using these tools and provide code examples to illustrate how to integrate them into your PyTorch projects.

Key Explainability Methods

1. Gradient-Based Methods

- **Grad-CAM (Gradient-weighted Class Activation Mapping):**
  Generates coarse heatmaps by computing the gradients of a target class with respect to the activations of a convolutional layer. This highlights the regions in the input image that are most influential in the model's prediction.
- **Integrated Gradients:**
  Computes the integral of the gradients along the path from a baseline (e.g., a black image) to the actual input. This method provides a more complete attribution by accumulating gradients over a continuum of scaled inputs.
- **Saliency Maps:**
  Use the gradient of the output with respect to the input pixels to identify which parts of the input are most sensitive to changes. Saliency maps can reveal the most critical regions that influence the output.

2. Model-Agnostic Methods

- **LIME (Local Interpretable Model-agnostic Explanations):**
  Approximates the model locally with a simple interpretable model (e.g., linear regression) to explain individual predictions. LIME perturbs the input data and observes the changes in predictions.
- **SHAP (SHapley Additive exPlanations):**
  Based on cooperative game theory, SHAP values represent the contribution of each feature to the prediction. It provides consistent and locally accurate explanations by averaging the contributions over all possible feature combinations.

Practical Code Examples

Example 1: Grad-CAM in PyTorch

Below is an example of how to implement Grad-CAM for a CNN model using PyTorch. This example demonstrates how to register hooks, compute gradients, and generate a heatmap overlay on the input image.

python

```python
import torch
import torch.nn.functional as F
import matplotlib.pyplot as plt
import numpy as np
from torchvision import models, transforms
from PIL import Image

class GradCAM:
    def __init__(self, model, target_layer):
        self.model = model
        self.target_layer = target_layer
        self.gradients = None
        self.activations = None

        # Hook the gradients and activations of the
target layer

self.target_layer.register_forward_hook(self.save_a
ctivation)

self.target_layer.register_backward_hook(self.save_
gradient)

    def save_activation(self, module, input,
output):
        self.activations = output.detach()

    def save_gradient(self, module, grad_input,
grad_output):
        self.gradients = grad_output[0].detach()
```

```python
    def generate_cam(self, input_image,
target_class):
        output = self.model(input_image)
        self.model.zero_grad()
        target = output[0, target_class]
        target.backward()

        # Global average pooling of gradients
        weights = torch.mean(self.gradients,
dim=[2, 3], keepdim=True)
        cam = torch.sum(weights * self.activations,
dim=1)
        cam = F.relu(cam)
        cam = cam.squeeze(0).cpu().numpy()
        cam = (cam - cam.min()) / (cam.max() -
cam.min() + 1e-8)
        return cam

# Load a pre-trained model and set up GradCAM for
the last convolutional layer
model = models.resnet50(pretrained=True)
model.eval()
target_layer = model.layer4[-1]
grad_cam = GradCAM(model, target_layer)

# Preprocess an example image
preprocess = transforms.Compose([
    transforms.Resize((224, 224)),
    transforms.ToTensor(),
    transforms.Normalize(mean=[0.485, 0.456,
0.406],
                          std=[0.229, 0.224, 0.225])
])
img_path = "path/to/your/image.jpg"
img = Image.open(img_path).convert("RGB")
input_tensor = preprocess(img).unsqueeze(0)

# Generate Grad-CAM for a specific target class
(e.g., class index 281 for tabby cat in ImageNet)
target_class = 281
```

```python
cam = grad_cam.generate_cam(input_tensor,
target_class)

# Resize and overlay the CAM on the original image
import cv2
img_np = np.array(img.resize((224, 224)))
heatmap = cv2.resize(cam, (224, 224))
heatmap = np.uint8(255 * heatmap)
heatmap = cv2.applyColorMap(heatmap,
cv2.COLORMAP_JET)
overlay = cv2.addWeighted(img_np, 0.6, heatmap,
0.4, 0)

plt.figure(figsize=(10, 5))
plt.subplot(1, 2, 1)
plt.title("Original Image")
plt.imshow(img_np)
plt.axis("off")
plt.subplot(1, 2, 2)
plt.title("Grad-CAM Overlay")
plt.imshow(overlay)
plt.axis("off")
plt.show()
```

Example 2: Using LIME for Explainability

Below is a brief example of using LIME to explain a PyTorch image classifier.

python

```python
from lime import lime_image
from skimage.segmentation import mark_boundaries

# Assume 'model' is a pre-trained PyTorch image
classifier and 'preprocess' is defined
def predict_fn(images):
    # Convert images to tensor and normalize
    images = [preprocess(Image.fromarray(img)) for
img in images]
    input_tensor = torch.stack(images)
    input_tensor = input_tensor.to(device)
```

```python
    with torch.no_grad():
        outputs = model(input_tensor)
    probabilities = F.softmax(outputs,
dim=1).cpu().numpy()
    return probabilities

explainer = lime_image.LimeImageExplainer()
explanation =
explainer.explain_instance(np.array(img.resize((224
, 224)))), predict_fn, top_labels=5, hide_color=0,
num_samples=1000)
temp, mask =
explanation.get_image_and_mask(target_class,
positive_only=True, num_features=10,
hide_rest=False)
plt.imshow(mark_boundaries(temp / 255.0, mask))
plt.title("LIME Explanation")
plt.axis("off")
plt.show()
```

Note: LIME works as a model-agnostic tool and can be used with any classifier by providing a prediction function.

Best Practices and Tips

- **Method Selection:**
  Choose explainability methods that best suit your application. For image models, Grad-CAM and Integrated Gradients are popular; for tabular or text data, consider LIME or SHAP.
- **Combining Methods:**
  Use multiple explainability tools in tandem to get complementary insights. For example, compare Grad-CAM heatmaps with Integrated Gradients attributions.
- **Visualization:**
  Visual representations of model explanations (e.g., heatmaps, segmentation overlays) are often more intuitive and can help identify issues such as overfitting to spurious features.
- **Interpretability vs. Performance Trade-off:**
  Some explainability methods can be computationally expensive.

Balance the need for interpretability with the performance requirements of your application.

- **Documentation:**
Document the explainability results alongside model performance metrics to provide a complete view of model behavior, especially for stakeholders and regulatory compliance.

Exercises

1. **Integrated Gradients Experiment:**
Implement Integrated Gradients for a PyTorch model and compare the resulting attributions with those from Grad-CAM on a set of sample images.

2. **SHAP Analysis:**
Use SHAP to explain the predictions of a PyTorch model on a tabular dataset. Visualize the SHAP values and analyze which features are most influential.

3. **Comparative Study:**
Apply LIME and Grad-CAM on the same image classification model and document the similarities and differences in the explanations provided.

4. **User Study:**
Present the explainability outputs (e.g., heatmaps or feature importance plots) to a group of users and collect feedback on their interpretability. Discuss how this feedback could guide further model improvements.

5. **Debugging Misclassifications:**
Use an explainability method (e.g., Grad-CAM) to investigate misclassified examples from your model. Analyze whether the explanations reveal any systematic issues or biases in the model.

Explainability is a crucial aspect of modern deep learning, providing insights into model behavior and building trust with end users. Tools such as Grad-CAM, Integrated Gradients, LIME, and SHAP allow you to understand which features or input regions drive your model's predictions. By integrating these methods into your workflow, you can diagnose model errors, ensure fairness, and improve transparency. Experiment with the provided exercises to further enhance your ability to interpret and explain your PyTorch models effectively.

10.4 Regulatory Compliance and AI Governance

As AI technologies become increasingly integrated into critical aspects of society, ensuring that these systems adhere to legal and ethical standards is paramount. Regulatory compliance and robust AI governance frameworks are essential for mitigating risks, protecting user privacy, and fostering public trust. This section explores the regulatory landscape, key principles of AI governance, and practical steps to implement compliance and oversight in AI deployments.

Key Regulatory Frameworks and Standards

1. Data Protection and Privacy Regulations

- **GDPR (General Data Protection Regulation):**
  Governs the collection, processing, and storage of personal data within the European Union. Key principles include data minimization, transparency, user consent, and the right to be forgotten.
- **CCPA (California Consumer Privacy Act):**
  Provides data privacy rights to California residents, emphasizing transparency and control over personal information.
- **Other Global Regulations:**
  Similar regulations exist in other regions (e.g., Brazil's LGPD, Canada's PIPEDA) and must be considered when deploying AI globally.

2. AI-Specific Guidelines and Ethical Standards

- **OECD Principles on AI:**
  Focus on inclusive growth, sustainable development, and respect for human rights. They advocate for transparency, robustness, and accountability.
- **EU's AI Act (Proposed):**
  Aims to establish a legal framework for trustworthy AI, categorizing

AI systems based on risk and imposing stricter requirements for high-risk applications.
- **IEEE and ISO Standards:**
  Provide technical standards and guidelines to ensure that AI systems are safe, ethical, and reliable.

AI Governance and Accountability

1. Establishing Clear Governance Structures

- **Ethical Review Boards:**
  Create multidisciplinary teams—including ethicists, legal experts, data scientists, and domain specialists—to review AI projects and ensure they adhere to ethical and regulatory standards.
- **Audit Trails and Documentation:**
  Maintain detailed records of data sources, model architectures, training procedures, and decision-making processes. This documentation is critical for audits and regulatory compliance.
- **Risk Management Frameworks:**
  Implement continuous risk assessments to identify and mitigate potential harms, including biases, privacy breaches, and security vulnerabilities.

2. Transparency and Explainability

- **Model Cards and Datasheets:**
  Publish comprehensive documentation (model cards for AI models, datasheets for datasets) that outline model performance, limitations, ethical considerations, and intended use cases.
- **Explainability Tools:**
  Use methods such as Grad-CAM, LIME, and SHAP to provide insights into model decision-making, making it easier for stakeholders to understand and trust the system.

3. Accountability Mechanisms

- **Legal Accountability:**
  Define clear responsibilities and liabilities for AI system outcomes. Organizations should be prepared to address grievances and correct errors.

- **Feedback Loops:**
  Establish channels for user feedback and mechanisms to update or recall models if they are found to cause harm or operate unfairly.
- **Third-Party Audits:**
  Engage independent auditors to review AI systems, validate compliance with regulations, and recommend improvements.

Implementation Guidelines and Best Practices

1. **Data Governance:**
   - **Ensure Data Quality and Diversity:** Implement robust data collection and preprocessing practices to avoid biases and ensure data represents the full spectrum of the target population.
   - **Anonymization and Encryption:** Protect personal data through techniques like anonymization and encryption to comply with privacy regulations.
2. **Model Development:**
   - **Bias Mitigation:** Integrate fairness audits and bias mitigation techniques during model development and deployment.
   - **Transparent Documentation:** Develop model cards and documentation detailing model behavior, assumptions, and limitations.
3. **Deployment and Monitoring:**
   - **Regular Audits:** Conduct periodic audits and performance reviews to ensure the model remains compliant as regulations evolve.
   - **Continuous Monitoring:** Use automated tools to monitor model performance, detect drift, and trigger retraining or rollback if necessary.
4. **Stakeholder Engagement:**
   - **Interdisciplinary Collaboration:** Involve diverse teams from technical, legal, ethical, and business backgrounds in the AI development process.
   - **User Communication:** Clearly communicate to end users how their data is used, the model's capabilities, and its limitations.

Exercises

1. **Compliance Checklist Development:**
   Create a comprehensive checklist that covers regulatory requirements (GDPR, CCPA, etc.), ethical guidelines (OECD, IEEE), and best practices for data governance, model development, and deployment. Use this checklist to audit a hypothetical AI project.
2. **Model Card Creation:**
   Develop a model card for an existing PyTorch model. Document its training data, intended use, performance metrics, potential biases, and limitations. Present the model card as if it were to be reviewed by an ethical review board.
3. **Risk Assessment Simulation:**
   Conduct a risk assessment for an AI system deployed in a sensitive domain (e.g., healthcare). Identify potential risks, propose mitigation strategies, and outline how you would monitor these risks post-deployment.
4. **Case Study Analysis:**
   Analyze a real-world example of an AI system that faced ethical or regulatory challenges (e.g., facial recognition technology). Identify the key issues, evaluate the responses taken, and propose alternative strategies based on the principles discussed.
5. **Develop a Governance Framework:**
   Draft a governance framework for your organization's AI initiatives, outlining roles, responsibilities, audit processes, and reporting mechanisms. Include guidelines for handling model drift, user feedback, and third-party audits.

Regulatory compliance and AI governance are not merely add-ons—they are integral to the responsible development and deployment of deep learning systems. By understanding and applying regulatory standards, establishing robust governance structures, and continuously monitoring model behavior, organizations can mitigate risks, build trust, and ensure that AI technologies benefit society as a whole. The strategies and exercises in this section provide a roadmap for developing ethical, transparent, and accountable AI systems.

10.5 Project: Bias Detection and Mitigation in Language Models

Bias in language models can manifest in numerous ways, often reflecting imbalances present in the training data or arising from the model architecture itself. This project focuses on two main tasks:

- **Bias Detection:** Identify and quantify biases using fairness metrics and explainability tools.
- **Bias Mitigation:** Implement strategies to reduce bias, such as data re-weighting, adversarial debiasing, or post-processing adjustments.

Through this project, you will gain hands-on experience with evaluating fairness in language models and applying interventions to ensure more equitable model behavior.

---

2. Project Objectives

- **Bias Detection:**
  - Evaluate model outputs across different demographic groups using fairness metrics (e.g., equal opportunity, demographic parity, and disparate impact).
  - Utilize explainability tools (e.g., SHAP, LIME) to visualize feature contributions and identify potential sources of bias.
- **Bias Mitigation:**
  - Apply data-level interventions such as re-sampling, re-weighting, or augmentation to balance training data.
  - Implement algorithm-level strategies (e.g., adversarial debiasing) to encourage the model to learn fair representations.
  - Explore post-processing techniques (e.g., calibrated thresholding) to adjust final predictions and reduce disparate impact.
- **Evaluation:**
  - Compare model performance and fairness before and after mitigation.
  - Analyze trade-offs between overall accuracy and fairness improvements.

3. Data Preparation

For this project, use a language dataset with known demographic attributes or synthetic data that simulates potential biases. For instance, if working with a sentiment analysis model, you might label samples with demographic identifiers or simulate different language styles.

Steps:

- **Data Collection:** Gather or generate text data with associated demographic or sensitive attribute labels.
- **Preprocessing:**
  - Clean and tokenize the text data.
  - Optionally, augment the data to balance representation across groups.
- **Splitting:** Create training, validation, and test sets ensuring balanced representation in each split.

4. Bias Detection Techniques

A. Quantitative Fairness Metrics

1. **Demographic Parity:**
   Ensure that the model's positive prediction rate is similar across different groups.
2. **Equal Opportunity:**
   Compare the true positive rates across groups.
3. **Equalized Odds:**
   Measure both true positive and false positive rates across groups.
4. **Disparate Impact:**
   Evaluate the ratio of favorable outcomes between groups.

B. Explainability Tools

- **SHAP (SHapley Additive exPlanations):**
  Use SHAP to determine the contribution of each feature to individual predictions.

- **LIME (Local Interpretable Model-agnostic Explanations):**
  Explain individual predictions by approximating the model locally with an interpretable model.

---

5. Bias Mitigation Strategies

A. Data-Level Interventions

- **Re-sampling and Re-weighting:**
  Adjust the training data distribution by over-sampling underrepresented groups or assigning higher weights to them during loss computation.
- **Data Augmentation:**
  Generate additional samples for underrepresented groups to improve balance.

B. Algorithm-Level Interventions

- **Adversarial Debiasing:**
  Train an auxiliary adversary to predict sensitive attributes from the model's representations and use its loss to penalize biased features.
- **Fair Representation Learning:**
  Incorporate fairness regularizers in the loss function to enforce similarity in representation distributions across groups.

C. Post-Processing Techniques

- **Threshold Calibration:**
  Adjust decision thresholds for different groups to equalize performance metrics like true positive rates.
- **Output Re-ranking:**
  Post-process model predictions to balance fairness across groups, for instance by reordering the ranked outputs.

---

6. Implementation Example

Below is a simplified example demonstrating bias detection with re-weighting for imbalanced data in a text classification setting, followed by a brief outline for integrating an adversarial debiasing component.

Example: Re-weighting to Mitigate Bias

```python
import torch
import torch.nn as nn
import torch.optim as optim
from torch.utils.data import DataLoader,
TensorDataset
import numpy as np

# Create synthetic imbalanced dataset
# Assume we have 1000 samples with a sensitive
attribute where class 0 is 90% and class 1 is 10%
num_samples = 1000
input_features = torch.randn(num_samples, 100)
labels = torch.cat((torch.zeros(int(num_samples *
0.9), dtype=torch.long),
                    torch.ones(int(num_samples *
0.1), dtype=torch.long)))
sensitive_attr =
torch.cat((torch.zeros(int(num_samples * 0.9),
dtype=torch.long),

torch.ones(int(num_samples * 0.1),
dtype=torch.long)))
dataset = TensorDataset(input_features, labels,
sensitive_attr)
dataloader = DataLoader(dataset, batch_size=32,
shuffle=True)

# Define a simple classifier
class SimpleClassifier(nn.Module):
    def __init__(self, input_dim, num_classes):
        super(SimpleClassifier, self).__init__()
        self.fc = nn.Linear(input_dim, num_classes)
```

```python
    def forward(self, x):
        return self.fc(x)

model = SimpleClassifier(100, 2)
criterion = nn.CrossEntropyLoss(reduction='none')
optimizer = optim.Adam(model.parameters(),
lr=0.001)

# Compute class weights inversely proportional to
class frequency
class_counts = np.bincount(labels.numpy())
class_weights = 1.0 / class_counts
print("Class Weights:", class_weights)

# Training loop with re-weighting
num_epochs = 5
for epoch in range(num_epochs):
    total_loss = 0.0
    for batch_data, batch_labels, _ in dataloader:
        optimizer.zero_grad()
        outputs = model(batch_data)
        loss = criterion(outputs, batch_labels)
        # Weight loss for each sample based on its
class
        batch_weights =
torch.tensor([class_weights[label.item()] for label
in batch_labels], dtype=torch.float32)
        weighted_loss = (loss *
batch_weights).mean()
        weighted_loss.backward()
        optimizer.step()
        total_loss += weighted_loss.item()
    print(f"Epoch {epoch+1}, Average Loss:
{total_loss/len(dataloader):.4f}")
```

Explanation:

- **Re-weighting:** The loss for each sample is scaled inversely to its class frequency, encouraging the model to pay more attention to underrepresented classes.

Outline for Adversarial Debiasing

1. **Main Model:**
   Train your primary language model (e.g., a text classifier) to perform the desired task.
2. **Adversary Model:**
   Simultaneously train a small adversary network that takes intermediate representations from the main model and predicts the sensitive attribute.
3. **Joint Loss:**
   Combine the main task loss with an adversarial loss that penalizes the main model if the adversary can accurately predict the sensitive attribute.
4. **Optimization:**
   Update the main model to minimize the primary loss and maximize the adversary loss (or minimize a combined loss), encouraging the main model to learn representations that are invariant to the sensitive attribute.

---

7. Best Practices and Tips

- **Iterative Refinement:**
  Bias mitigation is an iterative process. Regularly evaluate fairness metrics and refine your strategies based on the results.
- **Multifaceted Approach:**
  Combine data-level, algorithm-level, and post-processing interventions for robust mitigation.
- **Transparency:**
  Document all steps, including data preprocessing, model adjustments, and evaluation metrics, to provide a clear audit trail.
- **Stakeholder Involvement:**
  Engage domain experts and affected communities in the evaluation process to ensure that mitigation strategies are appropriate and effective.

8. Exercises

1. **Bias Metrics Implementation:**
   Select a dataset and implement fairness metrics (e.g., demographic parity, equal opportunity) to evaluate bias in a pre-trained language model.
2. **Adversarial Debiasing:**
   Implement an adversarial debiasing component for a text classification model. Compare the model's fairness and overall performance before and after applying adversarial training.
3. **Data Augmentation:**
   Experiment with data augmentation techniques to balance the representation of different groups in your training data. Evaluate the impact on model fairness.
4. **Post-Processing Adjustment:**
   Develop a post-processing method to adjust model predictions (e.g., calibrated thresholding) and measure its effect on fairness metrics.
5. **Comprehensive Report:**
   Create a report summarizing your bias detection and mitigation process, including quantitative results from fairness metrics, visualizations (e.g., confusion matrices or attribution maps), and a discussion of trade-offs between accuracy and fairness.

Mitigating bias in language models is critical for building ethical and equitable AI systems. This project provided a framework for detecting bias using quantitative metrics and applying various mitigation strategies—from data re-weighting to adversarial debiasing. By experimenting with these techniques and integrating explainability tools, you can gain deeper insights into your models and develop strategies that balance performance with fairness. The exercises are designed to reinforce these concepts and help you build robust, bias-aware models for real-world applications

10.6 Implementing Interpretability Techniques for CNN and Transformer Models

As deep learning models grow in complexity, understanding their internal decision processes becomes increasingly important for debugging, transparency, and building trust with end users. Interpretability techniques help uncover which parts of the input data drive the model's predictions. In this exercise, we focus on two popular model families:

- **CNN Models:**
  We will implement techniques such as Grad-CAM and Integrated Gradients to visualize which regions of an input image are most influential in the model's prediction.
- **Transformer Models:**
  We will explore methods to visualize attention weights and derive token-level attributions, helping to reveal how the model processes sequences and captures contextual relationships.

By implementing these techniques, you will be able to diagnose issues, understand model biases, and provide explanations that are valuable for stakeholders and regulatory compliance.

Interpretability Techniques for CNNs

Grad-CAM

Grad-CAM (Gradient-weighted Class Activation Mapping) uses the gradients of a target class flowing into the final convolutional layer to produce a coarse localization map highlighting important regions in the input image.

Key Steps:

- Register forward and backward hooks on the target convolutional layer.
- Compute the gradients and perform global average pooling.
- Generate a heatmap overlay on the input image.

Example Code Snippet:

```python
import torch
import torch.nn.functional as F
import matplotlib.pyplot as plt
import numpy as np
```

```python
from torchvision import models, transforms
from PIL import Image
import cv2

class GradCAM:
    def __init__(self, model, target_layer):
        self.model = model
        self.target_layer = target_layer
        self.gradients = None
        self.activations = None

self.target_layer.register_forward_hook(self.save_activation)

self.target_layer.register_backward_hook(self.save_gradient)

    def save_activation(self, module, input, output):
        self.activations = output.detach()

    def save_gradient(self, module, grad_input, grad_output):
        self.gradients = grad_output[0].detach()

    def generate_cam(self, input_tensor, target_class):
        output = self.model(input_tensor)
        self.model.zero_grad()
        target = output[0, target_class]
        target.backward()
        weights = torch.mean(self.gradients, dim=[2, 3], keepdim=True)
        cam = torch.sum(weights * self.activations, dim=1)
        cam = F.relu(cam)
        cam = cam.squeeze(0).cpu().numpy()
        cam = (cam - cam.min()) / (cam.max() - cam.min() + 1e-8)
        return cam

# Example usage:
```

```python
model = models.resnet50(pretrained=True)
model.eval()
target_layer = model.layer4[-1]
grad_cam = GradCAM(model, target_layer)

preprocess = transforms.Compose([
    transforms.Resize((224, 224)),
    transforms.ToTensor(),
    transforms.Normalize(mean=[0.485, 0.456,
0.406],
                         std=[0.229, 0.224, 0.225])
])
img =
Image.open("path/to/your/image.jpg").convert("RGB")
input_tensor = preprocess(img).unsqueeze(0)

target_class = 281  # Example: Tabby cat in
ImageNet
cam = grad_cam.generate_cam(input_tensor,
target_class)

img_np = np.array(img.resize((224, 224)))
heatmap = cv2.resize(cam, (224, 224))
heatmap = np.uint8(255 * heatmap)
heatmap = cv2.applyColorMap(heatmap,
cv2.COLORMAP_JET)
overlay = cv2.addWeighted(img_np, 0.6, heatmap,
0.4, 0)

plt.figure(figsize=(10, 5))
plt.subplot(1, 2, 1)
plt.title("Original Image")
plt.imshow(img_np)
plt.axis("off")
plt.subplot(1, 2, 2)
plt.title("Grad-CAM Overlay")
plt.imshow(overlay)
plt.axis("off")
plt.show()
```

Integrated Gradients

Integrated Gradients accumulate gradients along a path from a baseline input (e.g., a black image) to the actual input, providing a more comprehensive attribution for each input feature.

Key Steps:

- Define a baseline (e.g., a zero or blurred image).
- Compute gradients for interpolated inputs between the baseline and actual input.
- Sum and average the gradients to derive feature attributions.

For brevity, refer to existing libraries like Captum for Integrated Gradients implementations in PyTorch.

Interpretability Techniques for Transformer Models

Attention Visualization

Transformer models rely on self-attention mechanisms that can be visualized to understand how the model attends to different parts of the input sequence.

Key Steps:

- Extract attention weights from Transformer layers.
- Visualize attention distributions across tokens.
- Use methods like attention rollout to aggregate multi-head attention information.

Example Code Snippet:

```python
import torch
from transformers import BertTokenizer, BertModel
import matplotlib.pyplot as plt
import seaborn as sns

# Load a pre-trained BERT model and tokenizer
tokenizer = BertTokenizer.from_pretrained("bert-base-uncased")
```

```
model = BertModel.from_pretrained("bert-base-
uncased", output_attentions=True)
model.eval()

# Tokenize an example sentence
sentence = "The quick brown fox jumps over the lazy
dog."
inputs = tokenizer(sentence, return_tensors="pt")
outputs = model(**inputs)
attentions = outputs.attentions  # List of
attention matrices from each layer

# Visualize attention from the last layer, first
head
attention_matrix = attentions[-1][0,
0].detach().numpy()

plt.figure(figsize=(8, 8))
sns.heatmap(attention_matrix, cmap="viridis")
plt.title("Attention Weights (Last Layer, Head 1)")
plt.xlabel("Token Index")
plt.ylabel("Token Index")
plt.show()
```

Additional Methods

- **Attention Rollout:**
  Aggregate attention weights across multiple layers to obtain a global
  view of token interactions.
- **Token Attribution:**
  Methods like LIME or SHAP can also be applied to Transformers to
  understand which tokens contribute most to the output.

Best Practices and Tips

- **Select Appropriate Layers:**
  For CNNs, choose the last convolutional layers for Grad-CAM; for
  Transformers, analyze attention weights from both early and late
  layers for a comprehensive view.

- **Combine Multiple Methods:**
  Use a combination of gradient-based and model-agnostic techniques to obtain richer insights.
- **Visual Clarity:**
  Normalize and smooth attributions for better visualization and interpretation.
- **Evaluate Interpretability:**
  Validate that the explanations align with domain knowledge and do not indicate spurious correlations.
- **Documentation:**
  Document your interpretability analysis in model cards or technical reports to communicate findings with stakeholders.

Exercises

1. **Implement Integrated Gradients:**
   Use Captum or implement Integrated Gradients for a CNN classifier and compare the attributions with those from Grad-CAM.
2. **Attention Visualization in Transformers:**
   Visualize the attention weights for multiple layers of a Transformer model. Analyze how different layers focus on various parts of the input.
3. **Comparative Analysis:**
   Apply LIME to both a CNN and a Transformer model on the same dataset. Compare and contrast the explanations provided by the two methods.
4. **User Study:**
   Present the generated explanations (heatmaps, attention maps) to domain experts and gather feedback on their clarity and usefulness.
5. **Error Diagnosis:**
   Use interpretability techniques to analyze a set of misclassified examples from your models. Identify common patterns that may indicate model weaknesses or biases.

Interpretability is a key aspect of responsible AI development. By implementing techniques such as Grad-CAM and Integrated Gradients for

CNNs and attention visualization for Transformer models, you can gain valuable insights into your models' decision-making processes. These tools not only help in debugging and refining models but also play an essential role in building trust with end users. Experiment with the exercises provided to deepen your understanding of interpretability methods and to develop robust explanations for your PyTorch models.

Chapter 11: Real-World End-to-End Projects

Project 1: Healthcare Multimodal Classifier

Healthcare decisions often rely on diverse data sources such as medical images (e.g., X-rays, MRIs) and patient records (e.g., clinical notes, laboratory results). Integrating these modalities can lead to more accurate diagnoses and personalized treatments. In this project, you will build a multimodal classifier that leverages both visual and structured clinical data. The model will learn to combine features from medical images and patient records, producing predictions that could assist in tasks such as disease diagnosis, risk stratification, or treatment recommendations.

Project Objectives

- **Data Collection and Preprocessing:**
  - Gather medical images and corresponding patient records.
  - Clean, normalize, and augment the image data.
  - Preprocess and encode structured patient records (e.g., demographics, lab values, clinical notes).
- **Model Architecture:**
  - Build a CNN-based image encoder to extract visual features.
  - Construct a separate network (e.g., a fully connected network or a Transformer for text data) to process patient records.
  - Fuse the features from both modalities using early fusion (concatenation) or hybrid approaches.
  - Add a classification head to predict the target healthcare outcome.
- **Training Strategy:**
  - Train the multimodal classifier end-to-end.
  - Use appropriate loss functions and evaluation metrics that are relevant in the healthcare domain.
  - Implement regularization and fairness measures if needed.
- **Deployment:**
  - Containerize the model with Docker.
  - Deploy the model as a RESTful API (e.g., using FastAPI) for real-time predictions.

o Ensure the solution meets regulatory and performance requirements for healthcare applications.

Data Preparation

Medical Images

- **Collection:**
  Use publicly available datasets (e.g., NIH Chest X-rays) or synthetic data for demonstration.
- **Preprocessing:**
  - o Resize images to a consistent resolution (e.g., 224×224).
  - o Normalize pixel values (e.g., scaling to [0, 1] or [-1, 1]).
  - o Apply data augmentation techniques (e.g., rotation, flipping) to improve generalization.

Example Code:

python

```
from torchvision import transforms
from PIL import Image

image_transform = transforms.Compose([
    transforms.Resize((224, 224)),
    transforms.ToTensor(),
    transforms.Normalize(mean=[0.485, 0.456,
0.406],
                        std=[0.229, 0.224, 0.225])
])

# Load and preprocess a sample image
sample_image =
Image.open("path/to/medical_image.jpg").convert("RG
B")
processed_image = image_transform(sample_image)
```

Patient Records

- **Collection:**
  Utilize structured data such as demographics, lab results, and clinical notes. For demonstration, synthetic or anonymized data can be used.
- **Preprocessing:**
  - Clean the data by handling missing values and outliers.
  - Normalize numerical features.
  - Tokenize and embed text-based records if applicable (using techniques like word embeddings or Transformers).

Example Code:

```python
import pandas as pd
from sklearn.preprocessing import StandardScaler

# Load patient records from a CSV file
patient_data =
pd.read_csv("path/to/patient_records.csv")

# Fill missing values and standardize numerical
features
patient_data.fillna(method='ffill', inplace=True)
scaler = StandardScaler()
numerical_features = ['age', 'lab_value1',
'lab_value2']
patient_data[numerical_features] =
scaler.fit_transform(patient_data[numerical_feature
s])
```

Model Architecture

Image Encoder

- **CNN Architecture:**
  Use a pre-trained CNN (e.g., ResNet50) or a custom architecture to extract feature embeddings from medical images.

Example Code:

python

```python
import torch.nn as nn
import torchvision.models as models

# Load a pre-trained ResNet50 model and modify it
to extract features
class ImageEncoder(nn.Module):
    def __init__(self, embed_dim=256):
        super(ImageEncoder, self).__init__()
        resnet = models.resnet50(pretrained=True)
        modules = list(resnet.children())[:-1]   #
Remove the final classification layer
        self.feature_extractor =
nn.Sequential(*modules)
        self.fc = nn.Linear(resnet.fc.in_features,
embed_dim)

    def forward(self, x):
        features = self.feature_extractor(x)
        features = features.view(features.size(0),
-1)
        return self.fc(features)

image_encoder = ImageEncoder(embed_dim=256)
```

Patient Records Encoder

- **Structured Data Encoder:**
  Use a fully connected network for numerical data, or combine with
  an embedding layer for text data.

Example Code:

python

```python
class RecordsEncoder(nn.Module):
    def __init__(self, input_dim, embed_dim=128):
        super(RecordsEncoder, self).__init__()
        self.fc = nn.Sequential(
```

```python
            nn.Linear(input_dim, 64),
            nn.ReLU(),
            nn.Linear(64, embed_dim),
            nn.ReLU()
        )

    def forward(self, x):
        return self.fc(x)

# Assuming patient records have 10 features
records_encoder = RecordsEncoder(input_dim=10,
embed_dim=128)
```

Fusion and Classification Head

- **Fusion Layer:**
  Concatenate image and record embeddings, then pass through fully connected layers to output a classification decision.

Example Code:

python

```python
class MultimodalClassifier(nn.Module):
    def __init__(self, image_embed_dim,
record_embed_dim, num_classes):
        super(MultimodalClassifier,
self).__init__()
        self.fc = nn.Sequential(
            nn.Linear(image_embed_dim +
record_embed_dim, 128),
            nn.ReLU(),
            nn.Linear(128, num_classes)
        )

    def forward(self, image_features,
record_features):
        combined = torch.cat((image_features,
record_features), dim=1)
        return self.fc(combined)
```

```
# Assuming classification into 2 classes (e.g.,
disease vs. no disease)
classifier =
MultimodalClassifier(image_embed_dim=256,
record_embed_dim=128, num_classes=2)
```

Combined Model

Combine the encoders and classifier into one end-to-end model.

Example Code:

python

```
class HealthcareMultimodalModel(nn.Module):
    def __init__(self, image_encoder,
records_encoder, classifier):
        super(HealthcareMultimodalModel,
self).__init__()
        self.image_encoder = image_encoder
        self.records_encoder = records_encoder
        self.classifier = classifier

    def forward(self, image, records):
        img_features = self.image_encoder(image)
        rec_features =
self.records_encoder(records)
        return self.classifier(img_features,
rec_features)

model = HealthcareMultimodalModel(image_encoder,
records_encoder, classifier)
```

Training and Evaluation

- **Training:**
  Train the model using an appropriate loss function (e.g., Cross-Entropy Loss) and an optimizer (e.g., Adam). Use DataLoaders for both image and record datasets.
- **Evaluation:**
  Evaluate the model on a held-out test set using accuracy, precision,

recall, and other relevant metrics. Consider fairness metrics if appropriate.

Example Training Loop (Simplified):

python

```
import torch.optim as optim

criterion = nn.CrossEntropyLoss()
optimizer = optim.Adam(model.parameters(), lr=1e-4)

# Assume dataloader yields tuples (image_batch,
record_batch, label_batch)
for epoch in range(10):
    total_loss = 0.0
    model.train()
    for image_batch, record_batch, label_batch in
dataloader:
        optimizer.zero_grad()
        outputs = model(image_batch, record_batch)
        loss = criterion(outputs, label_batch)
        loss.backward()
        optimizer.step()
        total_loss += loss.item()
    print(f"Epoch {epoch+1}, Loss:
{total_loss/len(dataloader):.4f}")
```

Deployment

- **Containerization:**
  Use Docker to containerize your application, including the model and inference API (e.g., FastAPI).
- **REST API:**
  Deploy the model as a REST API for real-time predictions, ensuring secure and scalable access.
- **Cloud Deployment:**
  Optionally deploy your containerized application to cloud platforms such as AWS, GCP, or Azure.

Example FastAPI Endpoint for Inference:

python

```python
from fastapi import FastAPI, HTTPException
from pydantic import BaseModel
import torch
import uvicorn

app = FastAPI(title="Healthcare Multimodal
Classifier API")

class InferenceRequest(BaseModel):
    image_path: str  # For demonstration; in
production, accept image bytes
    record_data: list  # List of patient record
features

# Dummy function to load image and preprocess
(replace with actual implementation)
def load_and_preprocess_image(image_path):
    from PIL import Image
    from torchvision import transforms
    image = Image.open(image_path).convert("RGB")
    preprocess = transforms.Compose([
        transforms.Resize((224, 224)),
        transforms.ToTensor(),
        transforms.Normalize(mean=[0.485, 0.456,
0.406],
                             std=[0.229, 0.224,
0.225])
    ])
    return preprocess(image).unsqueeze(0)

@app.post("/predict")
async def predict(request: InferenceRequest):
    if not request.image_path or not
request.record_data:
        raise HTTPException(status_code=400,
detail="Invalid input data.")
```

```
    image_tensor =
load_and_preprocess_image(request.image_path)
    record_tensor =
torch.tensor(request.record_data,
dtype=torch.float32).unsqueeze(0)

    model.eval()
    with torch.no_grad():
        output = model(image_tensor, record_tensor)
    prediction = output.argmax(dim=1).item()

    return {"prediction": prediction}

if __name__ == "__main__":
    uvicorn.run(app, host="0.0.0.0", port=8000)
```

Best Practices

- **Data Synchronization:**
  Ensure that image and record data are correctly aligned for each patient.
- **Privacy and Security:**
  Implement strong data privacy measures and secure the API, particularly when handling sensitive medical data.
- **Robust Evaluation:**
  Use cross-validation and external datasets to validate the model's performance and generalizability.
- **Regulatory Compliance:**
  Ensure that the deployment meets healthcare regulatory standards (e.g., HIPAA, GDPR) when handling patient data.
- **Monitoring:**
  Continuously monitor model performance in production and set up mechanisms for model updates and rollback if necessary.

Exercises

1. **Data Augmentation for Medical Images:**
   Implement and evaluate different data augmentation techniques for medical images to improve the robustness of your image encoder.

2. **Feature Engineering for Patient Records:**
   Experiment with additional feature engineering on patient records (e.g., combining laboratory values or creating composite scores) and measure the impact on classification performance.
3. **Fusion Strategy Comparison:**
   Compare early fusion (concatenation) with hybrid fusion strategies (e.g., merging intermediate features) for combining image and record embeddings.
4. **End-to-End Testing:**
   Develop a test suite that evaluates the entire inference pipeline, from input preprocessing to final prediction. Use sample data to simulate real-world scenarios.
5. **Deployment Optimization:**
   Containerize the model using Docker, deploy it on a cloud service (e.g., AWS or Azure), and perform load testing to assess scalability and latency.

Building and deploying a healthcare multimodal classifier involves integrating diverse data sources, designing robust model architectures, and ensuring the system meets the strict requirements of the healthcare domain. This project provided a step-by-step guide to preprocess medical images and patient records, construct a multimodal model, and deploy it as a scalable API for real-time inference. Through iterative improvements, careful evaluation, and adherence to best practices, you can develop a system that enhances decision-making in healthcare while ensuring privacy, fairness, and compliance.

B. API Deployment and Integration with Hospital Systems

Integrating AI-driven models into hospital systems requires more than just building a high-performance model—it demands that the model be accessible via a secure, robust, and interoperable API. Hospital systems, such as electronic health records (EHR) and radiology information systems (RIS), often adhere to standards like HL7 (Health Level Seven) and FHIR (Fast Healthcare Interoperability Resources) for data exchange. In this section, you will learn how to:

- Package and deploy your healthcare multimodal classifier as a RESTful API using frameworks like FastAPI.

- Ensure that the API meets stringent security and privacy requirements (e.g., HIPAA compliance).
- Integrate with hospital systems through standard protocols and interfaces.
- Monitor and maintain the API for high availability and performance in a clinical environment.

Key Concepts

1. Secure API Deployment

- **Authentication & Authorization:**
  Use industry-standard protocols (e.g., OAuth 2.0, JWT) to secure API endpoints.
- **Encryption:**
  Ensure that data in transit is encrypted using TLS/SSL.
- **Compliance:**
  Adhere to regulatory requirements such as HIPAA by implementing strict access controls, audit logging, and data anonymization where necessary.

2. Interoperability with Hospital Systems

- **HL7 and FHIR Standards:**
  HL7 and FHIR provide structured data formats for exchanging medical information. Your API should be capable of processing, transforming, and returning data in these formats.
- **Integration Layers:**
  Use middleware or integration platforms that can bridge your API with hospital systems, ensuring seamless data flow.

3. Deployment Best Practices

- **Containerization:**
  Package your API in Docker containers for consistency and portability across environments.
- **Scalability:**
  Deploy using cloud services (e.g., AWS, Azure, or GCP) and configure auto-scaling to handle varying loads.

- **Monitoring and Logging:**
  Implement robust monitoring (e.g., via AWS CloudWatch, Prometheus) and logging to track API performance, security events, and system health.

Deployment Workflow

1. **Develop the API:**
   Build your API using FastAPI, incorporating security features (authentication, input validation) and ensuring it can handle HL7/FHIR formatted data if needed.
2. **Containerize the Application:**
   Create a Dockerfile to package your API along with its dependencies, ensuring that it can run reliably across different environments.
3. **Deploy on a Cloud Platform:**
   Use a cloud service (e.g., AWS Elastic Beanstalk, Azure App Service, or GCP App Engine) to deploy your Docker container. Configure load balancing, auto-scaling, and security groups as required.
4. **Integrate with Hospital Systems:**
   Use integration middleware or custom adapters to interface your API with existing hospital systems. This might involve converting JSON responses to HL7/FHIR messages or consuming HL7/FHIR inputs.
5. **Monitor and Maintain:**
   Set up logging and monitoring to ensure real-time visibility into API performance, detect anomalies, and manage errors effectively.

Practical Code Example: FastAPI Endpoint for Hospital Integration

Below is a simplified FastAPI example that demonstrates a secure endpoint. This endpoint receives patient data (e.g., an image path and structured record data), processes it using your multimodal model, and returns a prediction in a format that can be adapted for HL7/FHIR integration.

```python
from fastapi import FastAPI, HTTPException, Header
from pydantic import BaseModel
```

```python
import torch
import uvicorn
from typing import List

# Import your multimodal model (assume it is
defined and trained)
# from healthcare_multimodal_model import
HealthcareMultimodalModel, image_encoder,
records_encoder, classifier

# For demonstration, using a dummy model
class DummyModel(torch.nn.Module):
    def __init__(self):
        super(DummyModel, self).__init__()
        self.fc = torch.nn.Linear(10, 2)

    def forward(self, x_image, x_record):
        # Dummy fusion: simply combine two inputs
        x = torch.cat((x_image, x_record), dim=1)
        return self.fc(x)

model = DummyModel()
model.eval()
device = torch.device("cuda" if
torch.cuda.is_available() else "cpu")
model.to(device)

# Pydantic model for the API request
class PatientData(BaseModel):
    patient_id: str
    image_data: List[float]  # In practice, you may
pass image bytes or a URL to the image
    record_data: List[float]  # Structured patient
record features

app = FastAPI(title="Healthcare Multimodal
Classifier API")

# Endpoint to get predictions
@app.post("/predict")
async def predict(patient: PatientData,
authorization: str = Header(None)):
```

```python
    # Simple API key check for security
    if authorization != "Bearer
your_secure_api_key":
        raise HTTPException(status_code=401,
detail="Unauthorized")

    if len(patient.image_data) != 5 or
len(patient.record_data) != 5:
        raise HTTPException(status_code=400,
detail="Invalid input data format.")

    # Convert data to tensors (dummy conversion for
illustration)
    image_tensor =
torch.tensor([patient.image_data],
dtype=torch.float32).to(device)
    record_tensor =
torch.tensor([patient.record_data],
dtype=torch.float32).to(device)

    with torch.no_grad():
        output = model(image_tensor, record_tensor)

    prediction = output.argmax(dim=1).item()

    # For hospital integration, format response
according to HL7/FHIR requirements if necessary.
    # Here, we simply return a JSON response.
    response = {
        "patient_id": patient.patient_id,
        "prediction": prediction,
        "confidence": torch.softmax(output,
dim=1).cpu().tolist()[0]
    }
    return response

if __name__ == "__main__":
    uvicorn.run(app, host="0.0.0.0", port=8000)
```

Best Practices for Integration

- **Security and Compliance:**
  Secure your API endpoints with proper authentication (API keys, OAuth) and encrypt data in transit using TLS. Ensure compliance with healthcare regulations such as HIPAA.
- **Interoperability:**
  Design your API responses to be easily transformed into HL7 or FHIR formats, enabling seamless integration with hospital systems.
- **Error Handling:**
  Implement robust error handling and logging to capture issues in real-time, which is critical in clinical settings.
- **Scalability:**
  Use Docker and cloud deployment strategies (see previous sections) to ensure that your API can scale to meet the demands of a hospital environment.
- **Testing:**
  Perform extensive integration testing with simulated hospital data and workflows to ensure that your API functions reliably under real-world conditions.

Exercises

1. **HL7/FHIR Conversion:**
   Implement a middleware layer that converts your JSON API responses into HL7 or FHIR-compliant messages. Test this integration with sample data.
2. **Security Hardening:**
   Enhance your API by integrating OAuth 2.0 for authentication. Document the security configuration and test unauthorized access attempts.
3. **Load Testing:**
   Simulate high-volume traffic on your API using tools like Apache JMeter or Locust. Analyze performance metrics and adjust deployment configurations for optimal scalability.
4. **Integration Simulation:**
   Create a simulation of a hospital system that sends patient data to your API and processes the responses. Evaluate end-to-end latency and data consistency.

5. **User Interface Prototype:**
   Develop a simple web-based dashboard (using Streamlit or a JavaScript framework) that hospital staff can use to input patient data and view predictions, incorporating features like logging and error reporting.

Deploying an AI model as a secure, robust API and integrating it with hospital systems is a critical step in bringing advanced healthcare solutions into clinical practice. By following best practices in API security, interoperability, and scalability, and leveraging standards such as HL7 and FHIR, you can ensure that your model serves as a reliable tool for healthcare professionals. Experiment with the provided exercises to refine your integration and build a seamless end-to-end system that enhances patient care while meeting regulatory standards.

Project 2: Enterprise-Level Chatbot with Custom LLM

A. Fine-tuning Domain-Specific LLM with Proprietary Datasets

Enterprise chatbots require deep understanding of domain-specific language, terminology, and context. General-purpose LLMs may lack the nuance needed for specialized industries such as finance, legal, healthcare, or technology. Fine-tuning a pre-trained LLM on proprietary datasets enables the model to learn the unique linguistic patterns, jargon, and contextual cues relevant to your enterprise. This process not only improves the quality of responses but also enhances the chatbot's ability to handle complex, domain-specific queries.

Project Objectives

- **Adapt the LLM:**
  Leverage a pre-trained LLM (e.g., GPT, BERT, or LLaMA) and fine-tune it on your proprietary datasets to capture domain-specific language patterns and context.
- **Improve Domain Relevance:**
  Ensure that the chatbot accurately interprets and responds to

specialized queries by incorporating industry-specific terminology and data.

- **Optimize Performance:**
  Balance performance with resource constraints by using efficient fine-tuning techniques (e.g., LoRA, PEFT) to minimize computational overhead.
- **Ensure Compliance and Security:**
  Handle proprietary data with strict security protocols, ensuring compliance with internal policies and relevant regulations.

Data Preparation

1. Data Collection

- **Proprietary Datasets:**
  Gather datasets from your enterprise sources such as internal documents, customer service logs, email communications, chat transcripts, and domain-specific knowledge bases.
- **Data Privacy:**
  Ensure that all data is anonymized and complies with company privacy policies and regulatory requirements (e.g., GDPR, HIPAA).

2. Data Preprocessing

- **Cleaning and Normalization:**
  Remove noise, correct typos, and standardize formats. Consider using domain-specific lexicons for normalization.
- **Tokenization and Encoding:**
  Use the tokenizer associated with your chosen LLM. Customize the tokenizer if necessary to incorporate domain-specific vocabulary.
- **Formatting:**
  Format the data into prompt-response pairs or conversational threads. Include context if the chatbot is expected to handle multi-turn conversations.

Example Code for Data Preprocessing:

```python
import pandas as pd
```

```
import re
from transformers import AutoTokenizer

# Load your proprietary dataset (e.g., CSV with
'prompt' and 'response' columns)
data = pd.read_csv("enterprise_chat_data.csv")

# Basic preprocessing function tailored to your
domain
def preprocess_text(text):
    text = text.lower().strip()
    text = re.sub(r"[^a-z0-9\s\.,!?']", "", text)
    return text

data["prompt"] =
data["prompt"].apply(preprocess_text)
data["response"] =
data["response"].apply(preprocess_text)

# Save preprocessed data for further fine-tuning
data.to_csv("preprocessed_enterprise_chat_data.csv"
, index=False)

# Load the tokenizer (e.g., GPT-2 tokenizer)
tokenizer = AutoTokenizer.from_pretrained("gpt2")
# Optionally, add custom tokens for domain-specific
terms
special_tokens_dict = {"additional_special_tokens":
["<domain_token1>", "<domain_token2>"]}
tokenizer.add_special_tokens(special_tokens_dict)
```

Model Fine-Tuning

1. Model Selection

- **Choose a Pre-trained LLM:**
  Select a model that best aligns with your enterprise requirements.
  GPT-family models are suitable for generative tasks, while BERT-
  family models may be better for understanding tasks. For a
  conversational chatbot, a model like GPT-2, GPT-3, or a more
  efficient model such as LLaMA can be appropriate.

- **Efficient Fine-Tuning:**
  Consider techniques like LoRA or PEFT to fine-tune the model efficiently without updating all parameters. This reduces training time and computational resource usage.

2. Fine-Tuning Process

- **Define the Training Objective:**
  For a chatbot, the objective is to minimize the difference between the generated responses and the actual responses in your dataset. You may use language modeling losses (e.g., cross-entropy) and incorporate prompt engineering strategies.
- **Training Pipeline:**
  - Create a dataset and dataloader for your prompt-response pairs.
  - Set up a training loop using a framework like Hugging Face's Trainer API.
  - Monitor metrics such as perplexity and BLEU scores for generated responses.

Example Fine-Tuning Code Snippet (using Hugging Face Trainer):

```python
from transformers import GPT2LMHeadModel,
GPT2Tokenizer, TextDataset,
DataCollatorForLanguageModeling, Trainer,
TrainingArguments

model_name = "gpt2"
model = GPT2LMHeadModel.from_pretrained(model_name)
tokenizer =
GPT2LMHeadModel.from_pretrained(model_name)  # Use
GPT2Tokenizer in practice
# Adjust model for custom tokens if any
special_tokens_dict = {"additional_special_tokens":
["<domain_token1>", "<domain_token2>"]}
num_added_tokens =
tokenizer.add_special_tokens(special_tokens_dict)
model.resize_token_embeddings(len(tokenizer))
```

```python
# Prepare dataset (assumes the preprocessed data is
in a text file with prompt-response pairs)
train_dataset = TextDataset(
    tokenizer=tokenizer,

file_path="preprocessed_enterprise_chat_data.txt",
    block_size=128
)

data_collator = DataCollatorForLanguageModeling(
    tokenizer=tokenizer,
    mlm=False  # GPT models use causal language
modeling
)

training_args = TrainingArguments(
    output_dir="./enterprise_chatbot",
    overwrite_output_dir=True,
    num_train_epochs=3,
    per_device_train_batch_size=4,
    save_steps=500,
    save_total_limit=2,
    prediction_loss_only=True,
)

trainer = Trainer(
    model=model,
    args=training_args,
    data_collator=data_collator,
    train_dataset=train_dataset,
)

trainer.train()
model.save_pretrained("./enterprise_chatbot")
tokenizer.save_pretrained("./enterprise_chatbot")
```

Evaluation and Iteration

- **Qualitative Evaluation:**
  Test the chatbot with sample inputs from your domain. Gather
  feedback from domain experts and end users.

- **Quantitative Metrics:**
  Evaluate using metrics like perplexity, BLEU, ROUGE, or even user satisfaction scores if available.
- **Iterative Refinement:**
  Fine-tune further based on performance metrics and user feedback. Adjust training parameters, incorporate more domain-specific data, or experiment with different model architectures if needed.

Deployment Considerations

- **Integration with Enterprise Systems:**
  Deploy the fine-tuned chatbot as a REST API using frameworks like FastAPI. Ensure that it integrates with your enterprise communication tools and databases.
- **Security and Compliance:**
  Protect proprietary data and ensure that the chatbot adheres to enterprise security policies and regulatory standards.
- **Scalability:**
  Containerize the chatbot using Docker and deploy on scalable cloud infrastructure (e.g., AWS, Azure) to handle enterprise-level traffic.

Best Practices

- **Data Privacy:**
  Ensure that all proprietary data is handled securely, anonymized when necessary, and complies with relevant regulations.
- **Continuous Monitoring:**
  Implement logging and monitoring for the chatbot's interactions to identify and address any issues promptly.
- **User Feedback Loop:**
  Create channels for user feedback to continuously improve the chatbot's performance and domain relevance.
- **Documentation:**
  Maintain comprehensive documentation of the fine-tuning process, including data preprocessing, model adjustments, and evaluation results, to support ongoing maintenance and compliance.

Exercises

1. **Data Expansion:**
   Expand your proprietary dataset with additional conversation logs or simulated data. Fine-tune the model on the expanded dataset and evaluate improvements in domain-specific responses.
2. **Prompt Engineering:**
   Experiment with different prompt formats and special tokens in your training data. Analyze how these changes affect the model's ability to generate contextually relevant responses.
3. **Efficient Fine-Tuning:**
   Implement LoRA or another PEFT technique during fine-tuning to reduce the number of trainable parameters. Compare the performance and training time with full fine-tuning.
4. **User Simulation:**
   Develop a simulation of real enterprise user interactions. Collect model outputs, assess their relevance and accuracy, and refine your training process based on the findings.
5. **Deployment Test:**
   Build a simple web interface for the chatbot, deploy it in a staging environment, and perform load testing to ensure the solution can handle expected enterprise traffic.

Fine-tuning a domain-specific LLM using proprietary datasets is a crucial step in building an enterprise-level chatbot that meets the nuanced requirements of your organization. This project provided a detailed guide on preparing proprietary data, fine-tuning a pre-trained LLM, evaluating performance, and deploying the chatbot as a scalable, secure API. By following best practices and iterating based on user feedback and quantitative metrics, you can create a highly effective and specialized chatbot that enhances enterprise communication and decision-making.

B. Production Deployment Using Hugging Face APIs and Kubernetes

After fine-tuning your enterprise-level chatbot with proprietary data, the next step is to deploy it in a production environment where it can serve real-time requests. Hugging Face provides robust APIs and model hosting solutions that simplify model deployment, while Kubernetes offers scalable orchestration for containerized applications. By combining these technologies, you can achieve a highly available, scalable, and manageable deployment that meets enterprise standards.

In this section, you will:

- Package your fine-tuned chatbot model as a Docker container.
- Deploy the container using Kubernetes for automated scaling and management.
- Integrate with Hugging Face Inference APIs for seamless model serving.
- Implement monitoring, logging, and continuous deployment practices.

Key Steps for Production Deployment

1. Containerizing Your Chatbot Model

Before deploying on Kubernetes, you must package your chatbot application (e.g., a FastAPI-based service) along with your fine-tuned model into a Docker container.

Example Dockerfile:

```dockerfile
# Use an official Python base image
FROM python:3.9-slim

# Set the working directory
WORKDIR /app

# Install system dependencies
RUN apt-get update && apt-get install -y gcc

# Copy the requirements file and install
dependencies
COPY requirements.txt .
RUN pip install --upgrade pip && \
    pip install --no-cache-dir -r requirements.txt
```

```
# Copy the rest of your application code
COPY . .

# Expose the port that your FastAPI application
uses
EXPOSE 8000

# Command to run your FastAPI application using
Uvicorn
CMD ["uvicorn", "app:app", "--host", "0.0.0.0", "--port", "8000"]
```

Example requirements.txt:

plaintext

```
fastapi
uvicorn
torch
transformers
pydantic
```

Build and test the Docker image locally:

bash

```
docker build -t enterprise-chatbot .
docker run -p 8000:8000 enterprise-chatbot
```

2. Deploying with Kubernetes

Kubernetes automates the deployment, scaling, and management of containerized applications. Use Kubernetes manifests (YAML files) to define deployments, services, and scaling policies.

Example Deployment Manifest (`deployment.yaml`):

yaml

```
apiVersion: apps/v1
kind: Deployment
metadata:
```

```yaml
  name: enterprise-chatbot-deployment
spec:
  replicas: 3
  selector:
    matchLabels:
      app: enterprise-chatbot
  template:
    metadata:
      labels:
        app: enterprise-chatbot
    spec:
      containers:
      - name: enterprise-chatbot
        image: your-dockerhub-username/enterprise-chatbot:latest
        ports:
        - containerPort: 8000
        resources:
          limits:
            memory: "1Gi"
            cpu: "500m"
          requests:
            memory: "512Mi"
            cpu: "250m"
---
apiVersion: v1
kind: Service
metadata:
  name: enterprise-chatbot-service
spec:
  type: LoadBalancer
  selector:
    app: enterprise-chatbot
  ports:
    - protocol: TCP
      port: 80
      targetPort: 8000
```

Apply the manifest to your Kubernetes cluster:

bash

```
kubectl apply -f deployment.yaml
```

This configuration:

- Creates a deployment with three replicas for high availability.
- Exposes a service with a LoadBalancer to distribute incoming requests.
- Sets resource limits to manage cluster utilization.

3. Integration with Hugging Face APIs

Hugging Face offers a Model Hub and Inference API that can complement your deployment strategy. You can either:

- **Upload your Model:**
  Upload your fine-tuned model to the Hugging Face Model Hub, which provides endpoints for inference.
- **Hybrid Deployment:**
  Use Hugging Face Inference APIs as a fallback or for A/B testing while running your own Kubernetes deployment.

If you choose to upload your model:

- Use the Hugging Face CLI or API to push your model.
- Configure your deployment settings in the Hugging Face Model Hub.

4. Monitoring and Continuous Deployment

Set up monitoring and logging to ensure your chatbot API is performing optimally:

- **Monitoring Tools:**
  Integrate Prometheus and Grafana with Kubernetes to monitor metrics such as response times, CPU/memory usage, and error rates.
- **Logging:**
  Use centralized logging solutions like Elasticsearch and Kibana (ELK stack) or cloud-specific logging (e.g., AWS CloudWatch, GCP Stackdriver).
- **CI/CD Pipelines:**
  Integrate with GitHub Actions (as described in Chapter 8) to automate testing and deployment of new model versions.

Best Practices and Considerations

- **Security:**
  Secure API endpoints with authentication (e.g., OAuth, API keys) and use TLS for encrypted communication.
- **Resource Optimization:**
  Monitor resource utilization and adjust replica counts or resource limits in your Kubernetes manifests to balance performance and cost.
- **Scalability:**
  Implement auto-scaling policies in Kubernetes (Horizontal Pod Autoscaler) to dynamically adjust the number of replicas based on load.
- **Interoperability:**
  Ensure the deployed API adheres to enterprise integration standards for seamless connectivity with existing systems.
- **Documentation and Compliance:**
  Document your deployment process and ensure that it meets any regulatory or compliance requirements for your industry.

Exercises

1. **Containerization Challenge:**
   Create a multi-stage Dockerfile to minimize the final image size. Compare the size and performance of your containerized application before and after optimization.
2. **Kubernetes Auto-Scaling:**
   Configure a Horizontal Pod Autoscaler (HPA) for your deployment. Simulate high load using a load testing tool (e.g., Locust) and observe how the HPA scales the number of replicas.
3. **Hybrid Deployment Experiment:**
   Deploy your chatbot model both on your own Kubernetes cluster and on the Hugging Face Model Hub. Compare the inference performance, latency, and ease of integration between the two deployments.
4. **Monitoring Setup:**
   Set up Prometheus and Grafana in your Kubernetes cluster to monitor

API performance. Create dashboards that track key metrics such as request latency, error rates, and resource utilization.
5. **CI/CD Integration:**
Develop a GitHub Actions workflow that automatically builds, tests, and deploys your Docker container to your Kubernetes cluster whenever changes are pushed to the repository.

Production deployment using Hugging Face APIs and Kubernetes provides a robust, scalable solution for serving enterprise-level chatbot models. By containerizing your model, deploying it on a Kubernetes cluster, and integrating with cloud-based APIs and monitoring tools, you can achieve high availability, low latency, and secure operation. Experiment with the exercises to refine your deployment pipeline, optimize resource usage, and ensure seamless integration with enterprise systems.

Project 3: Real-Time Multimodal Search Engine

A. Multimodal Embeddings for Visual and Textual Queries

Multimodal embeddings are at the heart of any search engine that needs to bridge different data modalities. In a real-time multimodal search engine, both images and text are mapped into a shared embedding space, allowing for efficient similarity search and retrieval. For example, a user might submit a textual query like "sunset over the mountains," and the system retrieves images that best match this description.

In this project segment, we will focus on:

- **Theoretical Foundations:** Understanding the concept of joint embedding spaces and how models like CLIP achieve this.
- **Implementation:** Practical steps and code examples to generate embeddings for both images and text using a pre-trained model.
- **Best Practices:** Guidelines for fine-tuning, normalization, and efficient retrieval.
- **Exercises:** Hands-on challenges to deepen your understanding of multimodal embeddings.

Key Concepts

1. Joint Embedding Space

- **Definition:**
  A joint embedding space is a shared latent space where representations of different modalities (e.g., images and text) are aligned. In this space, semantically similar items from different modalities lie close to each other.
- **Benefits:**
  - **Cross-Modal Retrieval:** Enables querying across modalities (e.g., text-to-image, image-to-text).
  - **Semantic Consistency:** Ensures that the model captures high-level semantic information rather than modality-specific details.

2. Pre-trained Multimodal Models

- **CLIP (Contrastive Language–Image Pre-training):**
  CLIP is a popular model that jointly trains an image encoder and a text encoder using a contrastive loss. It learns to maximize the similarity between paired image-text examples while minimizing the similarity for mismatched pairs.
- **Other Models:**
  Similar approaches include ALIGN and Florence. For many applications, CLIP provides a robust starting point.

3. Embedding Extraction

- **Image Embeddings:**
  Derived from the output of the image encoder. Typically normalized to have unit length.
- **Text Embeddings:**
  Derived from the text encoder, often by taking the output of the [CLS] token (or an equivalent pooling operation), then normalized.
- **Normalization:**
  Normalizing embeddings is essential for computing cosine similarity, a common metric used in retrieval tasks.

Implementation

A. Using a Pre-trained CLIP Model to Generate Embeddings

We will use Hugging Face's Transformers library to load a pre-trained CLIP model and extract embeddings for both images and text.

Step 1: Install Dependencies

Ensure you have installed the `transformers`, `torch`, and `Pillow` libraries:

```bash
pip install transformers torch pillow
```

Step 2: Code to Extract Embeddings

Below is an example Python script to extract and normalize embeddings:

```python
import torch
import torch.nn.functional as F
from transformers import CLIPProcessor, CLIPModel
from PIL import Image

# Load the pre-trained CLIP model and processor
model_name = "openai/clip-vit-base-patch32"
clip_model = CLIPModel.from_pretrained(model_name)
clip_processor =
CLIPProcessor.from_pretrained(model_name)
device = torch.device("cuda" if
torch.cuda.is_available() else "cpu")
clip_model.to(device)
clip_model.eval()

def get_image_embedding(image_path):
```

```python
    """Load an image, preprocess it, and extract
the normalized image embedding."""
    image = Image.open(image_path).convert("RGB")
    inputs = clip_processor(images=image,
return_tensors="pt")
    inputs = {k: v.to(device) for k, v in
inputs.items()}
    with torch.no_grad():
        image_features =
clip_model.get_image_features(**inputs)
    # Normalize the embedding
    image_embedding = F.normalize(image_features,
dim=-1)
    return image_embedding.cpu()

def get_text_embedding(text):
    """Extract normalized text embedding from a
given text string."""
    inputs = clip_processor(text=[text],
return_tensors="pt", padding=True)
    inputs = {k: v.to(device) for k, v in
inputs.items()}
    with torch.no_grad():
        text_features =
clip_model.get_text_features(**inputs)
    text_embedding = F.normalize(text_features,
dim=-1)
    return text_embedding.cpu()

# Example usage:
image_path = "path/to/your/image.jpg"
text_query = "A sunset over the mountains"

image_embedding = get_image_embedding(image_path)
text_embedding = get_text_embedding(text_query)

# Compute cosine similarity between image and text
embeddings
cosine_similarity = torch.matmul(image_embedding,
text_embedding.t())
print("Cosine Similarity:",
cosine_similarity.item())
```

Explanation:

- **Model Loading:**
  We load a pre-trained CLIP model and processor from Hugging Face.
- **Embedding Extraction:**
  The functions `get_image_embedding` and `get_text_embedding` preprocess the inputs and obtain normalized embeddings.
- **Similarity Calculation:**
  Cosine similarity between embeddings is computed to evaluate how well the image matches the text query.

Best Practices

1. **Normalization:**
   Always normalize embeddings to ensure cosine similarity is a valid measure of semantic similarity.
2. **Batch Processing:**
   For large-scale applications, process embeddings in batches to improve efficiency.
3. **Fine-Tuning:**
   If necessary, fine-tune the CLIP model on your domain-specific data to improve performance in your specific context.
4. **Caching:**
   Cache embeddings for static data (e.g., images in your database) to reduce computation during search.
5. **Hardware Optimization:**
   Use GPUs to accelerate embedding extraction, especially when processing large datasets in real time.

Exercises

1. **Embedding Evaluation:**
   Collect a set of images and corresponding textual descriptions. Extract embeddings using the provided functions and compute the

cosine similarity for each pair. Analyze how well the similarities correlate with human judgments of relevance.

2. **Batch Extraction:**
   Modify the embedding extraction functions to handle a batch of images or texts. Benchmark the performance improvements over single-instance processing.

3. **Domain Adaptation:**
   Fine-tune the CLIP model on a small domain-specific dataset (e.g., art images with descriptions) and compare the retrieval performance before and after fine-tuning.

4. **Similarity Metrics:**
   Experiment with different similarity metrics (e.g., Euclidean distance, cosine similarity) for retrieval tasks. Document the impact on retrieval quality and computational efficiency.

5. **Integration with a Retrieval System:**
   Build a simple retrieval script that, given a textual query, ranks a set of images based on the cosine similarity of their embeddings. Test the retrieval quality using a small dataset.

Multimodal embeddings enable seamless retrieval across different data modalities by aligning images and text in a shared latent space. By leveraging a pre-trained model like CLIP, you can efficiently extract high-quality embeddings and measure their similarity to perform cross-modal search. The techniques, code examples, and exercises provided in this section lay the groundwork for building a robust, real-time multimodal search engine. As you progress, you can integrate these embeddings into a larger retrieval system that supports diverse query types and scales to enterprise-level applications.

B. End-to-End Deployment on Cloud Infrastructure (AWS/GCP/Azure)

Deploying a real-time multimodal search engine on the cloud involves several key steps: packaging the application into a Docker container, uploading it to a container registry, and orchestrating its deployment using cloud services like AWS Elastic Kubernetes Service (EKS), Google Kubernetes Engine (GKE), or Azure Kubernetes Service (AKS). These platforms offer robust solutions for scaling, security, and monitoring, ensuring that your application can handle high traffic, low-latency requirements, and regulatory constraints.

Key Deployment Steps

1. Containerization

- **Dockerization:**
  Package your search engine application—including your inference
  code, model embeddings extraction logic, and API endpoints (e.g.,
  built with FastAPI)—into a Docker container.
- **Dockerfile Example:**

```dockerfile
dockerfile

# Use a lightweight base image
FROM python:3.9-slim

# Set working directory
WORKDIR /app

# Install system dependencies
RUN apt-get update && apt-get install -y gcc

# Copy requirements and install them
COPY requirements.txt .
RUN pip install --upgrade pip && \
    pip install --no-cache-dir -r
requirements.txt

# Copy the application code
COPY . .

# Expose port for the API
EXPOSE 8000

# Run the FastAPI application using Uvicorn
CMD ["uvicorn", "app:app", "--host",
"0.0.0.0", "--port", "8000"]
```

- **Requirements File Example (`requirements.txt`):**

```plaintext
fastapi
uvicorn
torch
transformers
pillow
pydantic
```

- **Build and Test Locally:**

```bash
docker build -t multimodal-search-engine .
docker run -p 8000:8000 multimodal-search-engine
```

2. Uploading to a Container Registry

- **AWS ECR:**
  Push your Docker image to Amazon Elastic Container Registry.

```bash
# Authenticate Docker to your AWS ECR registry
aws ecr get-login-password --region us-west-2
| docker login --username AWS --password-stdin
<aws_account_id>.dkr.ecr.us-west-
2.amazonaws.com

# Tag your image
docker tag multimodal-search-engine:latest
<aws_account_id>.dkr.ecr.us-west-
2.amazonaws.com/multimodal-search-
engine:latest

# Push the image to ECR
docker push <aws_account_id>.dkr.ecr.us-west-
2.amazonaws.com/multimodal-search-
engine:latest
```

- **GCP GCR:**
  Use Google Container Registry (or Artifact Registry) to store your image.

  bash

```
gcloud auth configure-docker
docker tag multimodal-search-engine:latest
gcr.io/<project_id>/multimodal-search-
engine:latest
docker push gcr.io/<project_id>/multimodal-
search-engine:latest
```

- **Azure ACR:**
  For Azure, push your image to Azure Container Registry.

  bash

```
az acr login --name <acr_name>
docker tag multimodal-search-engine:latest
<acr_name>.azurecr.io/multimodal-search-
engine:latest
docker push <acr_name>.azurecr.io/multimodal-
search-engine:latest
```

3. Deploying with Kubernetes

- **Kubernetes Manifests:**
  Create YAML files for your deployment and service. Below is an example deployment manifest:

  yaml

```
apiVersion: apps/v1
kind: Deployment
metadata:
  name: multimodal-search-engine
spec:
  replicas: 3
  selector:
    matchLabels:
      app: multimodal-search-engine
```

```
    template:
      metadata:
        labels:
          app: multimodal-search-engine
      spec:
        containers:
        - name: multimodal-search-engine
          image:
<your_container_registry_url>/multimodal-
search-engine:latest
          ports:
          - containerPort: 8000
          resources:
            limits:
              memory: "1Gi"
              cpu: "500m"
            requests:
              memory: "512Mi"
              cpu: "250m"
---
apiVersion: v1
kind: Service
metadata:
  name: multimodal-search-engine-service
spec:
  type: LoadBalancer
  selector:
    app: multimodal-search-engine
  ports:
    - protocol: TCP
      port: 80
      targetPort: 8000
```

- **Deploy the Manifest:**

```bash
kubectl apply -f deployment.yaml
```

- **Cloud-Specific Deployment:**
  For AWS, use EKS; for GCP, use GKE; for Azure, use AKS. Each

platform has its own CLI (e.g., `eksctl`, `gcloud`, `az aks`) for cluster management.

4. Monitoring and Scaling

- **Auto-Scaling:**
  Configure Horizontal Pod Autoscalers (HPA) to adjust the number of replicas based on load.

  ```yaml
  apiVersion: autoscaling/v2
  kind: HorizontalPodAutoscaler
  metadata:
    name: multimodal-search-engine-hpa
  spec:
    scaleTargetRef:
      apiVersion: apps/v1
      kind: Deployment
      name: multimodal-search-engine
    minReplicas: 3
    maxReplicas: 10
    metrics:
    - type: Resource
      resource:
        name: cpu
        target:
          type: Utilization
          averageUtilization: 70
  ```

- **Logging and Monitoring:**
  Integrate cloud-native monitoring tools such as AWS CloudWatch, GCP Stackdriver, or Azure Monitor. Tools like Prometheus and Grafana can also be deployed on your cluster.

5. CI/CD Integration

- **Automate Deployment:**
  Integrate your deployment pipeline with GitHub Actions (as

described in previous chapters) to automatically build, test, and deploy changes.

Best Practices

- **Security:**
  Use secure container registries, enforce network policies, and ensure that your API endpoints are protected (e.g., using TLS, OAuth).
- **Cost Optimization:**
  Monitor resource usage and configure auto-scaling to handle variable load while managing costs.
- **Resilience:**
  Implement readiness and liveness probes in your Kubernetes manifests to ensure the health of your application.
- **Documentation:**
  Document your deployment process and maintain version-controlled manifests and CI/CD pipelines for reproducibility.
- **Testing:**
  Thoroughly test your deployment in a staging environment before going live.

Exercises

1. **Multi-Cloud Deployment:**
   Deploy your containerized application on at least two cloud platforms (e.g., AWS and GCP). Compare the deployment process, ease of scaling, and performance metrics.
2. **Auto-Scaling Experiment:**
   Configure and test a Horizontal Pod Autoscaler for your deployment. Simulate high traffic and observe how the HPA adjusts the number of replicas.
3. **CI/CD Pipeline:**
   Set up a CI/CD pipeline that automatically builds and deploys your Docker image to your Kubernetes cluster whenever changes are pushed to your GitHub repository.

4. **Monitoring Dashboard:**
   Create a monitoring dashboard using Prometheus and Grafana to track key metrics (CPU usage, memory, latency) for your deployment.
5. **Security Audit:**
   Perform a security audit of your deployed application, including vulnerability scans on your Docker image and configuration review for Kubernetes network policies.

Deploying a real-time multimodal search engine on cloud infrastructure requires careful planning and execution. By containerizing your application, leveraging Kubernetes for orchestration, and integrating with cloud-native monitoring and scaling tools, you can build a robust, scalable, and secure production system. Experiment with the exercises to deepen your understanding and optimize your deployment process, ensuring that your enterprise application meets performance, security, and cost-efficiency requirements.

Appendix

Appendix A: Troubleshooting & Common Errors

A.1 PyTorch Installation and Compatibility Issues

Installing PyTorch successfully is the first critical step toward building and deploying deep learning models. However, users often encounter issues related to operating system compatibility, CUDA versions, Python environments, and conflicting dependencies. This section outlines common installation problems, explains potential causes, and provides detailed solutions and best practices to resolve them.

Common Installation Challenges

1. **CUDA Version Mismatch:**
   - **Problem:**
     Installing a PyTorch version compiled for a specific CUDA version while your system has a different CUDA version (or none installed) can lead to runtime errors, such as "CUDA driver version is insufficient for CUDA runtime version."
   - **Solution:**
     - Verify your system's CUDA version using `nvcc --version` or `nvidia-smi`.
     - Choose the correct PyTorch build for your CUDA version from the PyTorch installation page.
     - If you don't have a GPU or want to use CPU-only mode, install the CPU-only version of PyTorch.

2. **Python Version and Environment Issues:**
   - **Problem:**
     Incompatibilities between Python versions and PyTorch releases or conflicts with other packages can result in installation failures or unexpected behavior.
   - **Solution:**
     - Use a supported Python version (commonly Python 3.7 to 3.10 are well-supported by recent PyTorch releases).

- Create an isolated virtual environment using `venv`, `conda`, or `pipenv` to manage dependencies and avoid conflicts.
- Example with `conda`:

```bash
bash

conda create -n pytorch_env python=3.9
conda activate pytorch_env
```

3. **Dependency Conflicts:**
   - **Problem:**
   Conflicts with other installed packages (e.g., NumPy, SciPy, torchvision) may cause installation errors or warnings.
   - **Solution:**
     - Update `pip` and use a requirements file to specify compatible versions.
     - Check the PyTorch compatibility matrix for recommended package versions.
     - Upgrade critical packages using:

```bash
bash

pip install --upgrade pip setuptools wheel
```

4. **Operating System-Specific Issues:**
   - **Problem:**
   Differences in library versions, missing system dependencies, or specific OS-related bugs (e.g., on Windows or macOS) can interfere with the installation.
   - **Solution:**
     - On Linux, install essential packages like `build-essential`, `cmake`, and `libopenblas-dev` if required.
     - On Windows, consider using the official Conda packages for easier management.
     - On macOS, use Conda or Homebrew to manage dependencies.

5. **Installation via Conda vs. pip:**
   - o **Problem:**
     Using pip in an environment where Conda is recommended can sometimes lead to issues with binary compatibility, especially for CUDA.
   - o **Solution:**
     - For CUDA-enabled installations, using Conda is often more reliable:

       ```bash
       conda install pytorch torchvision torchaudio cudatoolkit=11.3 -c pytorch
       ```

     - If using pip, ensure that you are installing the correct wheels that match your CUDA version.

Troubleshooting Steps

1. **Check CUDA Compatibility:**
   - o Run `nvidia-smi` and `nvcc --version` to confirm your installed CUDA driver and toolkit versions.
   - o Verify that the PyTorch build you install is compatible with your CUDA version.
2. **Create a Clean Environment:**
   - o Use virtual environments (e.g., Conda or venv) to isolate your PyTorch installation:

     ```bash
     conda create -n pytorch_env python=3.9
     conda activate pytorch_env
     ```

3. **Install PyTorch Using Official Commands:**
   - o Visit the PyTorch website to generate the correct installation command.
   - o For example, for CUDA 11.3 using Conda:

```bash
bash

conda install pytorch torchvision
torchaudio cudatoolkit=11.3 -c pytorch
```

4. **Resolve Dependency Conflicts:**
   o If errors arise during installation, consider updating pip and installing packages one at a time.
   o Use the `--no-cache-dir` option with pip to avoid issues with cached packages.
5. **Consult Logs and Error Messages:**
   o Carefully read error messages during installation to identify missing libraries or conflicting package versions.
   o Use online forums (e.g., PyTorch Forums, Stack Overflow) to search for similar issues and recommended fixes.
6. **Test Your Installation:**
   o Run a simple PyTorch script to verify that the installation works correctly:

```python
python

import torch
print(torch.__version__)
print("CUDA available:",
torch.cuda.is_available())
```

Additional Resources

- **PyTorch Forums:**
  A community where you can ask questions and find solutions to common installation issues.
- **GitHub Issues:**
  Check the PyTorch GitHub repository for reported issues and fixes related to installation.
- **Official Documentation:**
  The PyTorch installation guide provides detailed instructions and troubleshooting tips.

PyTorch installation and compatibility issues are common challenges that can usually be resolved by ensuring correct CUDA versions, using isolated environments, and carefully managing dependencies. By following the troubleshooting steps and best practices outlined in this section, you can mitigate these issues and set up a robust deep learning environment. This foundation is essential for developing and deploying high-quality PyTorch models in production.

A.2 GPU Memory Management

Efficient GPU memory management is critical for training deep learning models, especially when working with large models or high-resolution data. Insufficient or inefficient use of GPU memory can lead to out-of-memory (OOM) errors, slow performance, or underutilization of available resources. This section outlines strategies to monitor, optimize, and troubleshoot GPU memory usage in PyTorch environments.

Key Concepts and Techniques

1. **Monitoring GPU Memory Usage**
   - `torch.cuda.memory_allocated():`
     Returns the current GPU memory usage by tensors.
   - `torch.cuda.max_memory_allocated():`
     Provides the maximum memory allocated by the current device since the beginning of the program.
   - `nvidia-smi:`
     A command-line tool for real-time monitoring of GPU memory, utilization, and temperature.
2. **Efficient Data Loading and Memory Transfer**
   - **Pin Memory:**
     When using `DataLoader`, setting `pin_memory=True` enables faster data transfer from CPU to GPU.
   - **Multiple Workers:**
     Increasing `num_workers` in your DataLoader can overlap data loading with GPU computations, reducing idle time.
3. **Managing Memory During Training**
   - Use `torch.no_grad():`
     During inference or evaluation, disable gradient computations to save memory.

- Detaching Tensors:
  Use `.detach()` to break computation graphs and prevent unnecessary memory retention.
- Clearing Cache:
  Use `torch.cuda.empty_cache()` to release unoccupied cached memory back to the GPU for other applications. Note that this does not free the memory allocated by tensors but helps reduce fragmentation.
4. **Optimization Techniques**
   - **Mixed Precision Training:**
     Reduces memory usage by performing calculations in half-precision (FP16) while maintaining model accuracy.
   - **Gradient Checkpointing:**
     Trades compute for memory by recomputing intermediate activations during the backward pass instead of storing them.
   - **Memory Profiling:**
     Tools such as PyTorch Profiler and NVIDIA Nsight Systems help identify memory bottlenecks and optimize usage.

Practical Code Examples

Example 1: Monitoring GPU Memory Usage

```python
import torch

# Print current and maximum GPU memory usage
print("Current memory allocated:",
torch.cuda.memory_allocated() / (1024 ** 2), "MB")
print("Maximum memory allocated:",
torch.cuda.max_memory_allocated() / (1024 ** 2),
"MB")

# Reset the maximum memory counter for fresh
measurements
torch.cuda.reset_max_memory_allocated()
```

Example 2: Using `torch.no_grad()` for Inference

python

```python
# Assuming 'model' is a pre-trained PyTorch model
and 'input_tensor' is prepared
model.eval()  # Set model to evaluation mode
with torch.no_grad():
    output = model(input_tensor)
```

Example 3: DataLoader with Pinned Memory and Multiple Workers

python

```python
from torch.utils.data import DataLoader

# Assuming 'dataset' is already defined
dataloader = DataLoader(dataset, batch_size=64,
shuffle=True, num_workers=4, pin_memory=True)
```

Example 4: Clearing Cached Memory

python

```python
# After completing heavy computations, clear unused
memory
torch.cuda.empty_cache()
```

Best Practices and Tips

- **Profile Regularly:**
  Regularly monitor GPU memory usage during training and inference to identify memory leaks or inefficiencies.
- **Optimize Data Loading:**
  Use `pin_memory` and appropriate `num_workers` settings to accelerate data transfers and reduce CPU-GPU bottlenecks.
- **Use Context Managers:**
  Always wrap inference code in `torch.no_grad()` to avoid building unnecessary computation graphs.
- **Implement Mixed Precision Training:**
  Utilize `torch.cuda.amp.autocast` and `GradScaler` for

training to reduce memory consumption while preserving performance.

- **Gradual Memory Release:**
  Periodically call `torch.cuda.empty_cache()` during long-running experiments to mitigate fragmentation, especially in iterative development environments.
- **Monitor Memory with External Tools:**
  Supplement PyTorch's built-in functions with tools like `nvidia-smi` to get a real-time overview of GPU usage across processes.
- **Batch Size Management:**
  If encountering OOM errors, consider reducing the batch size or using gradient accumulation to simulate larger batches.

Exercises

1. **Memory Usage Experiment:**
   Run a training loop with and without `torch.no_grad()` during validation. Compare GPU memory usage and training speed.
2. **DataLoader Tuning:**
   Experiment with different values for `num_workers` and `pin_memory` in your DataLoader. Measure the impact on data loading time and overall training performance.
3. **Mixed Precision vs. Full Precision:**
   Train the same model using mixed precision training and full precision training. Compare memory usage, training speed, and model performance.
4. **Gradient Checkpointing Implementation:**
   Implement gradient checkpointing for a large model and observe the reduction in memory usage. Evaluate any changes in training time.
5. **Real-Time Monitoring Script:**
   Write a script that periodically logs GPU memory usage using `torch.cuda.memory_allocated()` and `torch.cuda.max_memory_allocated()`, and visualize the data to identify potential memory leaks.

Effective GPU memory management is essential for developing scalable and efficient deep learning models. By implementing monitoring strategies, optimizing data loading, using mixed precision training, and applying best practices for memory management, you can minimize OOM errors and ensure that your models utilize GPU resources effectively. Experimenting with the techniques and exercises provided in this section will help you fine-tune your memory usage and improve the overall performance of your PyTorch applications.

A.3 Debugging Model Convergence Problems

Achieving convergence in deep learning models can be challenging. Models may fail to converge, converge too slowly, or oscillate without reaching a stable state. Debugging these issues is crucial for building robust and efficient models. In this section, we discuss common causes of convergence problems, strategies for diagnosing them, and practical tips to improve convergence during training.

Common Causes of Convergence Problems

1. **Learning Rate Issues:**
   - **Too High:**
     An excessively high learning rate may cause the loss to diverge or oscillate.
   - **Too Low:**
     A very low learning rate can lead to extremely slow convergence.
   - **Solution:**
     Experiment with learning rate schedules, such as step decay, cosine annealing, or using adaptive optimizers (e.g., Adam, RMSprop).
2. **Improper Weight Initialization:**
   - **Problem:**
     Poor initialization can cause vanishing or exploding gradients.
   - **Solution:**
     Use recommended initialization schemes (e.g., Xavier/Glorot for tanh activations, He initialization for ReLU).
3. **Batch Size Selection:**
   - **Problem:**
     Very small batches can lead to noisy gradient estimates, while very large batches may result in poor generalization.

- o **Solution:**
  Experiment with different batch sizes and consider gradient accumulation if GPU memory is limited.
4. **Data Quality and Preprocessing:**
   - o **Problem:**
     Noisy, unnormalized, or imbalanced data can impede convergence.
   - o **Solution:**
     Ensure proper data normalization, outlier handling, and augmentation to create a robust training set.
5. **Loss Function and Objective:**
   - o **Problem:**
     A mis-specified loss function or one that doesn't align well with the task can hinder convergence.
   - o **Solution:**
     Verify that the loss function is appropriate for the problem and consider adding regularization terms if necessary.
6. **Gradient Issues:**
   - o **Vanishing/Exploding Gradients:**
     Deep networks are susceptible to vanishing or exploding gradients.
   - o **Solution:**
     Use gradient clipping, proper activation functions, normalization layers (e.g., BatchNorm, LayerNorm), or architectures designed to alleviate these issues (e.g., LSTM for sequential data).
7. **Overfitting or Underfitting:**
   - o **Problem:**
     Overfitting occurs when the model memorizes training data, while underfitting happens when the model is too simple.
   - o **Solution:**
     Adjust model capacity, incorporate dropout or regularization, and ensure the training data is sufficiently diverse.

Diagnostic Strategies

1. **Visualize Training Metrics:**
   - o Plot the training and validation loss over epochs. Look for patterns such as divergence, oscillation, or plateauing.

- o Monitor metrics like accuracy, precision, and recall if applicable.
2. **Learning Rate Finder:**
   - o Use a learning rate finder to identify an optimal learning rate range. Libraries like `fastai` offer built-in utilities for this purpose.
3. **Gradient Monitoring:**
   - o Track the magnitude of gradients during training. Sudden spikes or diminishing gradients can signal issues with learning rate or architecture.
4. **Layer-wise Analysis:**
   - o Check the outputs of individual layers to detect if certain parts of the network are not learning (e.g., consistently zero activations).
5. **Ablation Studies:**
   - o Gradually simplify the model or reduce the dataset to identify whether a specific component is causing convergence issues.

Practical Code Examples

Example 1: Plotting Training Loss

python

```
import matplotlib.pyplot as plt

# Assume loss_history is a list of loss values
recorded during training
loss_history = [0.8, 0.65, 0.55, 0.5, 0.48, 0.47,
0.46]  # Example values
epochs = range(1, len(loss_history) + 1)

plt.plot(epochs, loss_history, marker='o',
label="Training Loss")
plt.xlabel("Epoch")
plt.ylabel("Loss")
plt.title("Training Loss Over Epochs")
plt.legend()
plt.show()
```

Example 2: Using Gradient Clipping

```python
python

import torch.nn as nn
import torch.optim as optim

model = nn.Sequential(nn.Linear(100, 50),
nn.ReLU(), nn.Linear(50, 10))
optimizer = optim.Adam(model.parameters(),
lr=0.001)
criterion = nn.CrossEntropyLoss()

# Dummy training loop with gradient clipping
for epoch in range(5):
    optimizer.zero_grad()
    inputs = torch.randn(32, 100)
    targets = torch.randint(0, 10, (32,))
    outputs = model(inputs)
    loss = criterion(outputs, targets)
    loss.backward()
    # Clip gradients to a maximum norm of 1.0

torch.nn.utils.clip_grad_norm_(model.parameters(),
max_norm=1.0)
    optimizer.step()
    print(f"Epoch {epoch+1}, Loss:
{loss.item():.4f}")
```

Example 3: Learning Rate Finder

Utilize a learning rate finder to automatically suggest an optimal learning rate. (Refer to libraries like fastai for an out-of-the-box solution or implement your own.)

Best Practices and Tips

- **Experiment Systematically:**
  Change one variable at a time (learning rate, batch size, architecture) and observe its effect on convergence.

- **Regular Monitoring:**
  Continuously monitor both training and validation metrics to detect early signs of overfitting or underfitting.
- **Use Advanced Optimizers:**
  Adaptive optimizers like Adam or RMSprop can help stabilize training.
- **Keep Detailed Logs:**
  Maintain logs of hyperparameters, loss values, and gradient norms to facilitate debugging and reproducibility.
- **Leverage Community Resources:**
  Use forums, GitHub issues, and documentation for insights into common convergence problems and their fixes.

Exercises

1. **Learning Rate Experiment:**
   Use a learning rate finder to identify an optimal learning rate for your model. Plot the loss vs. learning rate and determine the range where the loss decreases most steadily.
2. **Batch Size Variation:**
   Train your model with different batch sizes. Analyze how batch size affects the convergence rate and stability.
3. **Gradient Norm Monitoring:**
   Modify your training loop to log the gradient norms of each layer at every epoch. Plot these norms to detect any exploding or vanishing gradients.
4. **Ablation Study:**
   Remove or modify specific layers (e.g., dropout, normalization) and observe the impact on convergence. Identify which components are critical for stable training.
5. **Overfitting and Underfitting Analysis:**
   Train your model on subsets of the data and with varying model capacities. Evaluate and compare training and validation performance to diagnose overfitting or underfitting.

Debugging model convergence problems requires a methodical approach that involves monitoring training metrics, experimenting with hyperparameters, and analyzing gradient behaviors. By applying the strategies and best practices discussed in this section, you can identify and resolve issues that impede your model's convergence, leading to more robust and efficient training processes. Experiment with the exercises provided to deepen your understanding and improve your troubleshooting skills for complex deep learning models.

A.4 Deployment-Specific Troubleshooting

Deploying deep learning models, particularly those built with PyTorch, involves more than just successful training. Production deployments may encounter a variety of challenges that are unique to the deployment environment, such as containerization issues, cloud integration problems, networking and latency concerns, and security or dependency conflicts. This section provides an overview of common deployment issues and offers practical strategies to diagnose and resolve them, ensuring that your model serving pipelines are robust and reliable.

Common Deployment Challenges

1. **Containerization Issues:**
   - **Image Build Failures:**
     Errors during Docker image builds can stem from missing system dependencies or incorrect base images.
   - **Dependency Mismatches:**
     Differences between the development environment and the container environment may lead to package version conflicts or missing libraries.
   - **Solution:**
     - Use multi-stage builds and minimal base images.
     - Verify that your `requirements.txt` or `conda` environment file accurately reflects all dependencies.
     - Test the container locally before deployment using commands like `docker run` and inspect logs with `docker logs`.
2. **Cloud Integration Problems:**
   - **Configuration Errors:**
     Misconfigured environment variables, IAM roles, or network settings can cause failures when deploying to cloud platforms such as AWS SageMaker, GCP Vertex AI, or Azure ML.

- o **Service Connectivity:**
  Endpoints may not be accessible due to firewall settings or misconfigured load balancers.
- o **Solution:**
  - Double-check configuration files and cloud service settings.
  - Use cloud-specific diagnostics (e.g., AWS CloudWatch, GCP's Stackdriver) to monitor and log errors.
  - Test connectivity with simple health-check endpoints.

3. **Network and Latency Issues:**
   - o **High Inference Latency:**
     Delays can occur due to inefficient data transfer, lack of batching, or inadequate resource allocation.
   - o **Scaling Challenges:**
     Under heavy load, the API may not scale properly, resulting in timeouts or dropped requests.
   - o **Solution:**
     - Implement batch processing and asynchronous inference.
     - Optimize your model (e.g., convert to TorchScript or ONNX) to reduce overhead.
     - Configure auto-scaling policies and load balancers.
     - Monitor performance using tools like `nvidia-smi`, Prometheus, or cloud-native monitoring services.

4. **Security and Compliance Issues:**
   - o **Authentication Failures:**
     Issues with API keys, OAuth tokens, or certificate configurations can block access.
   - o **Data Privacy Concerns:**
     Misconfiguration in data encryption (TLS/SSL) may expose sensitive information.
   - o **Solution:**
     - Validate security configurations and test API endpoints with proper authentication.
     - Use secure protocols and enforce strict access controls.
     - Review compliance requirements (e.g., HIPAA, GDPR) and ensure your deployment adheres to them.

5. **Logging and Monitoring Shortcomings:**

- o **Insufficient Logs:**
  Lack of detailed logs can make diagnosing issues difficult, especially in production environments.
- o **Monitoring Gaps:**
  Without proper monitoring, performance degradation and errors might go unnoticed.
- o **Solution:**
  - Integrate comprehensive logging within your application and container.
  - Set up monitoring dashboards and alerting systems using tools like Prometheus, Grafana, AWS CloudWatch, or Azure Monitor.
  - Periodically review logs and metrics to identify and resolve anomalies.

Practical Examples

Example 1: Checking Docker Container Logs

Use the following command to view logs from a running Docker container:

```bash

docker logs <container_id_or_name>
```

This command helps you diagnose issues that occurred during container startup or execution.

Example 2: Kubernetes Pod Logs

If you're deploying on Kubernetes, use:

```bash

kubectl logs <pod_name> -n <namespace>
```

This provides access to logs generated by your containerized application running in the cluster.

Example 3: Simple Health Check Endpoint

Implement a simple health-check endpoint in your FastAPI application to verify that the service is running correctly:

```python
python

from fastapi import FastAPI

app = FastAPI()

@app.get("/health")
async def health_check():
    return {"status": "ok"}

# Run the app as usual...
```

This endpoint can be used by load balancers or orchestration tools to monitor the health of your deployment.

Best Practices and Tips

- **Develop in an Isolated Environment:**
  Always test your container locally in an environment that mimics production as closely as possible.
- **Use Version Control for Configuration:**
  Keep your deployment configuration files (e.g., Dockerfile, Kubernetes manifests) under version control to track changes and facilitate rollback if issues arise.
- **Automate Testing and Deployment:**
  Integrate CI/CD pipelines (e.g., with GitHub Actions) that include steps for building, testing, and deploying your containerized applications. This helps catch errors early in the development cycle.
- **Implement Robust Logging and Monitoring:**
  Ensure that your deployment includes centralized logging and monitoring to track application performance and diagnose issues promptly.
- **Perform Regular Security Audits:**
  Regularly review and update your security configurations, including authentication mechanisms, encryption settings, and access controls.
- **Document Troubleshooting Steps:**
  Maintain detailed documentation of common issues and their

resolutions. This serves as a reference for future troubleshooting and aids team members in resolving problems efficiently.

Exercises

1. **Reproduce a Deployment Error:**
   Intentionally misconfigure an environment variable or dependency in your Dockerfile. Attempt to deploy the model and use the logs to diagnose and resolve the error.
2. **Load Balancer Simulation:**
   Deploy your API on Kubernetes and simulate network issues by misconfiguring the load balancer. Identify the symptoms in the logs and adjust the configuration to resolve the issues.
3. **Security Misconfiguration Test:**
   Deploy your API without proper authentication, then implement a secure authentication mechanism. Use penetration testing tools to ensure that unauthorized access is blocked.
4. **Monitoring Dashboard Setup:**
   Set up a basic Prometheus and Grafana dashboard to monitor key metrics (e.g., memory usage, CPU load, API response times) from your deployed application. Document how these metrics change under different load conditions.
5. **End-to-End Troubleshooting Scenario:**
   Create a scenario where multiple deployment issues occur simultaneously (e.g., high latency, missing dependencies, security misconfiguration). Develop a step-by-step troubleshooting guide to systematically diagnose and resolve each issue.

Deployment-specific troubleshooting is a critical aspect of ensuring that your PyTorch models run reliably in production environments. By understanding common issues, using appropriate tools to monitor and log performance, and following best practices, you can quickly diagnose and resolve deployment challenges. The exercises provided in this section will help you build practical troubleshooting skills and ensure that your deployments are robust, secure, and efficient.

Appendix B: Essential PyTorch Resources

B.1 PyTorch Documentation and Official Resources

Official PyTorch Documentation

The official PyTorch documentation is your primary resource for understanding the framework's extensive API. It provides:

- **API References:** Detailed explanations of modules, classes, and functions.
- **Tutorials and Guides:** Step-by-step tutorials for both beginners and advanced users, covering topics such as autograd, model building, optimization, and distributed training.
- **Release Notes:** Information on new features, bug fixes, and improvements for each version.

Visit: https://pytorch.org/docs/stable

PyTorch Tutorials

For hands-on learning, the PyTorch Tutorials offer a wide range of examples that cover:

- **Getting Started:** to PyTorch basics, including tensors and automatic differentiation.
- **Deep Learning with PyTorch:** In-depth guides on building neural networks, training models, and using advanced features.
- **Advanced Topics:** Tutorials on topics like TorchScript, distributed training, and model optimization.

Visit: https://pytorch.org/tutorials

PyTorch GitHub Repository

The PyTorch GitHub repository is the central hub for:

- **Source Code:** Access the latest codebase and contribute to the project.
- **Issue Tracker:** Report bugs or browse existing issues to learn from community discussions.
- **Pull Requests:** See ongoing developments and enhancements to the framework.

Visit: https://github.com/pytorch/pytorch

PyTorch Forums

The PyTorch Forums are a vibrant community where you can:

- **Ask Questions:** Get help with technical issues and best practices.
- **Share Knowledge:** Participate in discussions, share projects, and collaborate with other PyTorch users.
- **Explore Tutorials and Examples:** Learn from real-world case studies and community contributions.

Visit: https://discuss.pytorch.org/

PyTorch Blog

Stay updated with the latest research, tutorials, and success stories by following the PyTorch Blog. It features:

- **New Releases and Updates:** Information on new features and improvements.
- **Case Studies:** Real-world applications and success stories.
- **Technical Deep Dives:** Articles exploring complex topics and advanced techniques.

Visit: https://pytorch.org/blog/

TorchScript Documentation

For model optimization and deployment, TorchScript is an essential tool. Its documentation covers:

- **Compilation Techniques:** Learn about tracing and scripting.
- **Deployment Strategies:** Understand how to serialize models for production use.

Visit: https://pytorch.org/docs/stable/jit.html

Additional Resources

- **PyTorch Lightning:**
  While not an official PyTorch project, PyTorch Lightning provides a high-level interface for training and scaling models, emphasizing best practices and reducing boilerplate code.

  Visit: https://www.pytorchlightning.ai/

- **Community Contributions and Research Papers:**
  Explore recent research and community projects that leverage PyTorch for cutting-edge applications.

By leveraging these official resources, you can deepen your understanding of PyTorch, troubleshoot issues effectively, and stay up-to-date with the latest advancements in the framework. Whether you're a beginner or an experienced developer, these resources are indispensable for building, optimizing, and deploying your deep learning models.

B.2 Recommended Papers and Articles

Foundational and Influential Papers

- **Attention is All You Need (Vaswani et al., 2017):**
  This seminal paper introduced the Transformer architecture, which revolutionized natural language processing and laid the foundation for models such as BERT, GPT, and LLaMA.
  Direct link: http://arxiv.org/abs/1706.03762
- **Deep Residual Learning for Image Recognition (He et al., 2015):**
  This paper introduced ResNet, which addressed the degradation problem in deep networks and influenced the design of many modern convolutional architectures.
  Direct link: http://arxiv.org/abs/1512.03385
- **Generative Adversarial Nets (Goodfellow et al., 2014):**
  The original GAN paper that sparked significant interest in generative models by proposing an adversarial training framework.
  Direct link: http://arxiv.org/abs/1406.2661

- **Auto-Encoding Variational Bayes (Kingma & Welling, 2014):**
  This paper introduced Variational Autoencoders (VAEs), merging variational inference with deep learning to generate data and learn latent representations.
  Direct link: http://arxiv.org/abs/1312.6114
- **Denoising Diffusion Probabilistic Models (Ho et al., 2020):**
  An influential work advancing generative modeling through diffusion processes, achieving state-of-the-art results in image synthesis.
  Direct link: http://arxiv.org/abs/2006.11239
- **Language Models are Few-Shot Learners (Brown et al., 2020):**
  The GPT-3 paper demonstrates the power of large-scale language models and introduces the concept of few-shot learning, influencing subsequent research in language modeling.
  Direct link: http://arxiv.org/abs/2005.14165
- **BERT: Pre-training of Deep Bidirectional Transformers for Language Understanding (Devlin et al., 2018):**
  This paper introduced BERT, a groundbreaking model that leverages bidirectional training to achieve superior performance on various NLP tasks.
  Direct link: http://arxiv.org/abs/1810.04805
- **LLaMA: Open and Efficient Foundation Language Models (Touvron et al., 2023):**
  A recent work focusing on building efficient and accessible large language models, offering insights into scaling and resource efficiency.
  Direct link: http://arxiv.org/abs/2302.13971
- **LoRA: Low-Rank Adaptation of Large Language Models (Hu et al., 2021):**
  This paper proposes a parameter-efficient method for fine-tuning large language models, facilitating domain adaptation without excessive computational cost.
  Direct link: http://arxiv.org/abs/2106.09685

Practical Articles, Tutorials, and Blogs

- **PyTorch Official Blog and Tutorials:**
  The official PyTorch blog and tutorials offer hands-on guides, case studies, and updates on new features, making them essential for both beginners and advanced users.
  Direct link to blog: http://pytorch.org/blog/
  Direct link to tutorials: http://pytorch.org/tutorials

- **Hugging Face Blog:**
  Provides insights into state-of-the-art models and practical guides on fine-tuning and deploying transformer models.
  Direct link: http://huggingface.co/blog
- **Distill.pub:**
  Offers in-depth, interactive articles that explain deep learning concepts with visualizations, enhancing understanding of complex topics such as attention mechanisms.
  Direct link: http://distill.pub/
- **Towards Data Science and Medium Articles:**
  These platforms host a wide range of articles that cover practical tips, advanced techniques, and real-world applications of PyTorch.
  Direct link (Towards Data Science PyTorch tag): http://towardsdatascience.com/tagged/pytorch
- **Papers with Code:**
  Connects research papers with their code implementations, allowing you to explore and experiment with the latest advances in deep learning.
  Direct link: http://paperswithcode.com/

Keeping Up-to-Date

- **ArXiv and Google Scholar:**
  Regularly check for new preprints and research papers in deep learning.
  Direct link (ArXiv): http://arxiv.org/
  Direct link (Google Scholar): http://scholar.google.com/
- **Conferences and Workshops:**
  Follow conferences such as NeurIPS, ICML, CVPR, and ACL to stay informed about the latest research breakthroughs.
- **Social Media and Newsletters:**
  Follow key researchers and subscribe to newsletters that provide curated deep learning content.

B.3 Community Links and GitHub Repositories

Official and Community Forums

- **PyTorch Forums:**
  A vibrant community for discussions, troubleshooting, and sharing

projects.
Direct link: http://discuss.pytorch.org/
- **Reddit – r/MachineLearning and r/pytorch:**
  Subreddits for machine learning and PyTorch offer insights, project showcases, and discussions on the latest trends.
  Direct link to r/MachineLearning:
  http://reddit.com/r/MachineLearning/
  Direct link to r/pytorch: http://reddit.com/r/pytorch/
- **Stack Overflow:**
  A popular Q&A site for programming issues, including many questions related to PyTorch.
  Direct link: http://stackoverflow.com/questions/tagged/pytorch
- **Hugging Face Forums:**
  A community centered on transformers and NLP, providing support for PyTorch users working on language and multimodal models.
  Direct link: http://discuss.huggingface.co/

Key GitHub Repositories

- **PyTorch Repository:**
  The official PyTorch source code repository for updates, bug reports, and contributions.
  Direct link: http://github.com/pytorch/pytorch
- **TorchVision:**
  Contains models, datasets, and image processing tools for computer vision applications.
  Direct link: http://github.com/pytorch/vision
- **PyTorch Lightning:**
  A high-level framework for organizing PyTorch code, promoting best practices and scalability.
  Direct link: http://github.com/PyTorchLightning/pytorch-lightning
- **Hugging Face Transformers:**
  A repository of transformer models and tools for NLP and multimodal applications.
  Direct link: http://github.com/huggingface/transformers
- **DeepSpeed:**
  A library for optimizing large-scale deep learning training, with support for distributed training and efficient inference.
  Direct link: http://github.com/microsoft/DeepSpeed

Additional Community Resources

- **Papers with Code:**
  Links research papers with code implementations, helping you replicate and extend state-of-the-art methods.
  Direct link: http://paperswithcode.com/
- **Awesome PyTorch:**
  A curated list of PyTorch projects, libraries, and resources.
  Direct link: http://github.com/bharathgs/Awesome-pytorch-list
- **Kaggle:**
  A platform for data science competitions and community-shared PyTorch projects.
  Direct link: http://kaggle.com/
- **Medium – PyTorch Tag:**
  A collection of articles and tutorials tagged with PyTorch on Medium.
  Direct link: http://medium.com/tag/pytorch

The resources listed in Appendix B, Sections B.2 and B.3 provide a robust foundation for deepening your understanding of PyTorch and staying connected with the community. By engaging with these papers, articles, and community links, you can keep up-to-date with the latest research, find solutions to common problems, and contribute to the vibrant PyTorch ecosystem.

B.3 Community Links and GitHub Repositories

Official and Community Forums

- **PyTorch Forums:**
  A vibrant community for discussions, troubleshooting, and sharing projects related to PyTorch.
  http://discuss.pytorch.org/
- **Reddit – r/MachineLearning:**
  A community for discussing machine learning research, applications, and trends, including PyTorch topics.
  http://reddit.com/r/MachineLearning/
- **Reddit – r/pytorch:**
  A subreddit dedicated specifically to PyTorch where users share projects, ask questions, and discuss best practices.
  http://reddit.com/r/pytorch/

- **Stack Overflow:**
  A widely used Q&A site where many developers discuss and resolve PyTorch-related issues.
  http://stackoverflow.com/questions/tagged/pytorch
- **Hugging Face Forums:**
  A community focused on transformers and NLP that also covers PyTorch topics, particularly for multimodal and language model applications.
  http://discuss.huggingface.co/

Key GitHub Repositories

- **PyTorch Repository:**
  The official PyTorch GitHub repository where you can find the latest source code, contribute to development, and track issues.
  http://github.com/pytorch/pytorch
- **TorchVision:**
  Provides a collection of popular datasets, model architectures, and image transformations for computer vision, all built on PyTorch.
  http://github.com/pytorch/vision
- **PyTorch Lightning:**
  A lightweight wrapper for PyTorch that helps organize code and manage training routines more efficiently, promoting best practices and scalability.
  http://github.com/PyTorchLightning/pytorch-lightning
- **Hugging Face Transformers:**
  A repository offering a wide array of transformer models and tools for NLP and multimodal tasks, widely used in PyTorch projects.
  http://github.com/huggingface/transformers
- **DeepSpeed:**
  An optimization library developed by Microsoft for distributed training and efficient inference of large-scale deep learning models using PyTorch.
  http://github.com/microsoft/DeepSpeed

Additional Community Resources

- **Papers with Code:**
  Connects state-of-the-art research papers with their corresponding code implementations in PyTorch, facilitating exploration and replication of new techniques.
  http://paperswithcode.com/

- **Awesome PyTorch:**
  A curated list of projects, libraries, and resources related to PyTorch that can help you discover useful tools and community contributions.
  http://github.com/bharathgs/Awesome-pytorch-list
- **Kaggle:**
  A platform where data scientists and machine learning practitioners share projects, compete in challenges, and provide kernels (code notebooks) that often leverage PyTorch.
  http://kaggle.com/
- **Medium – PyTorch Tag:**
  A collection of articles, tutorials, and insights on PyTorch posted on Medium by practitioners and researchers.
  http://medium.com/tag/pytorch

Engaging with these community links and GitHub repositories will keep you updated on the latest developments, best practices, and innovations in the PyTorch ecosystem. Whether you're seeking help, contributing code, or exploring cutting-edge research, these resources are invaluable for your journey in deep learning with PyTorch.

Appendix C: Advanced Optimization Techniques

C.1 Hyperparameter Optimization with Optuna

Hyperparameter optimization is a critical component of building high-performing deep learning models. Selecting the best learning rate, batch size, network architecture parameters, and regularization techniques can significantly influence your model's convergence and generalization. Optuna is an open-source hyperparameter optimization framework that enables efficient and scalable searches over hyperparameter spaces using state-of-the-art algorithms such as Tree-structured Parzen Estimator (TPE).

Optuna's key features include:

- **Automated Search:** Define objective functions and let Optuna suggest hyperparameter values.
- **Pruning:** Automatically terminate unpromising trials to save computation time.

- **Flexible API:** Easily integrate with PyTorch training loops or high-level libraries like PyTorch Lightning.
- **Visualization:** Built-in tools to analyze the hyperparameter search and visualize results.

Key Concepts

1. **Objective Function:**
   The objective function defines the training process of your model and returns a value (e.g., validation loss or accuracy) that Optuna will minimize or maximize.
2. **Study:**
   A study is an optimization session where Optuna explores the hyperparameter space. It manages the trials, records results, and determines the best hyperparameters based on your objective.
3. **Pruning:**
   Optuna can terminate trials early if they are unlikely to yield promising results, making the search process more efficient.

Practical Code Example

Below is an example of using Optuna to optimize the learning rate and batch size of a simple PyTorch model.

```python
import torch
import torch.nn as nn
import torch.optim as optim
from torch.utils.data import DataLoader,
TensorDataset
import optuna

# Define a simple model
class SimpleModel(nn.Module):
    def __init__(self, input_dim=100,
hidden_dim=64, output_dim=10):
        super(SimpleModel, self).__init__()
```

```python
        self.fc1 = nn.Linear(input_dim, hidden_dim)
        self.relu = nn.ReLU()
        self.fc2 = nn.Linear(hidden_dim, output_dim)

    def forward(self, x):
        return self.fc2(self.relu(self.fc1(x)))

# Create a synthetic dataset for demonstration
def get_data():
    X = torch.randn(1000, 100)
    y = torch.randint(0, 10, (1000,))
    dataset = TensorDataset(X, y)
    return dataset

dataset = get_data()

# Objective function for Optuna optimization
def objective(trial):
    # Suggest hyperparameters: learning rate and batch size
    lr = trial.suggest_loguniform("lr", 1e-5, 1e-2)
    batch_size = trial.suggest_categorical("batch_size", [16, 32, 64])

    # Create data loader
    dataloader = DataLoader(dataset, batch_size=batch_size, shuffle=True)

    # Instantiate the model, loss function, and optimizer
    model = SimpleModel().to("cuda" if torch.cuda.is_available() else "cpu")
    device = next(model.parameters()).device
    criterion = nn.CrossEntropyLoss()
    optimizer = optim.Adam(model.parameters(), lr=lr)

    # Train the model for one epoch
    model.train()
    total_loss = 0.0
```

```
    for inputs, targets in dataloader:
        inputs, targets = inputs.to(device),
targets.to(device)
        optimizer.zero_grad()
        outputs = model(inputs)
        loss = criterion(outputs, targets)
        loss.backward()
        optimizer.step()
        total_loss += loss.item()

    avg_loss = total_loss / len(dataloader)
    return avg_loss

# Create a study and optimize the objective
function
study = optuna.create_study(direction="minimize")
study.optimize(objective, n_trials=20)

print("Best trial:")
trial = study.best_trial
print("  Loss: {:.4f}".format(trial.value))
print("  Best hyperparameters:
{}".format(trial.params))
```

Explanation:

- **Objective Function:**
  The function trains a simple model for one epoch using
  hyperparameters suggested by Optuna and returns the average loss.
- **Hyperparameter Suggestions:**
  Optuna suggests a learning rate (log-uniformly distributed between
  1e-5 and 1e-2) and a batch size (selected from [16, 32, 64]).
- **Study:**
  The study runs 20 trials to find the best hyperparameters that
  minimize the loss.

Best Practices

- **Early Stopping with Pruning:**
  Utilize Optuna's pruning features to terminate unpromising trials early, saving time and resources.
- **Incremental Testing:**
  Start with a smaller number of trials to validate your objective function before scaling up the search.
- **Logging and Visualization:**
  Use Optuna's visualization tools (e.g., `optuna.visualization.plot_optimization_history (study)`) to analyze trial performance and hyperparameter relationships.
- **Integration with Frameworks:**
  Consider integrating Optuna with high-level libraries like PyTorch Lightning for more streamlined hyperparameter tuning.

Exercises

1. **Extended Hyperparameter Search:**
   Expand the search space to include additional hyperparameters such as hidden layer sizes, dropout rates, or optimizer types. Analyze how these changes affect model performance.
2. **Pruning Implementation:**
   Implement Optuna's pruning mechanism by adding intermediate validation checks in your objective function. Compare the total optimization time with and without pruning.
3. **Visualization Analysis:**
   Use Optuna's visualization features to generate plots for optimization history, parameter importance, and parallel coordinate plots. Interpret the results and discuss any correlations between hyperparameters and performance.
4. **Integration Challenge:**
   Integrate Optuna with a real-world dataset and a more complex model (e.g., a CNN for image classification). Evaluate the benefits of hyperparameter optimization on model accuracy and convergence speed.
5. **Reproducibility Experiment:**
   Run your hyperparameter optimization multiple times and analyze

the variability in the best hyperparameters. Discuss strategies to improve reproducibility (e.g., fixing random seeds).

Optuna provides a powerful, flexible framework for hyperparameter optimization, enabling you to automate the search for optimal model configurations efficiently. By integrating Optuna into your PyTorch workflow, you can systematically improve model performance while reducing manual tuning effort. The practical code examples, best practices, and exercises in this section offer a solid foundation to start optimizing your models and achieving better performance in your deep learning projects.

Appendix C: Advanced Optimization Techniques

C.2 AutoML and NAS (Neural Architecture Search)

Designing optimal neural network architectures often involves significant trial and error, expert intuition, and time-consuming manual tuning. AutoML and Neural Architecture Search (NAS) seek to automate this process by exploring a large space of possible architectures and hyperparameters to find models that meet specified performance criteria. These techniques leverage optimization algorithms and reinforcement learning to automate model selection, potentially discovering novel architectures that outperform manually designed ones.

Key benefits include:

- **Efficiency:** Drastically reduce the time and expertise required for model design.
- **Performance:** Identify architectures that achieve state-of-the-art results by exploring combinations that might not be considered manually.
- **Scalability:** Adapt automatically to different datasets and tasks with minimal human intervention.

Key Concepts

1. **AutoML:**
   - **Definition:**
     AutoML encompasses a suite of tools and algorithms that automate the end-to-end process of applying machine learning to real-world problems, including data preprocessing, feature engineering, model selection, hyperparameter tuning, and deployment.
   - **Scope in Neural Networks:**
     In deep learning, AutoML frameworks often integrate NAS to optimize network architectures along with hyperparameters.
2. **Neural Architecture Search (NAS):**
   - **Definition:**
     NAS is a subfield of AutoML focused on automatically finding the best neural network architecture for a given task.
   - **Approaches:**
     - **Reinforcement Learning (RL)-Based NAS:**
       An RL agent selects architecture components (e.g., layers, operations) and receives rewards based on model performance.
     - **Evolutionary Algorithms:**
       Population-based search where architectures evolve over successive generations.
     - **Gradient-Based NAS:**
       Techniques like DARTS (Differentiable Architecture Search) allow for continuous relaxation of the architecture search space and optimize it using gradient descent.
   - **Challenges:**
     - **Computational Cost:**
       NAS can be resource-intensive due to the need to train and evaluate numerous candidate models.
     - **Search Space Design:**
       Balancing the flexibility of the search space with computational feasibility is crucial.

Practical Code Example: NAS with Optuna and PyTorch

In this example, we use Optuna to simulate a simple NAS experiment for a small CNN. Although real-world NAS can be far more complex, this example demonstrates the concept of searching for optimal architecture hyperparameters.

python

```python
import torch
import torch.nn as nn
import torch.optim as optim
from torch.utils.data import DataLoader,
TensorDataset
import optuna

# Define a simple CNN model with variable
parameters
class SimpleCNN(nn.Module):
    def __init__(self, num_filters, kernel_size,
dropout_rate):
        super(SimpleCNN, self).__init__()
        self.conv1 = nn.Conv2d(1, num_filters,
kernel_size=kernel_size, padding=kernel_size//2)
        self.conv2 = nn.Conv2d(num_filters,
num_filters * 2, kernel_size=kernel_size,
padding=kernel_size//2)
        self.dropout = nn.Dropout(dropout_rate)
        self.fc = nn.Linear((num_filters * 2) * 7 *
7, 10)

    def forward(self, x):
        x = torch.relu(self.conv1(x))
        x = torch.relu(self.conv2(x))
        x = nn.functional.max_pool2d(x, 2)
        x = x.view(x.size(0), -1)
        x = self.dropout(x)
        return self.fc(x)

# Create a dummy dataset (e.g., MNIST-like)
def get_dummy_data():
```

```python
    # 1000 samples of 1x28x28 images and labels
from 0 to 9
    X = torch.randn(1000, 1, 28, 28)
    y = torch.randint(0, 10, (1000,))
    dataset = TensorDataset(X, y)
    return dataset

dataset = get_dummy_data()

# Objective function for NAS using Optuna
def objective(trial):
    # Suggest hyperparameters for the CNN
architecture
    num_filters = trial.suggest_int("num_filters",
8, 32, step=8)
    kernel_size = trial.suggest_int("kernel_size",
3, 7, step=2)
    dropout_rate =
trial.suggest_float("dropout_rate", 0.1, 0.5)
    lr = trial.suggest_loguniform("lr", 1e-4, 1e-2)
    batch_size =
trial.suggest_categorical("batch_size", [32, 64])

    # Create DataLoader
    dataloader = DataLoader(dataset,
batch_size=batch_size, shuffle=True)

    # Initialize the model, optimizer, and loss
function
    device = torch.device("cuda" if
torch.cuda.is_available() else "cpu")
    model = SimpleCNN(num_filters, kernel_size,
dropout_rate).to(device)
    optimizer = optim.Adam(model.parameters(),
lr=lr)
    criterion = nn.CrossEntropyLoss()

    model.train()
    total_loss = 0.0
    # Train for one epoch (for demonstration)
    for inputs, targets in dataloader:
```

```
            inputs, targets = inputs.to(device),
targets.to(device)
            optimizer.zero_grad()
            outputs = model(inputs)
            loss = criterion(outputs, targets)
            loss.backward()
            optimizer.step()
            total_loss += loss.item()

        avg_loss = total_loss / len(dataloader)
        return avg_loss

# Run the NAS study with Optuna
study = optuna.create_study(direction="minimize")
study.optimize(objective, n_trials=20)

print("Best trial:")
trial = study.best_trial
print("  Loss: {:.4f}".format(trial.value))
print("  Best hyperparameters:
{}".format(trial.params))
```

Explanation:

- **Model Definition:**
  The `SimpleCNN` class takes hyperparameters for the number of
  filters, kernel size, and dropout rate.
- **Objective Function:**
  Optuna's objective function trains the model for one epoch on
  dummy data and returns the average loss.
- **Hyperparameter Search:**
  Optuna searches for optimal architecture parameters along with
  learning rate and batch size, simulating a simplified NAS process.

Best Practices and Tips

- **Define a Reasonable Search Space:**
  Limit the search space to a manageable size to reduce computational
  cost while still exploring meaningful architecture variations.

- **Use Pruning:**
  Implement Optuna's pruning feature to stop trials early if they are not promising.
- **Incremental Complexity:**
  Start with a simplified model and gradually add complexity as you validate the search methodology.
- **Leverage Pre-trained Models:**
  When possible, fine-tune pre-trained models with NAS techniques to benefit from transfer learning.
- **Monitor and Log Results:**
  Use Optuna's visualization tools (e.g., optimization history, parameter importance) to analyze how different hyperparameters affect performance.

Exercises

1. **Extended Search Space:**
   Expand the search space to include additional architectural parameters such as the number of convolutional layers or the use of pooling layers. Evaluate the impact on model performance.
2. **Comparative Study:**
   Compare the performance of models found via NAS with a manually designed architecture on the same dataset.
3. **Resource Management:**
   Experiment with different numbers of trials and measure the computational cost. Analyze trade-offs between search comprehensiveness and resource usage.
4. **Visualization and Analysis:**
   Use Optuna's visualization tools to plot the optimization history and analyze the relationships between hyperparameters and performance metrics.
5. **Real-World Application:**
   Apply the NAS approach to a real-world dataset (e.g., CIFAR-10) using a more complex model. Evaluate how the optimized architecture compares with standard models in terms of accuracy and efficiency.

AutoML and Neural Architecture Search (NAS) provide powerful approaches to automate the discovery of high-performing neural network architectures. By integrating frameworks like Optuna into your PyTorch workflow, you can efficiently explore the hyperparameter space and identify architectures that yield superior performance with reduced manual effort. The techniques, code examples, and exercises provided in this section form a strong foundation for leveraging AutoML and NAS in advanced deep learning projects.

C.3 Advanced Scheduler Usage (Cosine Annealing, Cyclical LR)

The learning rate is one of the most critical hyperparameters in training deep neural networks. Instead of using a fixed learning rate, advanced schedulers dynamically adjust the learning rate during training to improve convergence and avoid local minima. Two popular strategies are:

- **Cosine Annealing:**
  Gradually reduces the learning rate following a cosine function, often with restarts, to achieve smoother convergence.
- **Cyclical Learning Rate (CLR):**
  Cycles the learning rate between a lower and an upper bound throughout training, which can help escape shallow local minima and accelerate convergence.

These techniques can lead to improved performance and faster convergence, especially when training complex models.

Cosine Annealing Learning Rate Scheduler

Concept:
Cosine Annealing reduces the learning rate following a cosine curve. The learning rate starts at a maximum value and decreases to a minimum value over a predefined number of epochs or iterations. Optionally, with warm restarts, the learning rate can be periodically reset to a higher value to allow further exploration of the loss landscape.

PyTorch Implementation Example:

```python
python

import torch
import torch.optim as optim
import torch.nn as nn
import matplotlib.pyplot as plt

# Dummy model and optimizer
model = nn.Linear(10, 2)
optimizer = optim.SGD(model.parameters(), lr=0.1)

# Set up Cosine Annealing scheduler
scheduler =
optim.lr_scheduler.CosineAnnealingLR(optimizer,
T_max=50, eta_min=0.001)

# Record learning rates for plotting
lrs = []
for epoch in range(50):
    # Simulate one training epoch
    optimizer.step()
    lrs.append(optimizer.param_groups[0]['lr'])
    scheduler.step()

# Plot the learning rate schedule
plt.figure(figsize=(8, 4))
plt.plot(range(50), lrs, label="Cosine Annealing
LR")
plt.xlabel("Epoch")
plt.ylabel("Learning Rate")
plt.title("Cosine Annealing Learning Rate
Schedule")
plt.legend()
plt.show()
```

Key Points:

- `T_max`: Number of iterations/epochs for one cycle.
- `eta_min`: Minimum learning rate reached at the end of the cycle.

Cyclical Learning Rate (CLR)

Concept:
Cyclical Learning Rate (CLR) oscillates the learning rate between a lower and upper bound within a cycle. Common policies include:

- **Triangular:** Linearly increases and then decreases the learning rate.
- **Triangular2:** Similar to triangular but with a decreasing amplitude after each cycle.
- **Exp_range:** Scales the learning rate exponentially.

CLR can help the optimizer escape local minima and has been shown to improve training speed and generalization.

PyTorch Implementation Example:

```python
python

import torch
import torch.optim as optim
import torch.nn as nn
import matplotlib.pyplot as plt

# Dummy model and optimizer
model = nn.Linear(10, 2)
optimizer = optim.SGD(model.parameters(), lr=0.01)

# Set up Cyclical LR scheduler using the
"triangular" policy
scheduler = optim.lr_scheduler.CyclicLR(optimizer,
base_lr=0.001, max_lr=0.1, step_size_up=20,
mode='triangular')

# Record learning rates for plotting
lrs = []
for iteration in range(100):
    optimizer.step()
    lrs.append(optimizer.param_groups[0]['lr'])
    scheduler.step()
```

```
# Plot the cyclical learning rate schedule
plt.figure(figsize=(8, 4))
plt.plot(range(100), lrs, label="Cyclical LR
(Triangular)")
plt.xlabel("Iteration")
plt.ylabel("Learning Rate")
plt.title("Cyclical Learning Rate Schedule")
plt.legend()
plt.show()
```

Key Points:

- `base_lr`: The minimum learning rate.
- `max_lr`: The maximum learning rate.
- `step_size_up`: The number of iterations to increase the learning rate from `base_lr` to `max_lr`.
- `mode`: The policy to use (e.g., "triangular", "triangular2", "exp_range").

Best Practices

- **Experiment with Schedulers:**
  Test both Cosine Annealing and Cyclical LR schedulers on your specific task to see which offers better convergence and performance.
- **Warm Restarts:**
  For Cosine Annealing, consider using warm restarts (`CosineAnnealingWarmRestarts`) to periodically reset the learning rate and potentially escape local minima.
- **Monitoring:**
  Plot learning rate schedules alongside training metrics to visualize correlations between LR adjustments and model performance.
- **Integration with Early Stopping:**
  Combine learning rate schedulers with early stopping criteria to prevent overfitting and reduce training time.

Exercises

1. **Scheduler Comparison:**
   Train a model using both Cosine Annealing and Cyclical LR
   schedulers. Compare the convergence speed, final accuracy, and
   training stability.
2. **Warm Restart Experiment:**
   Implement `CosineAnnealingWarmRestarts` and compare its
   performance with the standard Cosine Annealing scheduler on a
   validation set.
3. **Hyperparameter Tuning:**
   Experiment with different values for `T_max`, `eta_min`, `base_lr`,
   and `max_lr` for each scheduler. Document how changes in these
   parameters affect model performance.
4. **Visualization:**
   Use Matplotlib to plot the learning rate schedules over training
   iterations. Overlay training loss curves to analyze the relationship
   between learning rate changes and loss reduction.
5. **Real-World Application:**
   Apply one of these schedulers to a complex deep learning model
   (e.g., a CNN or Transformer) on a real dataset. Evaluate its impact on
   training efficiency and model generalization.

Advanced learning rate scheduling techniques such as Cosine Annealing and
Cyclical LR can significantly improve the convergence and performance of
deep learning models. By dynamically adjusting the learning rate during
training, these schedulers help navigate the loss landscape more effectively,
avoid local minima, and enhance model generalization. Integrating these
methods into your training workflow, monitoring their impact, and
iteratively refining hyperparameters are key steps toward optimizing model
performance. Experiment with the provided code examples and exercises to
deepen your understanding of these techniques.